JUST
SAY
YES

JUST SAY YES

WHAT I'VE LEARNED ABOUT
LIFE, LUCK, AND THE
PURSUIT OF OPPORTUNITY

BERNARD L. SCHWARTZ

GREENLEAF
BOOK GROUP PRESS

Published by Greenleaf Book Group Press
Austin, Texas
www.gbgpress.com

Distributed by Greenleaf Book Group LLC

For ordering information or special discounts for bulk purchases, please contact Greenleaf Book Group LLC at PO Box 91869, Austin, TX 78709, 512.891.6100.

Design and composition by Greenleaf Book Group LLC
Cover design by Greenleaf Book Group LLC
Cover image copyright Elenamiv, 2014. Used under license from Shutterstock.com.

Cataloging-in-Publication data
Schwartz, Bernard L.
  Just say yes : what I've learned about life, luck, and the pursuit of opportunity / Bernard L. Schwartz.—1st ed.
     p. ; cm.
  Issued also as an ebook.
  ISBN: 978-1-62634-074-9
  1. Schwartz, Bernard L. 2. Aerospace industries--United States--Biography. 3. Industrialists—United States—Biography. 4. Executives—United States—Attitudes. 5. Loral Corporation—Biography. 6. Success in business. 7. Optimism. 8. Autobiography. I. Title.
HD9711.5.U62 S392 2014
338.4/76291/0973/092   2013957847

Part of the Tree Neutral® program, which offsets the number of trees consumed in the production and printing of this book by taking proactive steps, such as planting trees in direct proportion to the number of trees used: www.treeneutral.com

TreeNeutral

Printed in the United States of America on acid-free paper

14 15 16 17 18 19   10 9 8 7 6 5 4 3 2 1

First Edition

To Irene

Epigraphs

"I've been struck over the years by how there is almost no gap between the public and the private Bernard Schwartz. My father is the same man in both places—very much the leader, but also very down to earth. His story is the story of a man who accomplished great things in the world of business and finance, but who at heart is motivated more than anything else by what he values most: people. I have learned from my father that a trusted handshake and valued relationship count for a lot more than a contract."

—KAREN SCHWARTZ

"As long as I've known him, my father has been a man who brings elegance, glamour, and creativity to all of his pursuits. On the occasion of his retirement from Loral I wanted to memorialize his success and felt the best way to do that was through a book of pictures. If anyone could look up in the sky and see a vision of opportunities, it would be my father. So, I named the book *Throwing Dreams into Space: BLS and Loral*. It captured my image of my father."

—FRANCESCA SCHWARTZ

"The first thing I think of about Grandpa is his laugh: the way his mouth sneaks into a smile—his eyes engage and twinkle, effortlessly delighted. I've always loved when I could make him laugh.

I think of my grandpa as very gentle. He taught me how to play backgammon when I was about seven. I got the impression that there was no place he'd rather be. I suppose that speaks to his presence. I didn't understand that until recently—the importance of being present, both mentally and physically. I think my grandpa is a perfect example of that.

All of his employees that I have ever known have told me what a wonderful grandfather I have, and how great he is to work for. Even when I was a little girl I knew my grandpa was someone respected, revered, and even feared by some people. But, like Grandma, he's a deeply moral person with a tremendous sense of ethics and integrity, and he wants his businesses and his life to operate in a certain way. Ultimately he is a gentle and joyful man, even when things don't live up to his expectations. He understands better than anyone I know how to live in the moment, to be present in the present. I know he faced many challenges, but I don't think he ever really had any real failures in his career, because he always tried his best."

—JESSIE PADDOCK

"August sunshine, top down, Grandpa at the wheel. Barbra Streisand's rendition of 'Memories' blasting. This, especially if coupled with an acoustic encore of 'Anything Goes' and chocolate ice cream, is summertime heaven and among my favorite memories of my grandfather. In addition to his being my Cole Porter ambassador, he is also my partner in what has always been a very important thing for him and me. Backgammon.

Grandpa has taught every grandchild in the family to play, but I may be the most backgammon obsessed of us all. Upon finally making my move, I would often hear him say something like, 'You sure you want to do that?' which would send my little head into a tailspin. Rarely—in fact, I can't remember a single time—did he tell me what to do. Instead, he taught me how to look. And in doing so, I learned that the answer is often not in what you find out but in how you ask.

Gradually my wins would come about without any advice from my seasoned opponent ('play the position, do not let it play you,' I can hear him say), and I would learn the satisfaction of winning.

A certain degree of luck is imperative, but as my grandfather has taught me again and again, good luck is useless without the ability to know how to use it. And, in a sense, what I have come to realize is this counsel is ultimately an important guide to perspective in life: choosing optimism, even if the choice defies immediate sense. Because change happens every moment. And when the wind is in your favor, it is best you are ready with kite in hand. I have my grandfather to thank for reminding me to keep that kite in my back pocket. That and, of course, for showing me *The Maltese Falcon*."

—ALLIE PADDOCK

"Whenever I think about my grandfather, the sound of dice crashing together inevitably consumes my mind. From an early age, I have played my grandfather's favorite pastime, backgammon (taught by him of course), and through this game, I have learned so much about him. During play, his stern face creates a barrier between us, rightfully so as I am his opponent. His poker face is like no other. Yet, when I was just a novice to the game, before I would pull the trigger on a thoughtless move, my grandfather would let out a high-pitched 'OOP' noise. At first this noise startled me, as I would look up and only see his poker face blankly staring back at me. If I were to try the move again, he would utter the same sound. As I came to learn, this little yelp notified me about my carelessness and urged me to reconsider my move. Even when I was seven, my grandfather would never spoon-feed me the answers; rather, he made me search for them. But more important, this strange and hilarious noise opened the door to the world that is the playful Bernard Schwartz. Although he is a vital mentor in my life, I will always think of my grandfather as a high-spirited comic."

—NICHOLAS JACOBSON

"No one will ever have to justify my grandpa's greatness for me. I see it in the way he effortlessly captivates people with his words and his capacity to inspire those around him to strive for their own personal significance. I have seen his influence act as a guide for various members of my family and now I see it within myself. His presence offers a new lesson every time. I am constantly observing his work ethic and sensibility, incorporating certain traits into my identity. Throughout the years, I have felt his presence and experienced his influence, paving the way for my own significance."

—TESS JACOBSON

Contents

Preface   *xiii*

Part I: Outside the Box   1
Chapter 1: The $13-Billion Lunch   *3*
Chapter 2: Brooklyn Beginnings   *11*
Chapter 3: Moving Up, Taking Off   *21*

Part II: Let's Get Caught Trying   29
Chapter 4: Entry Level   *31*
Chapter 5: Full Partner   *41*
Chapter 6: New Opportunities   *49*
Chapter 7: Moving Upstairs   *61*
Chapter 8: A Near Miss   *73*
Chapter 9: Buying Loral   *81*

Part III: Not in the Conventional Way   93
Chapter 10: Running "My" Company   *95*
Chapter 11: Early Hurdles   *105*
Chapter 12: Problem-Solving   *117*
Chapter 13: Good News . . . and Better News   *133*
Chapter 14: Mickey Mouse and Good Management   *145*
Chapter 15: A Good Man   *159*
Chapter 16: Exceptional Growth in the 1980s   *167*
Chapter 17: Operation Ill Wind   *181*

Part IV: Choices and Decisions   189
Chapter 18: China Opening   *191*
Chapter 19: Satellites, Continued Growth, and Profitability   *201*
Chapter 20: Tough Questions and Short Answers   *209*
Chapter 21: The Win-Win-Win and Launching Globalstar   *217*

Chapter 22: The Chinese Contract and Its Aftermath   *231*

Chapter 23: Selling the Defense Business and
  Rewarding Shareholders   *239*

Chapter 24: A Day No One Can Ever Forget   *249*

Chapter 25: A New Chapter   *253*

Part V: Creating Jobs and Sharing the Wealth   265

Chapter 26: Bill Clinton and Infrastructure   *267*

Chapter 27: Giving Back   *285*

Chapter 28: A Warning . . . and a Challenge   *293*

Acknowledgments   305

Index   309

About the Author   317

Preface

You hold in your hands the autobiography of a lucky man.

The son of an occasionally prosperous Brooklyn sign maker, I have had the privilege of dining in the private quarters of the White House with the president and his wife. I have talked for long, late hours with political leaders in Europe, the Middle East, and the United States. I have sipped scotch and sake with some of the great business minds in modern Asia, Europe, and America. When you have that much good fortune, you can't help but learn a few things, and if you don't drink too much scotch and sake, you might even remember them.

We had a little inside joke at Loral, the company I ran for many years. The joke usually came up whenever the top management team gathered to discuss some critical issue. At these meetings, I would listen, ask questions, and choose a course of action—then we would move on. That's how we did things—no committees, no focus groups, no management by consensus.

Every so often, though, a team member might continue arguing the point, hoping to change my decision. I would smile sweetly, lean in the direction of the speaker, gently pat his or her arm, sigh deeply, and say, "Just say yes."

The line always got a laugh, but I wasn't kidding. As much as I appreciate passion, wisdom, and lively debate—and as seriously as I considered my colleagues' opinions in arriving at my decision—I wanted it understood that once I'd heard all the arguments pro and con and had made the decision, it was time to move forward. It was time to just say yes.

If I have more than a modicum of self-confidence it's because I base my judgments on certain values and principles that, over the decades, have served me well. I have a philosophy and I am decisive, each an important ingredient for success.

What is this philosophy?

It comes down to three elements I learned about from my father while I was still a young boy: hard work, a clear vision of what the entrepreneur wants to accomplish, and . . . luck. My thinking got refined, altered, and edited over the years, but at bottom it is very much a product of the extraordinary time and place in which I came up: Brooklyn—Bensonhurst, to be precise—of the 1930s and '40s. This was during the Great Depression, when disillusionment was always an option for many people, and yet I couldn't help noticing that more people chose hope. Despite widespread deprivation—perhaps *because* we couldn't avoid seeing the sad spectacle of breadlines, street-corner apple sellers, and men putting on a shirt and tie every day and pretending they had a job—a spirit of optimism prevailed. Millions of average citizens like my family pulled together against common enemies and toward common goals.

All the while, America, in the form of the federal government, was creating opportunities and nurturing us. It sounds odd today, doesn't it, to think of Washington as a font of wisdom and blessings? Not then. In my home and in many others, Franklin Roosevelt's New Deal was something like a religion.

When the Depression was over and World War II ended, the doors swung open on the American Dream—maybe not with one big whoosh, but steadily. My generation walked in and benefited from a new age of opportunity. Thanks to an improving economy and the GI Bill, which made it possible for working-class veterans like me to go to college, we felt as if anything was possible as long as we were willing to work hard and help each other. Success was out there for the having . . . if we just said yes.

Since then, this nation has never stopped changing. Most of that change has been for the better, but unfortunately in some ways we have regressed. I'm not one for nostalgia; as I see it, the question is not "how can we recapture the old days?" but rather "how can we keep improving what *has* gotten better (equality across race and gender lines, for example) while restoring some of the ideals that have all but disappeared?" Can we renew our country in the physical sense, hiring our unemployed millions to rebuild badly needed highways, tunnels, and bridges? Can we rekindle hope? Can we return to a society based on mutual trust and caring and a business environment based on human relationships, as opposed to the soulless torrent of computerized transactions that helped create the most recent financial crises?

I am by nature an optimist with an abiding faith in America's ability for growth and improvement, and I think we can. So with this book I'd like in some small way to contribute to the national conversation. I know that it is possible to run a multibillion-dollar corporation where handshakes are as dependable as contracts, because I did it for thirty-four years at Loral. We called our value system the "Loral culture," and that meant thinking in terms of relationships, not transactions. It meant being responsible, ethical, and fair—to our customers, our suppliers, our shareholders, our employees, our bankers, and ourselves. Profit was not a dirty word, but profit was always the end result of superior performance.

But in the years since I ran Loral, I've noticed a change in the way business is done—from a relational orientation to a transactional one—and that fundamental shift motivated me to write this book. Rather than criticizing others, however, I plan to tell my story, describing the approaches to life and business that have worked consistently well for me.

If you're seeking a ten-point system on how to become a billionaire, you've picked up the wrong book. But if you're interested in the kind of lessons you can learn by looking around at what's important to success and what's not, the way we did in Bensonhurst . . . of those I do have a few.

PART I

Outside the Box

"Bernard is not like a lot of self-made men. He doesn't think that just because he has money he knows everything. At the same time, he's very smart, and there are things about which he feels very strongly. You don't get conventional political or corporate thinking from Bernard. You don't get the party line or CEO talking points. He says what he thinks, and what he feels. Most of the time that winds up defining him as a Democrat, but not always, and if he's outside the box with a certain opinion he doesn't worry about that. Bernard would rather be right than be right in step with everyone else."

—RAHM EMANUEL, MAYOR OF CHICAGO

—————— ⧓ ——————

CHAPTER 1

The $13-Billion Lunch

To make the deal of a lifetime, you don't always need the meal of a lifetime.

On the day I'm talking about, lunch came to something like $20; my friend and I were seated in a run-of-the-mill diner in Virginia. Norman Augustine—the head of Lockheed Martin, the world's largest defense contractor—and I had met to discuss a deal in which Lockheed could acquire the greater part of my company, Loral. In the pages ahead, I'll relate the full story of exactly how I wound up at that diner with Norman. But what we did together that day over the course of two hours or so might be called the ultimate no-frills negotiation.

I wasn't desperate to sell and hadn't shopped the company around. I just felt it was time, for the sake of the shareholders, to monetize the success of Loral. I also believed that Lockheed, under a visionary person like Norm, was the kind of place that understood Loral's true value. So I called Norm. We both knew why we were there, and things never got tense. First, we chatted about the basic parameters of the deal; I intended to sell Lockheed everything except the satellite technology part of the business. After a while, I took an envelope from my inside suit-jacket pocket and wrote down the financial fundamentals, including the proposed selling price for Loral's defense business: $9.4 billion. Combined with the portions I intended to keep, that put the market value of Loral at $13 billion. I picked up the envelope, turned it around, and showed it to Norm. Sometimes you don't need PowerPoint.

As unglamorous as I've made it sound, this was hardly just another transaction. Loral for me represented a singular achievement in a life spent buying and running companies with the goal of adding to their value (as opposed to stripping out and selling off the assets in the manner of private equity investors). Loral reflected my philosophy and personality, especially my belief that capitalism can be a kind of art form—a beautiful thing that benefits *everyone* involved: rank-and-file employees, customers, executives, suppliers, and stockholders. Employing that philosophy, I had taken Loral from the brink of bankruptcy in 1972 to immense success by that day in 1996 when Norm and I sat across the table from each other in the diner.

When I took over Loral, I already knew something about making deals and money, but except for what turned up in my due diligence, I didn't know anything about the company's main business: high-tech electronic communication and defense systems for military aircraft. I also had zero experience with Loral's most important customer, the Pentagon. On top of that, as a New Yorker, an outspoken Democrat, and a man named Bernard Schwartz, I was—how should I put this?—not your typical member of the military-industrial complex.

But so what? I wasn't going to let any of those things get in the way. The economist John Maynard Keynes once wrote that "exuberant inexperience" was a key ingredient in success, and I certainly had plenty of *that*. Besides, where I grew up you had to be a quick study to make a living. You had to know how to reinvent yourself.

In retrospect I can see it was to my advantage that I was not steeped in the conventional wisdom, or even the basic facts, of the defense business. To quote the great Victorian novelist Samuel Butler, a little knowledge can be a dangerous thing. If I had been a hard-bitten veteran of the defense industry, I probably would have taken one look at Loral as it was in 1972 and run in the other direction. Imagine the opportunities, financial and otherwise, I would have missed!

I'll go into the details later, but for now, suffice it to say that when my best friend, Bob Hodes, asked me in 1971 if I'd take a quick look at a struggling company that he was involved with, I soon learned that the company—Loral—was doing miserably. Started in 1948 by an engineer named William Lorenz and an accountant named Leon Alpert (the *Lor* and *al* in Loral), the company was bleeding red ink. The stock was selling for around $2 a share, down from about $50 in palmier days. The New York Stock Exchange was threatening to delist the company, and banks were getting ready to cut off its credit.

Loral's main problem was lack of vision. By that time Lorenz had more or less checked out of the business, and the people left in charge, including Alpert, had built the company into a kind of crazy-quilt conglomerate: They had acquired a company that made toy soldiers, a wire company, a packaging company, and a few other unrelated firms. Mind you, the Vietnam War was raging at this time, and while that was horrible for America in so many ways, you might have thought it would at least be good for Loral's bottom line. If an established defense contractor can't profit during an extended period of armed conflict, when *can* it do well?

And yet, there were things about Loral that intrigued me. Furthermore, from a professional standpoint, the timing was right for me too. In 1971 I was president of Reliance Group and working with its CEO, Saul Steinberg. We had been very successful with a computer-leasing business and an insurance business among other enterprises. But I had reached a kind of comfort zone that I found unfamiliar and, well, uncomfortable. I needed a fresh challenge, a new chance to be creative—I needed a company I could run myself.

So I made what turned out to be the single best move of my professional career. On February 18, 1972, Loral announced that both of its founders were retiring and that I was taking over as chairman and CEO. I remember my friend Gershon Kekst, the head of one of the nation's top financial public relations firms, saying, "When Bernard Schwartz jumps into something, he doesn't do it with both feet, he does it with eight feet!" I'm not the octopus that Gershon apparently thinks I am, but it was true that transforming Loral into a profitable company became my sole professional focus.

Where did I get the courage, or maybe it was just the nerve, to think I could take a company that was headed so rapidly in the wrong direction—a company in an area in which I had no expertise—and turn it completely around? My hopes and plans for Loral came from something I saw when I assessed the situation in light of my previous experience as a businessman: hidden value. The business community in general looked askance at defense companies, and conglomerates that had divisions in that sector undervalued those divisions and considered them a drag on their stock price. In 1971 Wall Street saw high-tech electronics companies that were similar to but even much more successful than Loral as troublesome investments, and few analysts covered the industry. Despite all of the uncontrollable factors and cycles that made the defense industry such a challenge, when I looked at the same sector I saw a lot of undervalued companies that could be acquired at relatively low prices and then combined in a way that would build on their success and release their previously untapped synergies.

In other words, this is not the tale of the acquisitive businessman that you've heard a thousand times before. I wasn't one of those vultures that swoop in on ailing companies, firing most of the employees and selling off the assets. Such acquirers set a short-term sellout strategy, eliminating long-terms plans like R&D to realize huge returns on their investments. But my plan was about growth and empowerment: making the company profitable and less susceptible to business cycles and unpredictable events and putting into effect cross-synergies that could increase efficiencies and lead to dramatic growth even at a time when defense spending was likely to start declining.

I had my own very particular ideas about running a company and creating the right atmosphere. As determined as I was to turn Loral around financially, I was equally determined that it would reflect my philosophy and values—and it did. After a while people inside and outside of the company started talking about the "Loral culture." In the end it didn't just change Loral; it changed the entire defense industry and sent out ripples far beyond. The swift and enduring success of the Loral approach was a beautiful thing to behold, especially if you were a shareholder. Indeed, it would turn out to be the single most gratifying aspect of my professional experience.

The Loral culture meant a lot of things, but one key was keeping the management team small. At our height, when we were competing successfully with and subcontracting for industry giants such as Lockheed, Hughes, McDonnell Douglas, Boeing, ITT, IBM, and Northrop, we maintained a core leadership group of only about eight people— tiny in comparison with our rivals. But communication was free-form and constant. We had what I liked to call a "bias toward action." The company started growing in 1972, and it was still going strong when I sold the defense business to Lockheed in 1996. We had put together ninety-six consecutive quarters of growth, the second-longest streak in American corporate history, topped only by Jack Welch in a run at General Electric. From just over $32 million, sales from continuing operations grew to $5.5 billion. Our annual net income rose from negative $2.7 million to $288 million, and our net worth increased from $14.4 million to $1.7 billion. The stock split three times in the interim, we instituted an annual dividend, and the average price, adjusted for stock splits, rose from about $0.75 to more than $45 a share. Instead of thirteen hundred employees, we had nearly thirty-eight thousand. A $100 investment in Loral, made when I took over, would have been worth $17,799 in 1995.

For all those reasons and a few others, the deal I outlined on the back of that envelope and showed to Norm Augustine, although it wouldn't be signed and announced to the public for a few months, would be seen as excellent news for shareholders. At the same time, it was also a fair price for Lockheed to pay for a company that had become a major player in the defense industry. In fact, after the lawyers and other executives spent a couple of months screwing down the details, the number didn't change.

The sale of our defense businesses for more than $9 billion in cash was a crowning achievement in the history of Loral. Standard procedure for a CEO would have been to take the money and use it to invest in another venture, and it would have been perfectly legitimate to do so. But the stockholders, I realized, deserved to be rewarded. They had put their trust and their money in a very special company that had enjoyed an extraordinary run, and I wanted to acknowledge that.

So when the deal was announced on January 8, 1996, I did something unprecedented: I declared a special distribution of $38 per share, or $7 billion, in cash to the stockholders. In addition, for every Loral share they owned, they received one share—valued at $13.13 per share, or an aggregate $2.4 billion—in Loral Space & Communications, a new, smaller company that would concentrate on designing and manufacturing communications satellites and operating a satellite constellation for commercial and government purposes.

And I wanted to do one more thing.

Because of the sale, some Loral employees would soon be working for Lockheed, but for others the next step was less clear because of the possibility of redundancies. For them the future was uncertain. Norm had readily agreed with me that every effort would be taken to ensure that no one would lose a job, and I knew I could trust him to do his best.

Still, unexpected things happen in large-scale deals like ours. In order to provide some tangible comfort to those at risk, I set up an $18 million fund from my own personal resources for distribution to about forty of Loral's most vulnerable employees, top to bottom, with some top executives getting a million or more, and some secretaries getting as much as $100,000. It was my own money I was giving away, but I was happier when it became theirs. Why? Because for me the people have always been the most important part of any transaction.

Not long after the sale to Lockheed was announced, my wife, Irene, and I were in Paris, having lunch at one of our favorite cafés. Halfway through the meal, our waiter appeared with a beautiful bottle of white burgundy: a gift, he explained, from a fellow diner who had been a Loral stockholder and wanted to say thank you. That would turn out to be the first of quite a few bottles and desserts (my addiction to chocolate is well known) sent our way by happy investors over the years at restaurants around the world. I have also received many letters and other expressions of thanks from former or current Loral employees. They are part of my extended family and, truth be told, as much as I appreciate the fancy wine and sweets, I treasure their cards and snapshots even more. I gain deep satisfaction from knowing that the lunch Norm and I shared that day in Virginia resulted in good things for the people associated with this company that afforded me the deepest professional satisfaction of my career.

But there is much more to tell, of course, about how all this came about. As Wordsworth famously said, "The child is father of the man," and in order to understand my approach to finance, to business, or to anything else, it would be helpful to learn about the people, events, and circumstances that exerted the earliest, pivotal influences on my life. To tell that part of the story, I need to invite you to follow me back to Bensonhurst, in Brooklyn, during the years leading up to World War II.

CHAPTER 2

Brooklyn Beginnings

When I conjure up my childhood, I see myself in many different rooms. That's not because we lived in a large, rambling house or because my memory is shaky; it's because we moved around a lot.

In those days, Brooklyn landlords would paint an apartment for anyone who signed a two-year lease, and they would give a new tenant a concession ranging from two to six weeks on the rent for a three-year lease, depending on market conditions. In order to take advantage of those incentives, my five-person family would move every two to three years to an almost identical three-bedroom apartment with living room, dining room, and porch in a semidetached house. We always lived on the ground floor and the landlord lived on the second, just a few steps up the stairs. The arrangement made it clear to me early on that we live in a society built on relationships.

The Bensonhurst neighborhood of Brooklyn was a middle-class residential area with its own local shopping districts on Twentieth Avenue and on Eighty-Sixth Street. There were several six-story apartment houses, but the principal housing units were semidetached seven-room apartments, with two-car garages in the back of the house.

The only problem with our moving so much was that moving wasn't free. I remember how an appraiser would come to our place to make an estimate of what it would cost to move all our worldly goods, except for the piano. A piano was always $25 extra: no small consideration. We had one, and we hauled it around with us.

That should tell you something about the Schwartzes. On one hand, we felt it necessary to move often in order to save a little money. On the other, we felt the investment in our piano was an important part of our lifestyle. Even in the rough years, we never got rid of our old upright.

Looking back, I can't remember too many just plain old times in our household. We were either up or down, fat or lean. We had years when we went to Monticello, New York, in the summer and Lakewood, New Jersey, in the winter. Riding through the silent, snow-covered streets of Atlantic City in a one-horse open sleigh, complete with jingle bells, is something I'll never forget. But there were also years when we stuck to Coney Island. We had periods when my father drove a luxurious dark green Nash like you saw in the gangster movies and times when he had to trade it in for a plebian Plymouth.

My father, Harry Schwartz, was a sign maker by trade, self-employed. He started the business after working for Sheffield Farms, driving a horse-drawn milk wagon. As a sign maker he was mostly at the mercy of the cycles affecting the real-estate trade. With his stamping machines he made plastic signs that said things like "For Sale," "All Visitors Must Be Announced," "Deliveries to the Rear," and "No Soliciting," usually in his own neighborhood shop. He had as many as seven or eight employees, salespeople mostly, whom he tried to keep on the payroll in good periods and bad. Often, at the end of the week, the employees took home more money than he did.

He had good runs, too, and in the end, it amounted to a middle-class lifestyle for the Schwartz family. But while it was happening, Harry Schwartz didn't know how the story would turn out, so I imagine that, being the traditional father and provider, he must at times have felt a lot of pressure.

Once, for a period of two years or so, my mother, Hannah, had to get a job. That was no doubt an assault on my father's pride as well as a hardship for her. I don't remember what her job was, but I remember her leaving every morning to catch the subway. This was at the depths of the Depression, and everyone was doing what they could to survive. My brother Jules—who was ten years older than me and five years older than Harold, my middle brother—had to drop out of high school so he could get a job and help support the family. When Harold was old enough, he found part-time work, also contributing to the household. Stand-up guys, no doubt about it; good sons, *mensches*. Still, that was what was expected of them back then. Like the piano that always cost $25 to move, my brothers' sacrifice for the family was part of an unwritten Brooklyn code.

It may not have been a normal time, but my brothers and I were normal kids. When I wasn't in school, I was out in the street playing stickball or stoop ball, or I was roller-skating down an exit ramp of the still-unfinished Belt Parkway, my skate key flapping on a cord around my neck. I felt indestructible. I lived in a safe and secure world; I could go anywhere in the neighborhood without fear. Only once, when I was about fifteen, did I feel physically threatened. I had wandered into the Bay Ridge section for some reason, and I found myself suddenly surrounded by three older guys who pushed me around and made all the clichéd anti-Semitic put-downs. I stood my ground, and it didn't amount to much.

At home, meanwhile, it was understood in the family that whatever happened, "Bob"—that was me—would stay in school and someday go to college. In other words, Jules and Harold were expected to contribute to the household, which included my continuing my education. This was never spoken of as a sacrifice; it was part of what family members did for one another.

"Bob" is what everyone called me at home practically from the day I was born in our apartment of the moment, located on Nineteenth Avenue and Seventy-Sixth Street. (After having Jules in a hospital, my mother decided she didn't like such unfriendly places.) I had a girl cousin about three years older than I was who couldn't pronounce "Bernard"; it came out sounding something like "Bob." Everyone found this amusing, and it stuck. When I went to PS 86 for the first time, the teacher called out "Bernard Schwartz" and I didn't respond. Who was that? My name was Bob. Today almost everyone calls me either Bernard or Bob. Anyone who refers to me as "Bernie"—including some politicians—doesn't know me very well.

During those Bensonhurst days, being protected by the family wasn't the same thing as being given a free pass. I wasn't expected to contribute to the household, but I did occasionally take after-school and summer jobs so I could buy my own egg creams and pay my own way into movies and ball games. For a while I delivered contracts to various courthouses around the city for a lawyer in downtown Brooklyn (I did my homework on the subway), and later I ran a mimeograph machine for a man who served the legal trade. But the best job I ever had as a kid was being a delivery boy for a Schrafft's restaurant in the Garment District on West Thirty-Seventh Street in Manhattan.

That job was blissful for two reasons: First, Schrafft's success was built largely on its genuinely first-rate chocolate ice cream; second, I made a lot of deliveries at showrooms on Seventh Avenue that were often filled with professional female models. Frequently the girls were running around in nothing but their slips—hot stuff! They would taunt me: "Here's Bobby! Oh, Bobby!" Then they would giggle wickedly when I blushed. Schrafft's even provided a free lunch with this dream job, but the menu was extremely limited—no dessert included! Since the models weren't great tippers—to put it mildly—I wound up spending more on chocolate ice cream than I was making, so I had to quit. Ah, well, I have my memories.

The Schwartz family convened around the dining room table at the end of each workday and compared notes as we ate dinner. We would argue often, challenging one another's opinions about issues large and mundane. But the discussions were not always arguments; we talked about everything from the movies and politics to the day's events. Our discourse flowed from funny to serious. On Friday nights when he had a date, Jules would come to dinner with his hair carefully combed, wearing a shirt, tie, shoes, and socks . . . but no pants, because he didn't want to spoil the crease before going out for the evening. He would sit at the table and argue in his underwear.

All of us would participate, though my mother would often be going in and out of the kitchen carrying large platters of roast beef and potatoes, hard-boiled eggs, bread and butter, apple pie and, of course, chocolate ice cream. She performed miracles with simple ingredients, a great cook who learned from my grandmother. The bill of fare varied between basic American and German, the kind of diet that is considered a killer today. But despite the meat, potatoes, and chocolate diet, and despite my father's smoking two packs of cigarettes each day for his whole adult life, my parents and my brothers lived well into their eighties. Ask any Schwartz and they'll tell you that genes count.

Alone among us, my mother was openly conscious of doing things the American way, and with good reason: She was the only one of us who wasn't born here. Hannah Foreman started life in 1894 in rural eastern Poland. Her mother died in childbirth, and not long afterward her father left her in the care of her grandmother, making his way to this country to start a new life. When Hannah was eight years old he sent for her. Her grandmother put her on a train that took her across Europe to a big boat that took her across the Atlantic to New York, where she came to live with her father, whom she did not know.

Can you imagine what that must have been like for a little kid? She worked hard at assimilating and quickly learned to speak the language, with only a trace of the Old World in her *v*'s and *w*'s. She grew up strong, found a husband (probably at a dance on the Lower East Side; my parents never told us the story), and raised a family. My mother's one big regret was that she never finished high school; she was a girl and her education was not considered as important as her making a bit of money to support the family. Of course, my mother's was one of *millions* of similar stories that unfolded during the great immigration wave. But her experience had to be more challenging than that of many others, having made the long journey alone at such a young age, leaving behind everybody she knew, and having no understanding of the language of her new homeland.

My father was born in New York in 1888, but his family on his mother's side hailed from the American South. Matilda Manheimer was born in Memphis, Tennessee, during the latter part of the Civil War, the daughter of a prosperous merchant who came to the United States from Germany. Somehow she made it to New York and met and married Benjamin Schwartz, a German immigrant who was a junior functionary, probably what was known as a ward captain, for Tammany Hall, the Manhattan-based Democratic political machine. One of my grandfather's jobs was to stand on the street and make speeches promoting various candidates (and no doubt denouncing others), even in the dead of winter. One year, when my father was about fourteen years old, Benjamin, perhaps after making a speech on a street corner for the local Democratic candidate, caught pneumonia and died. After that, in recognition of my grandfather's loyal service, every year at Thanksgiving the Democratic Party sent his wife Matilda a turkey, and every Christmas she received a bag of coal.

Those annual gestures made a deep impression on the family. They showed that the Democrats stood for compassion, something my father, his mother, and his three sisters desperately needed with the family's breadwinner suddenly gone. Years later, when he had a wife and children of his own, my father's ardor for the bedrock ideals of the party remained palpable.

Religion was another topic we all felt pretty much the same about. My brothers and I had all been bar-mitzvahed and we considered ourselves Reform Jews. But apart from trips with my mother to synagogue on the high holidays, we were not very observant. Occasionally my father would remind us that he technically had the rights and privileges of a *kohen*, which in Judaism is a hereditary class of priests descended from Moses's brother Aaron. (Harry was a *kohen* because Benjamin Schwartz had been one.) This usually came up when an acquaintance or a distant relative passed away and my father was trying to avoid the ensuing social obligations. Because of the need for ritual cleanliness, a *kohen* is not allowed to enter cemeteries, and some Jewish scholars interpret the law to mean that even funerals are off-limits. "Ah, if only I wasn't a *kohen!*" he'd say, feigning regret at having to skip a service.

By the time my own children were growing up, my wife and I had developed stronger ties to our religion and our Jewish culture. This is true of my brothers' families as well. We became members of our neighborhood synagogue, attending services more often than just the high holidays. My daughters Karen and Fran and their children are also members of their synagogues and continue their involvement. We are proud of our Jewish heritage.

More than most people, Harry Schwartz was a study in contradictions. Short, skinny, but very strong, he was a man of surprising physical grace. Before he married my mother, he played semi-pro baseball for the Brooklyn Bushwicks, a highly regarded independent team known for its multiethnic lineup (good for the box office) and a dazzling array of drop-in guest stars (even better). The Bushwicks didn't really have a schedule; they played minor league and Negro League teams that barnstormed through town. I have a vintage picture in my office of my father wearing his Bushwicks cap, with its big blue *B*.

Years after he hung up his spikes, he would sometimes take my brothers and me to the local field and hit baseballs to us, and when he did this, you could see he was on another level from the other neighborhood dads. His swing was fluid, and he could hit the ball precisely to whatever spot on the field he wanted to, calling out the location beforehand, to our amazement. Harold and Jules were both strong all-around players; I was tall and rangy but what sportswriters of the day might have summed up as "good field, no hit." I never could have made the Bushwicks.

While I never saw my father play organized baseball, I did watch him compete in ballroom roller-skating, which was what it sounds like: fox-trotting, waltzing, and Peabodying on wooden-wheeled, indoor skates. When you consider that the rinks in those days were made of the same hard, highly polished wood as the wheels, you can perhaps begin to see how challenging ballroom roller-skating could be. One false step and you went from being Fred Astaire to Buster Keaton, lying in a heap by the sideboards. My mother and brothers and I would all go root for my father on Tuesday and Thursday evenings as he competed with a partner he found at the Rollerdrome. While I never reached the proficiency of my father or Harold at Rollerdrome dance skating, I was pretty good on my wooden wheels on the highly polished floor. I was a terror on steel-wheeled skates on the asphalt streets, racing and playing hockey: not good for the shins but inseparable from the neighborhood culture.

My father also had a real affinity for music. We'd go to see a movie like *Top Hat* or *42nd Street* at the Benson or Oriental theater, and as soon as we got home, he'd plop down in front of the piano and start plunking around with one or two fingers until, within twenty minutes or so, he could play the whole score of the film—and sing most of it too!

Heredity is a mysterious thing, isn't it? My brothers and I came from the same gene pool and had the same upbringing, but we turned out to be three distinct variations on a theme. Harold was the most flamboyant. If you could picture him as I can, striding confidently around the house in a pair of jodhpurs after a morning of horseback riding in Prospect Park, you would know exactly what I mean. He was a real risk taker in life.

Jules, in contrast, was decidedly risk averse. In later years, when we were playing the market together, I'd see one of our stocks going bad and I'd say, "Let's get out of XYZ," and he would say, "Yeah, I'll take care of it." But then two weeks later I'd say, "Jules, we're still in XYZ—what the heck's going on?" and he would respond, kind of sheepishly, "Bob, I don't want to take the loss." Thinking like that has always rankled me. One thing I've learned is that if you make an investment and it turns out to be bad, there is no use thinking twice about it: move on.

In terms of risk aversion, I fall squarely between Harold and Jules. Jules was shaped by a direct engagement in the Depression, which added risk aversion to his philosophy. And I'm sure Harold was affected by his experiences as a prisoner of war. At the young age of twenty-four, he survived the pressures of his responsibilities for other air force crewmen and his isolation in the hellish environment of prison camps through the self-determination and spirit of success and hope that shaped his attitudes forever. He was much more adventurous and flamboyant than either Jules or I.

Around the time I was thirteen, things started to change in our household. After all, it was 1939; a world war was looming. Jules met his future wife, Sylvia, moved out, and in due course they married and had a daughter, Barbara. Being a father and the sole support of his family—he worked for GE, a major defense contractor at the time—made him ineligible for the draft. Harold, who turned eighteen that year, enlisted in the US Army Air Corps and shipped out to basic training in Miami Beach. I can't say my parents were overjoyed by the prospect of his going off to war, but my mother proudly hung a blue star in our front window, showing she had a son in the service. Back then, Bensonhurst fairly shone because of these "blue-star moms."

And me? As the gears engaged in the war machine, I was dealing with slightly less significant worries, like the time I got called to the principal's office.

CHAPTER 3

Moving Up, Taking Off

My anxiety was short-lived.

As soon as I got to the principal's office and saw the three other boys who had been summoned there, I knew I wasn't in trouble; they were the smartest kids at PS 86.

"Have you ever heard of Townsend Harris?" said the principal.

A couple of the others may have nodded, but not me. In the 1840s, the New York merchant Townsend Harris founded the Free Academy, which later became the City College of New York; during the Abraham Lincoln administration, Harris also served as America's first ambassador to Japan. But when I was in the eighth grade, I had no idea who Harris was or that there was an exclusive public high school in Manhattan bearing his name. "It's got a special admissions test, very tough," he explained. "But we always manage to send a couple of boys there, and I'm proud of our record. I want you four to take the test and to represent our school well."

I was anxious about being included in that group, although I knew the math part of the exam would probably be a snap. I was always good with numbers, though at that stage probably not as sharp as my brothers. (When I went into the service, I remember Jules saying to me, "Bob, when the big boys sit down to play cards, go to the library.")

Anyway, I took the entrance exam and, as it turned out, I alone among the four kids from PS 86 scored high enough to get accepted. What an honor! But the Schwartz family had a big decision to make. On the one hand, Townsend Harris had a reputation as a superior school with small classes and a first-rate faculty; you did the usual four years' worth of work in three years and got a diploma that would impress any employer or college. On the other hand, it meant $6 a month in subway fare to and from Manhattan and eating lunch out every day, probably another $5 weekly. Twenty-six dollars was the kind of money that could make my parents stop and think in those days; and they did, but fortunately not for more than a few moments. "Don't worry, Bobby," my father said. "You're going."

My new school took up four floors (plus gymnasium) in a skyscraper at Twenty-Third Street and Lexington Avenue, in the same building as City College. At PS 86 I had been one of the brighter kids. But at Townsend Harris *everyone* was a bright kid, and for those who wanted to stand out, the competition was fierce.

I wanted to stand out, so I worked harder than I ever had before, and after a period of adjustment I did okay. Among many other things, my experience there taught me I was capable of succeeding on an elite level. If I had ever lacked confidence before I graduated from Townsend Harris, I never lacked it again, and that's really saying something. Confidence is not just another attribute; it's the quality that unlocks your intelligence, your creativity, and your powers of persuasion. In business, confidence is absolutely essential to success.

After three years at Townsend Harris, my pre-law classes at Brooklyn College seemed easy, and with military service on the horizon, I got lackadaisical. At the end of my freshman year, I was looking at some pretty mediocre grades. Still, I just couldn't get myself to care very much. I was distracted by the war that was by now raging in Europe and the Pacific. Like a lot of my contemporaries, I knew that the war would interrupt my college education eventually, I just didn't know when. Finally, a couple of months into my sophomore year, with my brother Harold training as a radar officer on B-24s, I was swept up in the spirit of the times; I just had to do something for my country. So I went down to the recruiting station in the Borough Hall section of Brooklyn and signed up.

My mother—proudly, but no doubt with a lump in her throat—placed a second blue star in our window.

Like Harold, I joined the US Army Air Corps, and I was accepted into the air cadet program. First, though, there was basic training at Keesler Air Force Base in Biloxi, Mississippi.

Basic training for pilots is all about pushing beyond your self-defined limits, learning to deal with sometimes harsh authority figures, feeling alone and a little frightened—and doing all those things in a place probably farther from home than you've ever been before. As such, it no doubt helped toughen up us raw recruits for the life-and-death challenges that lay ahead. But other parts of my early army experience were equally challenging, such as seeing signs in restaurant windows in Biloxi that read "Niggers and Jews Not Welcome." Obviously, America still had a lot of work to do at home once we defeated the Germans and the Japanese.

Air cadet training was mostly at Smyrna Army Airfield, outside Nashville, Tennessee, and at an airfield in Stuttgart, Arkansas. This was—at the start, anyway—a darn good gig. Learning to fly was fascinating; we had a sense of purpose. And on Saturday nights we used our A pass to go into Nashville, a cosmopolitan city compared to Biloxi. All duded up in our officer's uniforms (minus insignias), we basked in the admiration of the civilians we met, especially the ones in pretty dresses. It was all very glamorous and exciting, especially for a kid like me who grew up building model planes out of balsa wood, reading about hero pilots like Eddie Rickenbacker and Charles Lindbergh, and dreaming of "conquering the sky."

But then one day in the summer of 1944, the progress of our group suddenly stalled. Word had come down from on high that the army needed to "inventory" pilots, navigators, and bombardiers so they wouldn't run out in case the war lasted longer than expected. Our training classes abruptly ceased, and we spent our days doing calisthenics and working on the infrastructure of the air base. Other cadets, not so lucky, were washed out and immediately transferred to combat units. Now I felt antsy and slightly foolish, strolling around Nashville in my officer's duds while guys like my brother Harold were putting their lives on the line in Europe and the South Pacific.

I didn't know how extreme things would get.

Harold was assigned to a base near London. A normal tour of duty for those flying B-24s was thirty-five missions, but because of their special status, Harold and his crew only needed twenty-five missions before their tour was done, and they could either re-up or move on to different duties. The radar-equipped crew flew the safest spot in the formation— up in front. But they never knew when they were going to fly because their presence was only required on overcast days when ground targets were not visible with the naked eye.

Often the crew would assemble at the airfield outside London just after dawn and receive instructions but then be told to return to the base, and the other planes in the formation would fly without them. In the summer of 1944, Europe experienced about three consecutive weeks of nothing but sunshine, and so it took Harold and his pals a long time to get to even sixteen missions—which is the point they were at when someone in the crew suggested they sneak into London for a little nocturnal recreation.

Technically, this wasn't allowed on the night before a scheduled mission, but they thought they'd be all right, even if the day came up cloudy, as long as they got back in time for reveille. Before they left, they made a pact to meet the deadline and not get one another in trouble. It was going to be a big night. Harold's best friend, Avery Kay, the navigator on his crew, had a date with an American showgirl who was performing at a London theater, and she had arranged a blind date for Harold.

When they got to London, though, Avery found out that a few days earlier his showgirl had been swept off her feet by Jimmy Roosevelt, who had the advantage of being the president's son, and she was going out with her new beau that night. Of course, this also scuttled Harold's date. But what could they do? Shrugging off the loss, the two friends had dinner in London and headed back to the base early.

The next morning, though, when it came time to assemble (beneath cloudy skies) for their daily mission, everyone else in the crew was AWOL. So much for their pact. When the eight missing flyers finally showed up, they were told that ten missions had been added to their tour of duty. Instead of being nine missions from fulfilling their quota, they were now at *nineteen*.

It was better than being court-martialed, but it was a significant punishment. Harold and Avery, who hadn't broken any rules, were given the option of either taking on a new posting and finishing out their tour or staying with their original crew and flying the extra missions. Harold didn't hesitate. Out of loyalty and a belief that his old crew was lucky, he chose to stick with his wayward pals. Avery was ultimately assigned to another crew.

One day in December 1944 I was summoned to the phone at Smyrna. It was Jules, calling to inform me that Harold's plane had been shot down over Belgium. On his thirty-fifth and final mission, during the Battle of the Bulge, Harold's plane was shot from the sky. Twenty-four hours earlier the area where the parachutists landed had belonged to the Allies, but that very day the Germans had reclaimed it. According to the telegram that had arrived at our family home in Bensonhurst, Harold's fate was unknown. Three parachutes had been seen in the sky immediately afterward, but no one knew if one of them had belonged to Harold.

Even if he'd survived the landing, Harold was now behind enemy lines.

Back in Brooklyn, my mother, quite naturally, was distraught. I received leave to go home and be with her for five days, and I remember that she kept insisting that Harold was alive, that she just *knew* it. The rest of us, though we didn't contradict her, suspected otherwise.

The war suddenly felt personal; I wanted to fight for my country *and* avenge my brother. As soon as I got back to Tennessee, I told my commanding officer, "I want to wash out of the air cadets. Just make me a gunner in the air corps and send me to Europe so I can get into action."

"I understand how you feel," the officer said. "But I can't help you out. The army has frozen you in this status in case we need pilots in the future. Trust me, this is all part of the grand plan to win the war. And also trust me when I tell you that you're doing your part."

As the poet John Milton said, "They also serve who only stand and wait."

Six months after the arrival of the telegram saying that Harold was missing in action, another was delivered saying that he had been found by the US Army and would soon be transported back home. I received another furlough and flew up to visit Harold at Halloran General Hospital on Staten Island, where he was recuperating from a leg wound and malnutrition. As I sat at his bedside over the course of several days, he told me things about his time as a German prisoner that he would never repeat again, even to his children.

Harold was the only member of his crew to survive. He had thrown away his dog tags as soon as he hit the ground, as soldiers are instructed to do. This was especially important in his case because World War II dog tags listed your religion, and if the Germans had found out he was Jewish, they might have executed him on the spot. Even so, he was put in what was called an interrogation pulpit and questioned ceaselessly, his wounds unattended. Never once did he say anything beyond his name, rank, and serial number. Of course, the name Harold Schwartz made them strongly suspect he was perhaps of German-Jewish ancestry, but later on, one German soldier said, "I don't think he can be Jewish. He's an officer, and a Jew would never be allowed to be an officer in the air corps." When I asked Harold why a Nazi would speak up for him like that, he smiled and said, "That guy was a guard, and he and I used to play cards for cigarettes that the Red Cross sent to prisoners. I would make sure he always beat me."

Harold was not tortured by the Nazis, but he was often harshly treated, and food was meager and of poor quality. On the other hand, because he was in the US Army Air Corps, he went to a special hospital where the Germans operated on his leg and probably saved it from amputation. His captors' treatment of him, on balance, was nothing short of bizarre.

Although it meant suffering extreme pain, Harold would defy doctors' orders and limp around when he was supposed to be resting from surgery. He was trying to inflame his injured leg so the Germans couldn't force-march him, along with other American captives, back to prison camps in the Fatherland, where POWs would be especially difficult for Allied troops to find. One time a German doctor told Harold in English, "Look, soldier, I know what you're doing. You may lose your leg if you keep this up—I am warning you." But the doctor didn't report him, and Harold kept hobbling. Ultimately, his scheme worked. He was in a German hospital when Patton's Third Army arrived one day in April 1945 and liberated him.

Sitting by Harold's bedside and listening to his story about life behind enemy lines, I realized something that has stayed with me all my life: When setbacks happen, you can't panic. Whatever your situation, you have to *expect* setbacks and even embrace them. They are part of living and not necessarily a sign that you are doing anything wrong.

When you run a business, you're basically a problem solver. Things constantly go wrong—and that's actually a good thing. Problems lead to solutions, which foster innovation and progress. Finding your way out of difficult situations is how you get your satisfaction and how you build your career.

Another truth I saw played out in Harold's life is that there is a crucial difference between a problem and a disaster. I define a disaster as something you simply cannot survive: the nuclear bomb of problems. Such things do happen, but when you think about it, they are relatively rare. The end of the world can occur only once, so everything else is *not* the end of the world and thus can be recovered from. The vast majority of problems fall into this category. By taking advantage of his situation in any way he could, Harold solved his problems, avoiding disaster.

Harold also showed me something about luck. Harold's luck was that he hit the ground alive. He ultimately made it back home because he was able to exploit that one bit of good fortune so wisely.

The America that Harold returned to was in some ways a fundamentally different place. During the Depression a lot of people had to get by on almost nothing but faith in a better future, but now—with hard work, vision, and luck—a young man like Harold could turn a little into a lot. When he was honorably discharged, he received the standard military severance of $750. He had a friend from Brooklyn named Harry Fishman who also had just received $750 in mustering-out pay. The two pooled their money, and with that $1,500 grubstake they went into business for themselves. Starting out as two guys who sold swizzle sticks and cocktail napkins to local bars and restaurants, they ended up millionaires running a Fortune 500 firm.

What can I tell you? Harold and Harry were excellent businessmen, and this was America in the late 1940s. Conditions were never more conducive to success.

PART II

Let's Get Caught Trying

"I've known and admired Bernard for more than twenty years. Every time we talk, I learn something new. Bernard is always focused on solutions. He doesn't just complain about a problem or hope someone else will fix it. He takes a stand and actually gets things done. He brings the breadth and depth of his practical business experience, and his unsurpassed record of success, to every project. Bernard is a true patriot. He loves America and is grateful for all this country has given him.

In my family we have an expression, 'Let's get caught trying.' Bernard subscribes to that same philosophy. And we're all better off because Bernard gets caught trying, doing, fixing, and solving."

—HILLARY RODHAM CLINTON

CHAPTER 4

Entry Level

Patience is not one of my virtues. When the war ended, I couldn't wait to get back home, go back to college, and then begin my career.

I was hardly the only one who felt that way. In the late 1940s, something was happening—in society, in the economy, in Brooklyn, in America; you could just feel it. Because of the two world wars and a depression in between, the nation had been deprived of consumer goods for almost three decades, and even when goods were available, people often didn't have the means to acquire them. And so by the time of the armistice in 1945, there was an unprecedented pent-up demand, not just for things people had been denied but also for new products and services driven by the technologies that had been developed in the prior twenty years. This included everything from refrigerators, televisions, portable radios, and telephones to such newly available options as commercial air travel, affordable homes, and advanced medical techniques.

At the same time, those veterans lucky enough to return were pouring into schools and the workforce, eager to rise to the challenges of a revitalized marketplace and a new way of living. It wasn't simply a boom time, easy for everyone. It was a highly competitive environment, especially for people my age. But that was okay; the air crackled with excitement, and as fast as I could, I wanted to become a part of what was happening.

So intent was I on streamlining my reentry that I changed my basic career plan. Instead of becoming a lawyer, I decided to study accounting. If that meant my college major had slightly less cachet, that was fine with me. Switching gears got me out of college and into "real life" two years sooner, and that was all that mattered.

I was still taking my final exams as a senior at City College in June 1948 when I began stopping by the employment counselor's office to see about job leads. The day of my last exam, the counselor told me he might have an opportunity for me, but I should check back with him in a few hours. As it turned out, that same day, post-test, I was having my second official date with my future wife, Irene, a fellow student at CCNY, though a few years younger than me.

I took her to lunch at a pizza place in downtown Manhattan, and toward the end of the meal I excused myself so I could use the pay phone to check in with the school's employment office. The job had come through. "There's a place called Markel, Schnee that has an opening for a junior accountant," the counselor told me. "It's at 29 Broadway." That address was only a short walk from the pizza place. After I said goodbye to Irene—making sure to add that I hoped we could see each other again—I went directly there.

In life, you never know when you're going to come to a crossroads, and that afternoon I reached two: one personal and one professional. I wish I could remember the exact date because, based on the paths I wound up taking, I could make a case for that being my single luckiest day.

In fact, I had been on a winning streak for a while, going back at least to my discharge from the army air corps. Allow me to explain.

The various divisions of the armed services worked from a points system in those days: A serviceman got points for how long he served, points for being stationed overseas, points for being in combat, and so forth. The more points you accumulated, the higher you were on the list for early discharge. I had been eager to serve my country, but once the war was over and the right side had won, I had no interest in being a professional soldier.

As I mentioned earlier, I had spent my active duty time in training in Mississippi, Arkansas, and Tennessee. That wasn't exactly a great formula for gaining points, so I was worried about how long I was going to be stuck in the army. Before I could fret too much, though, an edict came down from the Pentagon saying that for some mysterious but wonderful reason the points system wouldn't apply to the air cadets. We were mustered out promptly. What a break!

As soon as I was officially a veteran and eligible for the Servicemen's Readjustment Act of 1944—a wonderful, life-changing piece of legislation for millions, more popularly known as the GI Bill—I applied to Wharton Business School at the University of Pennsylvania. I was conditionally accepted, but only if I was willing to forgo the year of credit I'd earned at Brooklyn College before I enlisted. Because of a backlog of Wharton students returning from the war, they told me, the sophomore class was already overcrowded, and I couldn't start at that level. Since I was a young man in a tremendous hurry, I said thanks, but no thanks, and I applied to City College instead.

If Harvard is for the best and the brightest, CCNY has always had a reputation as a place that attracts people with savvy and street smarts as well as academic commitment. The alumni list is actually much more distinguished: Colin Powell, Bernard Malamud, Felix Frankfurter, Ira Gershwin, Bernard Baruch, and nine Nobel laureates are among the most notable graduates. It's a very good school.

CCNY was in the same tall building on Twenty-Third Street where my high school, Townsend Harris, had been, but it had the best campus anyone could ever wish for: Manhattan. My friends and I went to the opera, sporting events, the ballet, concerts, and Broadway shows. Even a student could afford New York in those days; tickets for the original production of *Oklahoma* started at $1.75, for example. We found cheap but good restaurants in Greenwich Village, hung out in the parks on beautiful days, and availed ourselves of the world-renowned public library (though not nearly enough).

Thanks to all of those urban distractions, I was not the greatest student, but I *was* involved in student affairs—not as a fraternity boy but as an activist. In my three years at CCNY, I founded the campus's largest student organization—the American Veterans Committee—ran the National Student Organization of America, and was elected vice president of the student body as a senior.

I wasn't on the staff of the CCNY school newspaper, but I found myself gravitating toward the offices of the weekly known as the *Ticker*. The small band of students who put it out had an appealing, intellectual bent, and the girls were not just smart but quite pretty. Irene Zanderer—stunning and always smartly dressed, straight-talking but compassionate—was one of those *Ticker* girls. On Friday nights the staff would put the paper to bed in an office on Broome Street; then they would all go out for dinner, and sometimes I'd come along.

Irene and I had actually met a couple of years before this, when we were both taking the same course, Economics 101. I had asked her out for a drink almost immediately and then escorted her home on the IRT, but for some reason nothing more came of it. Our next date, lunch at the pizza joint, didn't happen until quite a few semesters later. When we reconnected, though, I guess you could say that things kind of clicked, because that was 1948, and as I write this I'm hoping my wife of all these years will like the way I'm telling this part of the story.

What I learned when I showed up for that job interview at 29 Broadway was that Markel, Schnee was a small but prestigious certified public accounting firm with a diversified list of middle-sized New York City–based clients. In those days, Markel, Schnee mostly prepared certified statements for bank credit and did tax work for the companies that comprised its clientele.

The check-in area for job applicants was a typical scene in those highly competitive times. When I walked in, about a dozen young men were waiting to be interviewed, and on my way out, I noticed perhaps six additional applicants. My interview with Abe Schnee went well, but according to the CCNY employment counselor, there was only one open position. I didn't have to be an accountant to see that the odds were against me and that I shouldn't get my hopes up. What I didn't realize, though, was that when Arnold Markel interviewed candidates, he strongly favored guys (they were virtually all guys) from his alma mater, NYU, and that when Abe Schnee talked to people, he gave graduates of CCNY, where *he'd* gone, a decided edge. A few days later I got a call asking me to come in for a second interview and, a short time later, another phone call offering me the job.

I was thrilled to have the spot, but it did not pay spectacularly well and it was hard work, especially during tax season. In those days you had to file your return by March 15, and very few extensions were granted. As a result, between December 15 and the tax deadline, an accountant at Markel, Schnee worked six days a week, sometimes seven, and he often worked nights.

Schnee was the best accountant I ever met: a superb natural teacher, a man generous with advice, but a stern taskmaster. He was probably about forty-five, a middle-aged man with a couple of young kids, but I viewed him as the venerable old sage whom I very much wanted to please. Which wasn't always easy. If you made a mistake, he could be tough. He didn't yell, but the way he spoke to you if you did something that might make the firm look bad was something you didn't quickly forget. "There are only two ways to do things—the right way and the wrong way," he used to say. "Do it the right way."

But at the same time, he went to the trouble to make sure that I understood the client must always come first; that I needed to arrive at work in a timely fashion (I've always been willing to work hard and long, but a nine-to-five guy I'm not); and that I should always wear a tie (except on Saturdays during tax season). Abe taught me that accounting should have a purpose: to inform the client of his choices and to show the implications of each choice. Even today, I still say to myself sometimes, "Abe, you would like the way I did that." Because of him, it wasn't long before I was rising within the firm, taking responsibility for particular clients, and starting to think and work more creatively.

I also learned a lot from Arnold Markel who, it turned out, didn't hold it against me that I was not an NYU graduate. The president of the Merchants Bank of New York and the senior partner of the accounting firm, he was a successful man who had great connections. As head of the bank, Arnold oversaw a committee of four or five businessmen charged with reviewing and assessing loans in distress. The board of directors was required by the bank's charter to have an expert help them make a financial analysis of the loans under review, and that became my job.

At the start I was the kind of "expert" who still had a lot to learn—but what an educational experience that proved to be! It was better than graduate school. The men on that committee were sharp, confident guys—successful owners and managers of New York City businesses—and they understood how to run a company, not just in theory, but in the real world. When they were reviewing a problem loan, they knew exactly what to look for to see if the borrower had any chance of turning things around.

I took it all in and basked in their abundant expertise. They taught me how to carry myself in the business world, how to treat other people—even where I should buy my shirts! I learned the value of keeping business on a human scale and never underestimating the importance of relationships. Every so often, when they were reviewing the file of a borrower who had fallen behind in his payments, they would call the loan officer from the banking floor to ask some questions. Their inquiries, I noticed, always focused on the specific people involved and their histories and character, not just on the numbers. In fact, sometimes numbers weren't mentioned.

It was not unusual to hear the loan officer say of the borrower, "Look, this is basically a good guy. He's having a little trouble right now, and it might continue for a while, but he's been with the bank for a long time, and I have faith in him. I'll keep an eye on him, but I think he'll be all right." And most of the time the board members, based on that assurance and what they saw in the file, would say, "Okay, we'll go along with that, as long as you trust him." I can't imagine that being done today, when everyone wants to just take his cut from a transaction and move on.

Listening to those veterans of the business wars, I was getting wealthy in terms of wisdom—though not in any other way. I may have known where to buy shirts, but coming up with the money for a new batch—that was another matter.

I'll never forget what happened when word got around the office that I was about to take the domestic plunge. "Mr. Markel would like to see you," one of his assistants said to me one day when I was working at Merchants Bank. At first I was nervous; Markel could be an intimidating man. He had a huge corner office, and after I got to his door, it was still a long walk to his desk. I made the journey with trepidation.

"So, I hear you're getting married, Bernie," he said to me.

"Yes," I said.

"How much are you making at the moment?"

Now my heart soared. So this would be good news, I thought, and at just the right time!

"Forty-five dollars a week," I said.

He thought for a moment and then said, "Well, you must have a lot of faith in the firm."

And that was that.

Irene and I got married on June 17, 1950, a magnificent sunny Saturday in New York City. I was all of twenty-four years old and Irene was twenty-one. (We have the same birthday, December 13. When I first told her that, early in our courtship, Irene thought I was just trying to get in good with her. Finally, my mother had to assure her it was true.) About five hours before the ceremony would start, Harold and Jules picked me up in the middle of the afternoon in Harold's car—a brand-new green Chrysler convertible with lots of chrome and the top down because of the perfect weather.

They drove me to downtown Brooklyn, where I bought a bottle of White Shoulders perfume for Irene. Then my brothers took me to her parents' house in East Flatbush so I could deliver it to her. When we got there, the street outside her two-family home was buzzing. Everyone in Flatbush seemed to know that Irene Zanderer was getting married.

People were hanging from the windows, watching Harold's car pull up and me get out and go inside to see my bride. It was one of those New York moments like you see in an old movie musical.

The wedding itself, at Tree of Life Temple on Eastern Parkway, was grand. I had wanted to elope and asked Irene's father if he could give us the money he would spend on a wedding as a gift, but he wouldn't hear of it. "I want a black-tie affair!" he said, so that's what we had. Our honeymoon was two weeks in Cape Cod, which was *the* romantic destination in those days, a few years before Patti Page famously sang about falling in love there. The trip was a real extravagance for us: We couldn't leave until the Monday following the wedding because, to fund the excursion, I had to go to the bank and deposit the money we had received as gifts.

We returned from Cape Cod to a one-and-a-half room apartment on Ocean Avenue. I had my job, and Irene worked on the staff of Henry Morgenthau, secretary of the treasury under FDR, who was then devoting his life to managing Jewish philanthropies. Irene and I didn't have a lot, but our financial situation didn't get us down, as Irene reminded me recently. "When we had very little," she said, "you never worried about money. You never went around saying, 'We have to save up!' or 'We have to sit down and discuss our finances!'" And she was right. It's not that I was stupid and carefree or bought things I couldn't afford. (Neither of us was like that.) I just felt that the money would come eventually if I stuck to the principles I knew were right and true.

As busy as I was during this time as a junior associate in the accounting firm and being a new father—Karen was born three years after Irene and I got married—I stayed involved in Democratic politics. In the mid-1950s, I joined the Democratic Progressive Club of Brooklyn and worked for the election of Adlai Stevenson, who in 1956 ran for president against the incumbent Dwight Eisenhower. Stevenson, a former governor of Illinois, had been the Democratic presidential candidate four years earlier, without success; he had a somewhat professorial, patrician air, but he was in fact a canny liberal who called for a "new America" and had an agenda that recalled FDR's New Deal and anticipated JFK's and LBJ's programs.

Stevenson was a huge underdog in the 1956 race, but he was a Democrat, he had the support of Eleanor Roosevelt, and I liked him a lot. The Progressive Club asked me to go out several evenings each week to the New Lots Avenue subway station, the last stop on the IRT line, on a flatbed truck all done up in red, white, and blue bunting with signs that read, "All the Way with Adlai." The truck had a loudspeaker that blared out "Happy Days Are Here Again," and we would park by the station from four-thirty to seven in the evening to catch people as they poured out on their way home from work.

Every time a train arrived and a wave of people hit the streets, we'd turn down the music and I would start speaking about Stevenson, saying why they should vote for him. New Lots was a heavily Hispanic neighborhood, and I got the impression that a lot of people who passed by didn't speak English. I, meanwhile, didn't speak Spanish. But though most of the commuters just rushed by me on their way home, about 25 percent stopped to listen to my spiel. I don't know how we connected, but somehow we did, and they stood around the truck for a few minutes and cheered for Stevenson.

Even though poor Adlai was destined to lose again in a landslide that long-ago November, I do think back on that time and sometimes find myself humming "Happy Days Are Here Again."

CHAPTER 5

Full Partner

During the 1950s, when I was in my late twenties and early thirties, I made steady progress at Markel, Schnee. Ten years after graduating from college, I became a junior partner, which was and is one of my proudest accomplishments. You always hear about the squeaky wheel getting the grease, but the way you got ahead in that firm was to do things that made the business grow, which is really the best way to climb the ladder in any company.

Years later, when I was running Loral, we had a slogan that we splashed across the covers of annual reports and other stockholder publications: "Performance is the best strategy." It became one of my favorite sayings, and I think it applies as much to an employee trying to work his or her way up in a firm as it does to a chairman or CEO communicating with the company's stockholders. What it means in a nutshell is this: It's nice to have a plan for success, but it's even better to have a track record.

One way I distinguished myself at Markel, Schnee was by getting in early on a trend of the late 1950s and early '60s that saw small, private companies going public. I didn't start this phenomenon—it was happening all over—but I saw how we could broaden the scope of our firm and bring in new business. It was really a win-win-win situation: For our clients, going public was a way of monetizing ideas and raising money to pursue and expand their vision; for investors, it was a way of participating selectively in the post-war economic boom by backing the companies and concepts they found most interesting; for the investment banks that underwrote the deals we did, it gave them an important role to fulfill and turn a profit by screening, scrutinizing, and—if they passed muster—promoting these new companies that proposed to sell shares to the public.

Going public was not the right move for every corporation. If a company's leadership lacked a vision of what it wanted to accomplish, the only thing they'd gain in the end was additional oversight and increased costs. But when I looked at our client list to see who might benefit from such a move, the first company I struck upon was Admiral Plastics (APL), the firm run by my brother Harold and his partner, Harry Fishman.

By the late 1950s, APL had come a long way from the days when Harold and Harry were knocking on doors and selling swizzle sticks inscribed with the name of local bars and restaurants. The partners had long since sold their primitive old stamping machine and now oversaw both a plastics business that made housewares and containers for industry and consumers as well as a company that distributed nonfood products to supermarkets nationally.

They were doing so well for themselves, in fact, that when I first suggested to Harold and Harry that they consider going public, they weren't enthusiastic about the idea. Harry, especially, wondered if such a move was worth making. "I don't know, Bob. Why should we fool with success? I have a home. I have a country club. Who needs to go public?" Harold, always more the adventurous type, and perhaps with more of a vision to grow the business, was more open to the move, but I understood their initial skepticism.

They were a small company—they had less than $7 million in annual sales—and in 1959 small companies seldom went public. But APL was growing fast, and I kept talking to them about the prospect until finally one day Harry said, "I'll tell you what, Bob. If we each can realize a million dollars after tax from this move, we'll make it." That demand sounds quaint by today's standards, but it still wasn't the lifetime cushion that Harry seemed to think it was.

When you take a company public, there are always certain hurdles you must get over with your investment bankers to convince them that you are offering the investors something worthwhile. And in those days the hurdles were higher. With APL, one thing that was likely to cause skepticism about an initial public offering (IPO) was the size of the company. In preparation for going public, you had to show five years of complete financials, with the last three certified, and to do that with APL took us back to a time when it was *really* tiny.

I couldn't disguise that it was such a small company, but I could make a more important point, I thought, if I could show how quickly and dramatically it was growing. I came up with the idea of comparing the most recent four-month period with the same four-month period from the previous year. By doing that, I was able to project an annual growth rate for the company of 40 percent. I thought that figure was impressive and reliable, eye-catching but fair.

I'm not sure if I was the first person to show growth this way, but no one at my accounting firm had ever heard of doing such a thing, so they couldn't say if it would fly with the Securities and Exchange Commission (SEC). Even Ed Heft, who was a senior partner at Touche Ross, one of the Big Five accounting firms, said the method was new to him, but that it sounded interesting and could prove popular at a time when so many small firms were ripe for going public. He suggested a trip to Washington and a meeting with the SEC.

Today, such a visit would never even be contemplated. The SEC has become too big and bureaucratic to be approachable by a couple of mere mortals. But even then, paying a call on the SEC was an unusual move because the agency was used to dealing with the GEs and the GMs of the world, not the APLs. But you'll never know if something is possible unless you ask; we explained what we were planning on doing, and the head accountant agreed to see us. Looking back, I have to give that fellow credit. It would have been easy for him to say no, to shoot down my new, creative approach, especially from a company our size. But instead he listened intently and then said he thought our idea would be acceptable. "I think we can do this, as long as there is full disclosure to the public."

My next challenge was to find an investment house to underwrite the public offering. I knew I wanted a bank that could handle a small company like APL without relegating it to second-class status. For our deal I chose Hardy and Company, a firm located on Broad Street. I made an appointment and told the several bankers who sat down with me what we intended to do. Jim Hodes, the lead partner of the banking firm, frowned a bit when I explained that Harold and Harry each wanted to realize a million dollars from the deal, but I was delighted when he and the others indicated, at the end of our meeting, that they were interested enough to take the next step. "Please bring in the principals," Jim Hodes said, "so we can explore this further." So I came back a few days later with my brother and his partner.

After hearing what they had to say about their company, Jim was impressed with them and their optimism about APL's future, but he was straightforward about his biggest concern: the money they wanted to take out at the start. It wasn't the amount that concerned him as much as the message it sent. "The hardest part of taking this firm public," he said, "will be explaining why the principals are selling some of their stock. That will definitely lessen confidence among the clients to whom we'd want to recommend buying stock in APL. Still," he added, standing up to signal that he had come to a decision and the meeting was over, "I think we can do this."

As we walked down the hall on the way out, Jim put his arms around Harold and me and said, "You're going to need a good lawyer with SEC experience. Do you have one?" We told him we didn't and asked if he could make a recommendation. "Well," he said, "as a matter of fact there's a firm right across the street called Willkie, Farr, and Gallagher. They are one of the top firms in the city, and my son has just become a partner. Let's go over right now and meet Bob Hodes."

We crossed the street and met the guy who eventually would become my best friend. Bob, who like me was in his early thirties, was the Willkie, Farr partner specializing in tax matters. He was tall and handsome, a witty man with a confident mien. "I want you to meet our SEC partner," he said after chatting with us for a bit, and he ushered us in to meet an older man named Jim Carroll.

We could see instantly that Carroll was a senior presence at Willkie, Farr, and a classic representative of a white-shoe law firm. His clothing and manners were conservative and impeccable, his office was orderly, and his desk was pristine and empty except for a few brass accessories and an expensive-looking fountain pen. You got the distinct feeling that you should not crack your knuckles or chew gum in Jim Carroll's presence. He was a charming man, but at the same time a little intimidating.

Carroll started to advise us about certain things regarding a public offering, and we were nodding and taking it all in. At one point Harold broke in and said, "Excuse me, can I get something to drink?" I winced a bit when that happened, thinking my brother had perhaps violated some taboo, but Bob Hodes said, "Certainly!" and asked us what we wanted. In a few minutes he was back with coffee and Cokes. Harold put his bottle of soda near Jim Carroll's leather-bound appointment book, which made me a little more nervous, and then a minute later he proceeded to *knock over* the bottle, spilling Coke onto Carroll's exquisite mahogany desk.

For one or two long seconds, we all watched this big brown puddle spreading in every direction. Then people jumped up, got paper to sop up the mess, shouted for secretaries, and lifted things from the desk— with Bob all the while insisting everything was under control. It was pandemonium.

I had to wonder if the Schwartz brothers and Harry Fishman hadn't made a devastatingly bad first impression. But Carroll did not show a trace of emotion. He just fell silent and sat impassively looking into the middle distance. When the last secretary had left the room with her paper towels and the door had clicked shut, he finished the sentence he had started perhaps five minutes before, kept on talking about his philosophy of going pubic, and discussed how he envisioned our deal happening.

In time, everything he said would happen came to pass, with his and Bob Hodes's help. In a straightforward fashion, we addressed the potentially tricky issue of Harold and Harry selling their stock simply by saying that their each realizing a million dollars was a condition of the offering and that they would simply not go public any other way. They were selling off just 20 percent of their stock, not 100 percent, after all, and that should have conveyed something to the bankers and the investing public about their confidence in APL. Our argument worked, and the public offering of APL was an immediate and outstanding success.

In short order, I followed that offering with IPOs for several other companies I attracted to Markel, Schnee, and Hauer (Arthur Hauer had recently been added as a partner). Thanks to these transactions the firm was growing rapidly. The only problem, as far as I was concerned, was that as a junior partner I wasn't earning an appropriate share. Irene and I had Karen and Francesca by this time, and our apartment in Forest Hills was starting to feel cramped. My basic notion that performance is the best strategy was being put to the test, and I thought it was time to have a chat with the boss.

I knew Abe Schnee was a no-nonsense guy, so when I went to see him about my future with the firm I got directly to the point. "Abe, I just can't make it here," I said. "I've got a family to support, and Markel is taking so much out of the firm for his share of the income that there's not enough for the rest of us. It's not that I don't want to work here; it's just that I can't figure out how to live on what I'm taking home."

"Well, so what do you want to do?" Schnee said.

I swallowed hard and spoke my mind. "I'd like to become a full and equal partner." After a beat or two of silence, Schnee said, "I'll get back to you."

The next day he came into my office and said, "We're going out to dinner tonight: you and me and Markel and Hauer. We'll have dinner together and then we'll go back to Markel's hotel to talk."

This did not sound to me like a fun evening. Arnold Markel was not the easiest man to spend time with; he had a brilliant mind but was socially awkward. Still, I had to figure they had something to say to me, perhaps in the form of a counteroffer.

After dinner the four of us strolled to the Hyde Park Hotel for our chat in Markel's room. For the most part, though, Markel and I did the talking.

"Abe said that if you can't be a full partner, you'll have to leave the firm," he said to me.

"Well, I wouldn't put it that way," I said. "I like the firm. I feel like it's my firm. I started here, and you made me a junior partner. That's no small thing, but I just don't make enough money."

"What do you suggest?"

"I don't know how to answer you," I said. "If I had a magic wand, I would buy your share."

It was either a bold or a stupid thing to say—I wasn't sure which. But Markel didn't seem shocked by my comeback.

"Mmm. That would cost a lot of money. How would you pay for that?"

"Frankly, I don't know. But I would borrow or figure out something."

And then suddenly we were done. "Okay, maybe we can work something out," he said, standing up and patting me on the shoulder. "We'll talk about it again; good night."

I was baffled, but not for long. Fortunately, Abe Schnee and Arthur Markel had worked something out, and as soon as I got on the elevator with him and Arthur Hauer, Schnee turned to me and told me, "We're going to arrange for you to buy Markel's position. He's decided to retire, and you, Arthur, and I are going to be equal partners. Further, we negotiated the price with Markel, which we think is fair."

I was ecstatic. I knew it would cost a lot, but I hoped they would let me pay for my partnership over time—probably, I figured, by deducting money from my paycheck. It would take a few years of sacrifice, but so be it. This was an investment in my future. I thanked Abe sincerely.

Abe had more news, though. "Bernie, I also want you to know that

Arthur and I have decided to take the money out of the firm to pay for your partnership."

For a moment I actually wondered if I'd heard correctly. Was Abe saying, in his usual matter-of-fact way, that I wouldn't have to pay a nickel to become a full partner? As a matter of fact, yes, he was! I knew I was helping the firm grow, but this was an act of generosity and a vote of confidence that nearly overwhelmed me. This would not be the only time in my career when a mentor stepped forward with a truly beneficent offer.

I went home that night to Irene and my daughters feeling the most secure I had felt since I was a child. I was a principal in a successful, established accounting firm, ready to settle in for the long haul at Schnee, Hauer . . . and Schwartz.

Of course, fate has a way of deciding just how long any particular haul is going to be, doesn't it?

CHAPTER 6

New Opportunities

I'll never forget being marched into that cavernous, cold meeting room in Worcester, Massachusetts, to explain why APL was having trouble repaying a certain large loan. Harry Fishman had stayed behind, so it was just my brother Harold and me, in my capacity as the company's accountant and advisor, who showed up to do the talking that gray winter's day. We'd already had a pretty dismal two-and-a-half-hour drive from New York.

It was not a particularly happy time for any of us. There was a problem with APL, which, though temporary, was well known. And now, at the request of the president of the Massachusetts Protective Association, an insurance firm that made investments in companies like Harold's, we were entering a stark, windowless chamber, with dozens of empty chairs around the periphery, to try to put a good face on a difficult situation. Our intention was not to deny reality but rather to make the point that we were, in spite of everything, still optimistic about this company that had just recently gone public with such great success.

The president of the insurance firm and two of his colleagues sat down on one side of the gigantic room and he gestured for us to take seats at the other side. Our creditor rose and spoke first.

"Not long ago, you came in here and said this was your business," he said in a decidedly unfriendly tone, holding up the APL prospectus. "On the basis of this, and the passion and commitment you talked about at our meeting that day, we made a loan to you. Now you're saying you can't make your loan payments."

I thought he would ask what happened or say *something* further, but he stopped right there and sat down. I guessed that meant it was our turn to respond.

Since I was the one who had arranged for the loan, I stood up and started speaking. Partly out of anxiety and partly because I truly believed what I was saying, I didn't stop for quite a while. I tried to explain that Harold's and Harry's core business—the distribution of nonfood items like housewares, drug products, and cleaning supplies to thousands of supermarkets around the country—was actually doing very well. Sales were up. We were even *exceeding* the projections we had made in the prospectus. To keep their healthy market share and manage the business better, the company had contracted to build a big warehouse in Linden, New Jersey, and consolidate all of its various distribution divisions there. APL was growing!

The problem was that we were switching from our old system to a new one and we had to do this while seamlessly servicing our customers. It was a tricky transition to pull off, and we wound up rushing our consolidation plans and moving into the new warehouse too soon. One ramification of this was that we temporarily lost control of the inventory, and a lot of it wound up going out the back door: stolen by an assortment of unscrupulous construction workers who had access to the warehouse site.

My brother and his partner had made an honest mistake, but for doing so, they were taking a short-term financial hit. There was absolutely no risk of them going under, but to show the financial community they had confidence in the long-term prospects of APL, they each loaned the business a million dollars—the same amount they had realized at the time of the IPO. I contributed to the business, too, by taking a second mortgage on my house in Great Neck and making a loan to the company.

Today, I can't imagine a scenario where the principals of a small firm like APL would be so personally involved, their identities and hopes so caught up in their company's destiny that they would put their own nest eggs on the line, as Harold, Harry, and I did. Furthermore, we did it without being ordered by creditors or pressured in any way. We did it because we believed in our own long-term goals and dreams. Yet even so, APL still had temporary trouble making the monthly loan payments to Massachusetts Protective.

Sometimes in business all you have is your faith, but if your faith is in the right place, then that is enough. "This is still a good company," I told the men from the insurance company. "We can solve this problem—and we will. We have built our plant in New Jersey, and we're going to repay the loan."

There was a moment's pause, and then the president of Massachusetts Protective stood up again, followed by his two colleagues. Another pause. Was he going to walk out of the room?

He strode toward us, with his hand extended. "Okay," he said. "We've made bad loans and good ones, and we'll make more of both. I just wanted to see if you guys knew what you were doing."

As we walked down the hall toward the front door, he said to Harold, "You do realize, of course, that your brother Bob is in effect your chief financial officer? I want you to take a step and make Bob's involvement in APL official. I want you to formally take him into the firm and appoint him your CFO, because we need to know who to send to jail if things go wrong again."

Was he kidding? Even now I don't know.

"And I want to be clear about this," he continued. "Either you make Bob your chief financial officer or we will appoint a chief financial officer for you."

Neither Harold nor I knew what to say. Our silence continued all the way back to New York as Harold drove. At last, when we got to my door, Harold pulled up to let me out and said, "Well?"

"Well, what?" I said.

"What about the question?"

"You know, Harold," I said, "I'm doing okay. I'm a partner in the firm. I'm comfortable. I like what I'm doing. I want to stay where I am. Let me think about it."

We were, after all, brothers.

"I'm not going to pressure you," he said. "The choice is yours. But pretty soon you'll have to tell me: Is it yes or no?"

I talked to Irene. She's an excellent listener and opinionated about a lot of things, but she usually leaves the business decisions to me. She paid close attention but said little, probably because we both knew what I was eventually going to do.

In truth, while it was a big decision for me, it was also an easy one. I had worked my way to a good position at Schnee, Hauer, Schwartz, but when your brother needs you, you go to him. If I didn't join APL, Harold might lose control of the business, and that would be a shame, because once he solved the problem and stopped the pilferage, I believed he'd be tremendously successful. So my joining was more or less inevitable.

Still, an awkward conversation loomed just ahead; I had to discuss compensation with my brother. It never happened, though, because when I finally told him I was signing on, Harold gave me a meaningful look and said, "You'll have to talk about *that* with Harry." We both knew what "that" was.

But the salary discussion with Harry was even easier. He said, "Whatever you want, Bob."

Abe Schnee took the news of my resignation like the gentleman that he was; he understood how close-knit the Schwartz brothers were. Still, for a guy who prided himself on being financially savvy, I was in a strange place in 1961. I'd voluntarily left a good position and taken a less secure and less lucrative one. But I didn't mope or have trouble sleeping. I've always been able to view business problems as part of professional life: something to be dealt with and learned from, not to be defined or defeated by.

When APL went public, it drew the attention of Julius and Michael Steinberg. Like Harold and Harry, they were in the housewares business. The Steinberg brothers' Ideal Rubber Company manufactured plastic and rubber items similar to those made by Rubbermaid. My brother and his partner were actually competitors with the Steinberg brothers, but despite these complications, or maybe because we were similar in so many ways—they came from a background much like the Schwartz brothers'—everyone got along fine.

Intrigued by APL's successful IPO, Julius and Michael Steinberg looked at the prospectus I'd put together and were impressed by what we'd done; they decided they wanted to go public with Ideal Rubber. It was a bigger company than APL in terms of net worth and annual sales and revenue, so they thought they would have no problem getting in on the trend that was allowing so many smaller businessmen to monetize their success and grow their companies. The Steinbergs and my brother and his partner were together at a housewares show in Chicago when Harry had first told them about his experience with an IPO and how I'd facilitated matters for him, and Michael had immediately left his booth at the convention and called me.

"Can you come to Chicago right away?" he said.

"No."

"But we're only going to be here two more days, and then we have to go home to Brooklyn."

"Good," I said. "I'll come over and see you then."

Julius, I soon learned, was used to getting his way, but in general he and Michael needed to be more patient about going public, if indeed that was ever going to happen for them. When I went over their financial records, I told them that even though their company was successful and a lot bigger than Harold's and Harry's, they would not be able to go public for at least a year. They were not running Ideal Rubber like a public company. And the SEC wasn't even the biggest hurdle you had to get over in those days. The toughest problem was to convince the investment bankers that the offering was a good, honest deal with solid prospects. The bankers negotiated the deal with the investor in mind and also decided the initial public offering price. They truly represented the public, not just their client.

"You'll have to show five years of complete financials, the last three certified, and otherwise behave like a public company," I told them, and I began working to get them ready for an IPO. No one said anything about me getting paid, but we all knew we'd come to some kind of terms down the road.

While working with the Steinberg brothers, I met someone who would become an integral and permanent part of my personal and professional life: Julius's son Saul. One of the smartest people I've ever known, as well as one of the funniest, Saul Steinberg was then nineteen years old and had already graduated from Wharton, which he'd finished in only two years. Saul was a true child prodigy. He'd worked in his father's and uncle's rubber factory since he was fourteen, learning the business from the ground up, and he was the sort of kid who read the *Wall Street Journal* every morning and would consume annual reports like mystery novels.

Although he was about fourteen years younger than I was, I felt we had a lot in common. For one thing, we were both fascinated with and excited by all the possibilities opening up in the business world, including the trend of relatively small companies going public. As things turned out, Ideal Rubber would never get itself to the point where it was able to do an IPO, but Saul and I spent a lot of time talking. "I don't want to be in the housewares business," he would say. It was pretty obvious, if you knew the young Saul, that he was not destined to be stamping out sink plugs and spatulas in Greenpoint.

Saul was fascinated by the leasing business. Although he was still a teenager, he was one of the first to understand its potential. At Wharton he'd written his senior thesis on the subject, saying that IBM, as big as it was, would not be able to fund the conversion of American business from its previous methods to high-speed computers. Another source of credit would be needed, Saul argued, and leasing companies could fill this gap. He turned out to be prescient about that. But how would he get the capital to buy the equipment that he intended to lease?

Saul had a plan for raising money. In addition to their rubber housewares firm, Julius and Michael had a side business making loans to local businesses like coffee shops, newspaper stands, and candy stores in Brooklyn and Queens, especially those located near a subway stop. These weren't good loans, truth be told. They were, in fact, high-risk, high-interest third mortgages made at the rate of 12 or 13 percent: about twice the rate they could have gotten from a bank had these little businesses been able to go that route.

The key to the Steinberg brothers' loan business, however, was that they took as collateral the only thing that was really important in this scenario: the lease. Banks and other people who were loaning money to these kinds of places traditionally took the furniture and fixtures as collateral, but the Steinberg brothers understood that there would always be a candy store, newsstand, or coffee shop at these spots. If a particular business failed, it didn't matter; another would soon come along, and the owners would have to deal with Julius and Michael. This was a dependable model, but not a growth business. Saul asked his father and uncle to divert all excess cash—some $250,000, as well as the additional capital to be earned as loans were repaid—to Saul to invest in his new leasing venture. With that capital he could get into the business of leasing IBM and other new and expensive data-processing equipment and technology, which even for a small company could cost quite a few million dollars.

Saul's biggest obstacle, he knew, was his father. Julius was an old-school thinker who did not understand his son's brilliant approach to leasing. He could also be extremely tight with a buck. Julius would have been shaking his head "no" before Saul even finished asking him about investing the profits from the loan company into his newfangled start-up. "I need you to speak to my father on my behalf," Saul said to me one day. "He'll never listen to me, but he trusts you and will listen to you." So I met with Julius and convinced him to let Saul run with his idea. As I was leaving, Julius said, "Saul won't do as I say. He won't listen to me, but he will listen to you." For a few years I wound up being a go-between for father and son.

By 1960 Saul had accumulated enough capital to borrow from the bank, and he had Leasco Data Processing Equipment Corporation, as he called the company, up and running. Acting with tremendous confidence and maturity, he'd found office space, hired a sales force, and was going out on the more important calls himself. He was, in short, developing a business at the age of twenty-one. Julius was the treasurer of Leasco, and I was the accountant.

In the first years of Leasco's existence, it became clear that we needed more operating capital, so Julius and Michael decided to put $500,000 into the business, no small sum then. I set it up so that in exchange for their investment they received preferred stock, convertible to common stock at any time. It was a sweetheart deal, because the price of the stock was very likely to go up if the company went public. But it was perfectly permissible, because Leasco was still a private company.

I thought this was a good time to speak up for myself, so I went to Saul. "As you know, I've put a lot of time into the company, and I don't have any equity in it. I would like to buy some of that preferred stock." But Saul thought it was not his deal to make and suggested I approach Julius and Michael myself.

I went to them the next day. "This is an opportunity for me," I said, "and I'd like to take advantage of it."

"How much stock do you want?" Julius said.

"As much as you want to sell me."

"Do you have the money?" Mike said.

"No, but I'll get it, even if I have to borrow it. I believe in this company."

A few days later Julius called me up and offered me 20 percent of the issue, or $100,000 of the preferred stock. Equity is a wonderful thing, and Julius and Mike were being very generous in giving me a chance to acquire that much. I was the first non-Steinberg to be financially involved in Leasco, and that was no small thing. Although I had to lay out a good deal of money for the stock, this is yet another example of my having led a charmed life. If Julius had offered me just 5 percent of the preferred stock, I would have been delighted. That preferred stock was like gold, and when the company went public, it was very lucrative.

I was not yet working at Leasco; I was a floor above Saul in the same office building in Great Neck serving as the CFO for APL. But we ate lunch together often and came up with ideas, one of which I am particularly proud of since it played a key role in Leasco's growth.

Typically, a company in those days might say, "We need a 360 IBM computer that's going to cost a million bucks. We could pay IBM a million dollars and own the machine, or we could go to a company like Leasco and lease the machine for, say, $1.3 million payable in equal monthly amounts for four years." For a lot of companies, the latter was going to be the more attractive alternative.

What the leasing company would normally do when it got an order for a 360 IBM computer was go to the bank and borrow 75 percent of the col-lateral—the machine itself. In this case, if the 360 cost $1 million, the loan would be $750,000. The leasing company would put up the difference, $250,000, and then lease the computer to the customer for a period of time for at least $1.3 million. The difference between the cost of the com-puter and what they charged for leasing it, more than $300,000, would be the leasing company's profit after interest and operating expenses.

It occurred to me that one of the beautiful things about the business was that virtually all our customers were big, solid AAA companies that were never going to go bust or default on their commitment. "If we have an airtight business lease with, say, General Electric," I thought, "that's a guaranteed $1.3 million–plus and ought to be regarded as such." I told Saul that as with his father and uncle and the candy stores, the *lease*, not the computer, should be the collateral. He loved the idea. The ultimate test, however, would be how the bank reacted.

I went into the Manufacturers Hanover bank on Forty-Second Street and Eighth Avenue, gave our balance sheet to the vice president who was overseeing our business, and told him what we planned to do. His decision was crucial, because borrowing against the lease meant we wouldn't have to put up *any* of our own money when we purchased a new computer, giving Leasco an opportunity for enormous expansion.

I remember the Manny Hanny vice president looking up from the balance sheet and saying, "I think the leasing business is a terrible idea, but I'm going to give you a loan on these terms anyway, and I'll tell you why. We've done business together, and I know and respect you. Also, the Steinberg family is long established in Brooklyn, and we'd like to get more of their business. And lastly, I think Saul Steinberg is a brilliant young man who is going to be a good customer in the future." In other words, he was more interested in the relationships than in the specifics of the present transaction.

A couple of years later that same banker would say to me, "Boy, was I wrong about Leasco." It turned out to be a terrific business, and his bank was one of the beneficiaries. At its height in the 1990s, Leasco, which later became Reliance Group Holdings, was a diversified financial services company with nearly nine thousand employees and more than $10 billion in assets.

But Saul did not become a rich man from Leasco right away. He took very little money out of the company for himself. By the time he was in his mid-twenties, he was married and had a child but was still only drawing expense money as he needed it. One day he came to me in my office at APL and said, "Bernard, I need more money."

"What are you telling me for?"

"I don't know how to get it."

"What do you mean? You take it out of the company. Start paying yourself a salary."

"My father won't let me do that. Can you please go tell Julius that I need more money?"

"No, I won't do that, Saul," I said. "And let me give you some advice. I don't think either of us should ask him if you can have more money. Leasco is a whole separate business from his, right?"

"Yeah."

"It's in a different building, right?"

"Yeah."

"The people here work for you, right? And it was you who hired the bookkeeper?"

"Yeah."

"Well, tomorrow morning I think you should go to your bookkeeper and say you want a salary, whatever amount you want."

"My father will kill me."

It's interesting to note the things money *doesn't* change—like a family dynamic. Saul was extremely successful; he was traveling to Latin America, Europe, and Hong Kong for his burgeoning business. But he had the same relationship with his father as he would have had if he were still living in his parents' basement. "Saul," I said, "you're never going to really own this company until you control the money."

It took Saul a couple of days, but finally he screwed up his courage and went to see that bookkeeper and got his salary. Julius, as treasurer of the company, no doubt noticed what had happened, but he never said a thing. After that, things were different, both with family and finances. Saul became a man, the boss. And before he turned thirty, he was a millionaire many times over.

As for me, I was the senior vice president of my brother's firm, APL. And after several years of working with Saul, I was still the only non-family stockholder in his company. This seemed fine with all the concerned parties—at least for a while.

CHAPTER 7

Moving Upstairs

My brother's company grew right along with Saul's firm. Harold and Harry were on their way to building their $1,500 investment into a Fortune 500 company. As APL's senior vice president, I had a full plate of duties, but Saul and I were frequently in each other's offices or on the phone to each other, talking mostly about matters involving Leasco.

One day in 1967 he called me at about two o'clock in the afternoon and said, "Do you have a moment to come up and meet someone?"

"Not really," I said. "My schedule is very crowded today."

"Just come to say hello," he said, and so I went.

As things turned out, I would go without dinner and not leave Saul's office until eleven o'clock that night.

Saul's visitor that day was a man named Ed Netter. An affable guy who appeared to be in his mid-thirties, Netter was an associate in an investment banking and brokerage firm that was then called Carter, Berlind & Weill. Ed's specialty was property and casualty insurance.

Carter, Berlind & Weill was an impressive outfit, a coalition of powerful business minds: Arthur Carter had been a French literature major at Brown and a serious classical pianist who'd gone on to become a legendary Wall Street investor; Roger Berlind, after banking, went on to become a Broadway producer and a director at Lehman Brothers; Sandy

Weill was the future CEO and chairman of Citigroup, one of the world's largest banking organizations. Two other partners were Marshall Cogan, who later founded United Automotive Group, once the world's largest association of car and truck dealers, and Arthur Levitt, who became the chairman of the SEC.

Netter came to talk to us that day about a situation developing in his field of expertise. Most property insurance companies, he explained, were sitting on mountains of excess cash—money they didn't need to run their businesses. Acquiring one of these firms would allow you to use the cash that came with it to pay down debt or finance other ventures.

Saul and I were fascinated, and when Netter left, Saul said to me, "This really sounds like something I should do." One thing Saul always said he liked about the insurance business was that it relied heavily on computers, and by that point Leasco had a lot of experience in that field and access to a lot of equipment. "Bernard," he said, "could you do an analysis to verify what Netter's telling us and also to see specifically where we might get involved?" Within a week I presented a report suggesting that Saul might look into four companies, though the best by far in my opinion was one called Reliance Insurance.

Saul was extremely eager to diversify. Leasco was one of the major players in its field, with $14.4 million in annual revenue. It was also an extremely innovative and aggressive company: As part of our diversification efforts, for example, we developed groundbreaking software for airline reservation systems, election-night projections, and many other things. Many of the top grads from MIT and Cal Tech wanted to work for us.

As a computer leasing executive, Saul had a unique insight: As successful as Leasco was, he understood our vulnerability to IBM. That company set prices, controlled the inventory, and introduced new technology as it saw fit. Leasing companies like ours existed at IBM's sufferance. Saul understood that by changing the price of its equipment, IBM could cut into Leasco's profits or even put us out of business. We tried to make the situation less perilous by negotiating for long-term leases; by developing the software that our clients needed to make their $5 million IBM computers work; and by increasing our maintenance capability as a hedge against IBM deciding one day that they wouldn't service our machines. Nonetheless, we had made a huge investment in the leasing concept: At the time, Saul owned something like $500 million in IBMs and other computers and had more than two thousand employees.

When I talked to him about Reliance Insurance Company, Saul liked what he heard. Reliance had been founded in Philadelphia in 1817, so it was certainly well established, if somewhat stodgy. It also had a strong balance sheet and, bearing out Ed Netter's general observation of the business, plenty of excess cash. They were the perfect fit for us. We had a hundred ideas for every dollar we had; they had a hundred dollars for every idea. Furthermore, a good amount of the company's stock was already in the hands of Carter, Berlind clients.

I was not the only person to see the value of Reliance, but a lot of people, including some of our own Leasco board members, said we would never be able to pull off an unfriendly takeover of a blue-blooded Philadelphia firm like Reliance, nearly ten times Leasco's size. "You're just a Brooklyn guy," they told Saul. "That's not the way these things work." But the world was changing. In fact, as one writer put it, "Minnows believed they could swallow whales." In those heady days of the late 1960s, Saul believed that he could accomplish anything. After we discussed a takeover of Reliance, he said to me, "I need to do this, Bernard, but I *can't* do this with you outside the company. Besides, I'm going to be acquiring more companies, and this is what you're good at: finding the best acquisitions, structuring the deals, and raising the capital to make them happen. But you have to finally become part of Leasco. I'll make you president and I'll be chairman of the board."

I talked to Harold the next day and told him I had an opportunity I couldn't pass up. He understood that the time was right for me to go down a different path; the crisis period for APL had long since passed. So I became president of Leasco, with a great salary and no moving expenses. All I did was snap closed my briefcase and go upstairs.

The first meeting I had at Carter, Berlind to discuss Reliance may not have been the strangest meeting I've had in my years as a businessman, but it definitely was the shortest; I'm guessing it lasted less than two minutes. At precisely nine in the morning, Saul and Bob Hodes (who had become Leasco's lawyer—another good thing I arranged) went with me to the offices of Carter, Berlind down on Wall Street. But instead of ushering us in, Arthur Carter stalked out into the vestibule where we were standing and handed us each a single sheet of paper. It was a list of seven or eight demands he had in order for him to do the deal. "Let me know what you think," he said before turning on his heel and going back inside.

I thought he was pompous and rude. The first of his demands was that we give him a gigantic fee. Another was that he would be able to appoint two of his people to our board. Saul thought he was being outrageous, but because Carter's firm controlled so much of the stock of our target company, he did have some leverage over us. The question was how much we'd have to concede. "I can swing the fee," Saul said. "But there's no way I'm going to put his people on our board."

But Carter wasn't finished. He had one more demand that wasn't on his sheet. After we thought we had come to an understanding on the various issues that would allow him to represent us, he paid a visit to Saul one day and said, "I really would like to represent Leasco. I trust you, Saul, but I don't trust Bernard Schwartz. If he is part of your company, I cannot deal with you. And if we wind up not representing you, I want you to know why."

Saul was baffled. "Do you even know Bernard?" he asked.

"No, but I know enough about him to not trust him," Carter said.

Saul couldn't get him to say more specifically what his problem was, so he finally suggested that Carter come next door and meet me. "Believe me, there is no reason for you to distrust Bernard Schwartz, and if you meet him and talk to him, you'll see what I mean."

When Carter walked into my office, I was surprised but happy to see him. "Welcome!" I said. "Sit down, take your coat off." But he just glared at me.

"What I have to say doesn't require me to sit down or take my coat off," he said. "I want you to know that I like the deal we have been talking about with Reliance, but I will not do business with you personally. I don't consider you trustworthy. I will have nothing to do with this deal or the company if you're involved."

Now it was my turn to be baffled. "Arthur, you don't know me well enough to say those things about me," I said. "You don't know me at all. Why are you saying these things?" But by that point he was already halfway out the door.

I have never been able to learn the cause of Arthur Carter's animosity toward me in those days. He happens to be a brilliant man. He later went on to own the New York *Observer* and now he's an accomplished sculptor. Maybe he had me confused with another Bernard Schwartz; I don't know. But I do know that he launched his odd attack on me without discussing it beforehand with any of the other members of his banking firm, and that a few days after he left my office he was no longer part of the firm—which was thereafter called Cogan, Berlind & Weill.

A short time after that I got a call from Marshall Cogan, asking to see me. When he came in, he said, "I want to apologize for the way you were treated by Arthur Carter. We're on our way to becoming an important investment house, and that's not the way we want to do business. We'd love to represent you in this deal, and I'm here to negotiate terms that would be good for you. You should also know that Arthur Carter is no longer associated with our firm."

I accepted Cogan's apology, and Saul put together what turned out to be a successful bid for Reliance Insurance. Leasco's equity capital promptly increased from $70 million to $236 million.

After their split with Carter, the firm of Cogan, Berlind became one of the most important banking houses in New York City. Arthur Carter, as I've mentioned, had his subsequent triumphs too. But I didn't see him for a long time after that.

Fade out, fade in to the late 1980s, nearly twenty years later. A group of people I know, all of them heavy hitters in the financial world, had a

Monday night poker game, and they kindly invited me to join. I knew and liked several people in the group, and I love poker, but I was very busy at the time and often worked late. Charles Lazarus, the founder and president of Toys "R" Us, urged me to give it a try. "We're having the game at my house this week. Come by, play cards, maybe you'll like it," he said.

"I can't pledge to be with you every week," I said. "But I'll be there on Monday."

That afternoon I asked my secretary to go to the bank and get $5,000 in cash for me to take to the poker game. I figured these guys were serious players, and when I got to Charles's house that night and sat down, they gave me three stacks of chips, telling me each red chip was worth 100, the white 50, and the blue 25. I nodded. About an hour into the game, I realized we were talking about *cents*. You would have to work hard to lose $200 or $300 in an evening with this room full of millionaires. It was just for laughs.

For me, though, there was considerable tension at the table because the player sitting directly across from me was Arthur Carter. We hadn't seen each other since he had stalked out of my office that day almost two decades earlier. When everyone was saying hello to one another at the start of the game, we hadn't shaken hands; we'd just nodded to each other. I didn't expect anything more to happen, but then when it was Arthur's turn to deal, he put the cards down and loudly cleared his throat. "I'd like to say something to everyone here tonight," he began. "I have something to tell you about Bernard."

"Oh, my God," I thought. "Here we go again."

Arthur started off by telling the story of the Reliance deal exactly the way it happened, that he came to Saul Steinberg's office and told Saul he insisted on my leaving the firm because I was not trustworthy. At that point the laughter stopped and the room grew quiet. But what came next surprised me.

"I just want to say now that I was wrong," Arthur said. "I made a mistake. There is nothing about Bernard Schwartz that is not trustworthy."

With that, he picked up the cards, began to deal, and we never said another word about our past problems. In fact, we've become quite good friends since then, and we'll occasionally have lunch at the Four Seasons or dinner together with our wives. Sometimes I am tempted to ask him why he once found me so unreliable, but then I think, "Why go back there?" Forward is always a better direction.

After Leasco took over Reliance in 1968, we entered the big leagues. As one analyst noted, "As of December 31, 1968, the price of Leasco stock had, over the five years preceding, appreciated by five thousand four hundred percent, making it the greatest percentage gainer of all the five hundred largest publicly owned companies during that period." We were a major insurance company and an important leasing company.

Around that time we also took over a shipping container company called CTI, which became even more successful under our management; we eventually owned one-quarter of all the shipping containers in the world. We were still a very lean outfit in terms of top-level executives, but we'd outgrown the outer boroughs. We changed our name from Leasco to The Reliance Group and moved into big and sumptuous offices on Park Avenue. People knew who we were and just about every bank in the country wanted to do business with us. Saul told *Forbes* magazine that nothing could stop him—and for quite a while he was right. He had truly become a star.

It was about six months after we acquired Reliance that Saul came to me one day and said, "Bernard, we ought to own a bank." Saul, a true visionary, wanted to take down the walls among insurance companies, leasing companies, and banks, which were, in his opinion, really in the same business—"the money business," as he put it. "We shouldn't be different companies doing insurance financing, leasing financing, and investment financing. All that should be part of one company." He believed that taking over a bank was the key to making this happen.

But which bank? At Saul's request, I did a study of the industry and came up with a likely candidate: Chemical Bank. Founded in 1824, Chemical, like Reliance, was a venerable institution run by old-school thinkers. It was the sixth-largest bank in the country at that time, with assets of more than $9 billion. And also, just like Reliance, it definitely did *not* want to be acquired. Saul actually liked it as a takeover candidate because it was the *least* forward-looking of any of the major banks, and thus the ripest for improvement. Equally important, it was not one of the institutions we already did business with; we would not be attacking one of our friends.

Saul agreed that Chemical was a good choice, and we began to put together a plan for taking it over. Our interest in the bank was a highly confidential matter. Even in our internal memos and phone conversations, we referred to Reliance as "Raquel" (for the voluptuous Ms. Welch) and Chemical Bank as "Faye" (for the lovely Ms. Dunaway) to confuse any snoopers. But somebody must have been leaking information, because one early February morning we opened the *New York Times* and saw a headline that read, "Leasco Eyeing Chemical Bank." I don't know where the writer, Robert Metz, got his information, but there was no denying it—he was spot on.

After that story, it was open season on Reliance. It seemed that the entire banking community was against us. We were turned into villains, portrayed as un-American. William Renchard, the chairman and CEO of Chemical Bank, was quoted in the papers as "sounding like a Marine Corps colonel" when he said, "We intend to resist this with all the means at our command!" And so he did. Chemical hit us where it hurt—in our stock price. So many companies came to the bank's rescue, divesting our stock out of their pension plans and selling us short, that by the twentieth of February our share price, which had started the month at $140, was down to $99 and still sinking fast.

The *New York Times* followed the story closely. "Bankers have been deeply shaken by the attempt," it said. "They want it made plain that banking is something special, off-limits to the corporate movers who currently are riding high on Wall Street." In an effort to calm the fears of the bankers, Saul and I met with some commercial bank leaders. I had lunch with John McGillicuddy, the soon-to-be chairman of

Manufacturers Hanover, and several of his associates. I did my best to explain our position, telling McGillicuddy that we might be newcomers but we cared very much about his industry and had plans to make Chemical an even stronger bank.

He listened very politely and attentively, then leaned in to ask the question that was most prominently on his mind: "Bernard, why did Saul choose Chemical to take over and not Manufacturers?" I told him there were two reasons. In the first place, Manny Hanny was one of *our* banks, which we would never attempt to take over. And in the second place, his bank was a better-run institution than was Chemical; Manny Hanny didn't need us as badly. I thought my response was both diplomatic and truthful—but our stock price continued to drop.

Saul was angry at the way we were being rejected out of hand by the banks, but he, too, could be diplomatic. In an attempt to keep the deal moving forward, he arranged a meeting at which he, Bob Hodes, and I sat down with certain members of the Chemical Bank board. At that meeting Saul explained that we were not doing anything illegal or inappropriate, and that benefits could be gained by working together. Renchard, when he dealt with us face to face, treated us with absolute respect. "Let us think about this and schedule another meeting," he said.

At the second meeting, though, he dug in his heels. "I think we know how to run this bank, thank you, and we're going to continue running this bank," he said. "I'm not going to allow this takeover to happen. If I can defeat you, I will defeat you." At least he was talking to us, which wasn't true of everyone who attended. Renchard had a vice chairman who came to all our meetings but wouldn't say hello to us beforehand or talk to us during the meetings, so offended was he by our proposed bid.

It seemed that the matter was over—and then Saul proposed a third meeting, to which Renchard agreed. "I've got a suggestion," Saul said. "I really believe that your bank and our company would be good for each other, so why don't *you* take *us* over? That way you could continue to run the bank." Talk about out-of-the-box thinking! Saul was willing to do this, I knew, because he thought that we were so much smarter than them that if we got together, Saul would be running the show in a couple of years. I think Renchard thought that, too, because he dismissed the idea out of hand, saying, "No, no, that won't do."

Finally, reeling from the downward pressure on our stock price—it was down to $7 by the end of May—we gave up on our plan. Even Man o' War got beat once. We would survive and thrive. Saul was philosophical about it. "I always knew there was an Establishment," he told the *Times*. "I just thought I was part of it." Looking back, Saul had the satisfaction of knowing that once we dropped our bid, Chemical did wind up adopting many of the ideas we put forward at the time and became a stronger bank as a result. Still, it was a very public defeat, and people remembered it.

A few months after our bid fell short, I was coming back from lunch one day and saw my secretary Merry Rich, who was six months pregnant, crying at her desk. "Merry, what's wrong?" I said. She was sobbing so hard she couldn't talk, so I pulled over a chair and sat down next to her.

"I'm going to lose the baby," Merry sobbed.

"Why do you think that?"

"I can't tell you," she said.

"Nonsense, you can tell me anything."

More sobs, and then, "I'm bleeding."

"Well, the first thing we're going to do is get you to a doctor," I said. "You're going this afternoon. And I want to tell you something else, Merry. You're going to be okay. The doctor is going to check you, and he's going to tell you that you are fine."

Suddenly she stopped crying and looked up at me. "How do you know that?" she asked.

"Because I'm older than you, I have two children, and I'm very, very smart."

"You were wrong about Chemical Bank!" she said, resuming her sobs.

I've often heard Saul describe the late 1960s as "tremendously fun times," and they were. We were wrong about Chemical Bank, or at any rate overconfident of our ability to pull it off. But most things, including Merry Rich's delivery of a healthy baby, went as planned or predicted, if not better, and a lot of people at Reliance did very well for themselves. As the 1960s ended and the '70s began, I became aware that I had reached the point where I could walk away from the business world if I wanted to, and my family and I could live comfortably on what I'd already made.

But instead of being happy, I felt discontented—not with my professional life, but with the world. My country in particular was letting me down and making me angry. The Vietnam War, a tragic mistake in the first place, was dragging on endlessly, and then on May 4, 1970, we heard the news that National Guardsmen had fired upon unarmed students at Kent State University. Some of those students had been peacefully marching in protest against the American invasion of Cambodia, which had been announced a few days before by President Richard Nixon. Others had merely been watching the demonstration or making their way to their next class. In thirteen seconds of wild gunfire, the National Guardsmen killed four students and wounded nine others. One young man was paralyzed for life.

I was so disgusted by the thought of this happening in the United States that I seriously considered quitting my job, taking my daughters out of school, and moving us all to France. Over the course of many evenings, Irene and I talked about the logistics of transplanting the family. Ultimately, though, we never made the move. I decided over time that I could be more effective as an agent for change if I stayed home and worked with and through the Democratic Party.

To run away from it all was a passing impulse; ultimately, curiosity trumped outrage. I have an insatiable desire to be part of the scene, I realized, to see what will happen next, and for that, a cozy pad in Paris did not afford the best perspective.

CHAPTER 8

A Near Miss

I don't usually dwell on the so-called good old days, but writing an autobiography has forced me to do exactly that. I've had to haul out the old appointment calendars, travel diaries, and annual reports and page through them. My memory doesn't need all that much jogging, but seeing a line that says "Meeting with Hillary Clinton" or simply "Lincoln Center" sometimes helps. I can't believe the over-packed schedule I kept: business trips to Paris, political gatherings in Washington, evenings out in New York City at the theater and ballet, long office hours, summer breaks in the Hamptons, parties at home, board meetings, movies, working lunches, skiing vacations out west with Irene, Karen, and Francesca, then back to our offices in New York.

It was nothing for me to visit thirteen different countries in one year (some of them more than once) on business. I loved it all—and what I remember best is that, even when I was sitting in a meeting in Israel and checking my watch to see if I could still make the tail end of a dinner party in New York, I was having so much fun.

"Did we really enjoy ourselves as much as I think we did?" I asked Saul Steinberg not too long ago during lunch at the Four Seasons.

"Without a doubt," he said, "and I'll tell you why. We knew how to laugh at ourselves—and we understood that there is a potential mistake around every corner. That helped us keep our sense of humor."

For Saul and me in 1969, one potential mistake was named Robert Maxwell—an oversized man, tall and round, whose personality was even bigger. He had that same quality his countryman Winston Churchill had, namely, that when he entered a room, he filled every corner. In Maxwell's life everything was on a grand scale; he ran a sprawling international business, lived in a gigantic house, and had nine children.

Maxwell was the owner of Pergamon Press, a major publisher of textbooks, encyclopedias, and scientific journals, and he was actively in the market for other publishing properties. He was also a member of Parliament representing the Labour Party. This was an unlikely affiliation for a multimillionaire like him, and Maxwell often had clashes with his own political colleagues as well as the opposition. But that was Maxwell: a self-made man who lived by his own rules and always played the maverick. Unfortunately, he was also a scoundrel.

By virtue of Saul's involvement with Leasco and then Reliance and the groundbreaking success he had with both, he was something of a celebrity businessman himself in those days. We had a London office and went there frequently. The British press was fascinated by Saul Steinberg, and I remember mornings when we'd walk out of Claridge's to see paparazzi snapping his picture and reporters peppering him with questions. Saul sometimes had meetings with Harold Wilson, then the British prime minister, and he got invited to all kinds of functions, lunches, conferences, and dinners. At a gala dinner one evening, Saul found himself seated beside Robert Maxwell.

It was not a particularly good moment for the publishing mogul. He had just lost a very public battle with the then-upstart Rupert Murdoch for control of the *News of the World* and was still quite upset about it. (In those days Murdoch was turning his attention away from his native Australia and starting to get heavily involved in the British newspaper business.) Maxwell also felt the leading bankers of London had turned against him and had rallied around Murdoch, giving the Australian interloper all the advantages. Saul was impressed with Maxwell—you almost had to be—but never intimidated by him the way a lot of people quite understandably were in those days. Though his story had elements of genuine tragedy to it, Maxwell was, at least in the minds of some people, a kind of mysterious, swashbuckling figure, a man of misty origins, multiple names, and uncertain connections.

He was born Ján Ludvik Hyman Binyamin Hoch in a small Czecho-slovakian village that is now part of the Ukraine. His parents had six other children, but his mother and father and most of Maxwell's siblings were killed in Auschwitz in 1944. By that time Maxwell was fighting for the Czech army, in exile in southern France. Somehow he managed to be transferred to the British army, saw action all over Europe, and rose through the ranks to become a captain. For his valor in battle he received the Military Cross from Field Marshal Montgomery and the Victoria Cross from the future Queen Elizabeth II. In 1945 he married Elisabeth Meynard, the daughter of the French minister of finance. British intel-ligence changed his name several times, finally settling on the one the world now knew him by.

After the war Maxwell got involved in publishing and distributing books and periodicals, building Pergamon Press into a large and lucrative business. As he gained success, he also acquired a reputation as someone who often had brilliant ideas but didn't always do the right thing. "Both in business and politics, he is not well regarded," Jacob Rothschild, the head of the Rothschild bank, told Saul and me.

Toward the end of his dinner conversation with Saul, Maxwell suddenly stopped talking about the *News of the World* affair and shot Saul a meaningful look. "I know who you are," Maxwell said. "You're doing things with computers that are very creative, and you're way ahead of the curve in the business world. I want you to learn about my Pergamon Press."

"Why is that?" said Saul.

"Because I want to buy your company and merge it with mine."

Saul's eyebrows must have gone up about two inches.

"I will explain," Maxwell said. "You have the technology—the computers you own through Leasco—and Pergamon Press has the printed content." He then went on to give a detailed scenario of how the traditional reading of paper books would decline in the future, how people would instead get their reading material from computers, and how wonderful and profitable it could be if Leasco and Pergamon were united. There is no denying that Maxwell was a visionary. Still, Saul was not going to part with Leasco, a company that had grown from an idea he'd nurtured and had become his only important asset. "I'm not interested in selling," Saul said, "but thank you anyway."

When they parted company that evening, Maxwell told Saul, "I'm leaving soon on a round-the-world trip to sell a new encyclopedia I'm publishing. But you'll be hearing from me again. Our companies should be put together somehow—because they're both unique."

He was right about that. Pergamon Press was an unusual and highly profitable operation. It was one of the world's leading publishers of scientific journals, all highly prestigious. Maxwell himself was not a scientist, but he had conceived and developed a system for producing these journals very efficiently. He would come up with a topic that some group of scientists wanted more information about—sometimes by relying on his own hunches but usually by asking professors at places like Cambridge, the University of Texas, and UCLA whom he was paying as consultants—and then create an advisory board of experts in that topic.

Those people would write articles and edit the publication. He paid the advisors relatively little, but they were delighted to do it for the prestige of publishing in an esteemed journal. There was nothing second-rate or shoddy about these publications, owing largely to the quality of the people who wrote them. People and institutions were willing to pay a premium price for Pergamon Press journals and that made it a vibrant business with excellent potential for growth.

But that wasn't the whole story. Maxwell very cleverly made additional money on the same material by overprinting the first run of the journals and holding on to the inventory. After two years or so, when the information in the journals would be considered somewhat dated, he sold the overstock, for a pittance, to a company that he happened to own, called Robert Maxwell LTD. That company then resold the old journals, for something more than a pittance, to individuals, colleges, high schools, and, most importantly, public libraries that might still have a use for them or who wanted to own every issue of a journal on a certain subject. It was perfectly legal, good for both companies, and especially good for Maxwell.

He had a typically ingenious plan for making money from his encyclopedia publishing company, Caxton. He promised customers that Caxton would produce twenty-two independent volumes of the *Caxton Encyclopedia*. He sold these by subscription; you'd buy the first four volumes as a group, and then every month thereafter the company would send you another volume. The initial price was quite reasonable.

Truth be told, there were some fairly significant problems with Caxton's program, which was essentially a Ponzi scheme. Maxwell clearly had cut a few corners. Still, he had produced seventeen of the planned twenty-two volumes by 1969, and he told anyone who'd listen that even before its completion it was already a huge success. But it couldn't be a success unless he produced *all* the volumes; he'd promised a full set in his contracts, and if he didn't meet that obligation, Caxton would not be able to collect the entire receivable for which it had contracted.

When Maxwell got to his first port of call on his sales tour, he cabled Saul. "We must do this deal," his message said. "If it's a question of you continuing to be involved, suppose I buy 80 percent of Leasco and leave 20 percent with you? You can be a stockholder." Saul wasn't going for that either. He didn't answer the cable.

Saul got another cable from the next port of call. "Saul, I keep thinking of all the things we could do if we could make this deal. What do you say we split the business, each take 50 percent? Together we could revolutionize the publishing world!"

Saul cabled back this time: "Thanks, Bob, but I really don't want to do that."

But Maxwell was a tremendously persistent man. Not long after that, he called Saul at our Park Avenue offices, said he was just a few blocks away at the Regency Hotel, and asked Saul to come over right away and meet with him. "I have to catch a plane to London in a couple of hours," he explained. "I'd like to talk to you immediately."

When Saul got there, Maxwell was still dressing and a butler was hurriedly packing his bags. Maxwell welcomed him warmly and said, "I'm changing my offer. I believe our companies should be united, and I believe it so strongly that I'm proposing that we turn around the whole deal. What if you buy Pergamon Press?"

That got Saul's attention, because he very much liked what he knew about the company's basic business. He just didn't want to be partners with Maxwell in Leasco.

"Okay, I'm willing to talk about that," Saul said.

"Excellent! But can we get it done right here? I've really got to leave for the airport."

Saul was flabbergasted. Maxwell was known for stepping up the slower-than-stately pace of the British publishing industry, but this was ridiculous. "You want to do a deal *now*? Here in your room? You haven't even met my colleague Bernard Schwartz. He is in charge of advising on the way we structure acquisitions; he would play an important part in putting something together."

"Can you get him over here right now?" Maxwell said.

Saul called the office and said, "I'd like you to come to the Regency and meet Bob Maxwell." I said, "Who is Bob Maxwell?" That's how little I knew about the situation. Still, I was at the hotel in about fifteen minutes. The door to Maxwell's room was open, maids were cleaning up, bellmen and butlers were rushing around packing and removing bags, and there in the midst of it all were Saul and Maxwell. It was the first time I'd ever seen Maxwell, but he turned and greeted me with a huge bear hug that almost broke my ribs.

"Bernard Schwartz, I've heard so much about you!" he said. Frankly, I doubted that he had ever heard of me before. "Please come in and help us conclude this deal." Then he looked at his watch. "Unfortunately, I only have about fifteen minutes. Please have a seat and let's see if we can make a deal."

"A deal to do what?" I said.

"To buy Pergamon Press."

I looked over at Saul and saw he was smiling. I was pleasant as could be, but I told Maxwell that was not how the sale of a company works. "I don't know how to do what you're asking me to do," I said. "At the moment I know absolutely nothing about Pergamon Press." I explained that we would need to do our due diligence, look at the financial records, and talk to people who worked for and with him; it would all take a while, several weeks at the very least. He took the news relatively well, seeming slightly disappointed but, on balance, cheerful enough. He was a man who'd had a lot of successes and a lot of setbacks, and he seemed to take both in stride.

"Okay, if you insist, that's the way we'll do it," he said. "Come over to Oxford, Bernard, and see me and the company, and we'll work all of this out, I'm sure. Bring your wife!"

"Uh, okay, when would be good for you?" I asked.

"How about the end of the month? "

And with that he was out the door, along with his bags and all the service people.

And so it was that at the end of that month, Irene and I visited Bob Maxwell's magnificent estate at Headington Hill Hall in Oxford. Maxwell and I spent several days discussing the operation of Pergamon Press, Robert Maxwell LTD, and Robert Maxwell Communications, a private company. I proposed to Maxwell that Reliance purchase Robert Maxwell LTD and Pergamon Press, which was traded on the London Stock Exchange. I proposed that we enter into an agreement that provided Reliance with the opportunity to complete due diligence, vetting the public numbers that had been issued by Pergamon Press. The importance of this approach was that we at Reliance maintained both control of the due diligence process and the opportunity to cancel the deal if things were not up to snuff. The transaction provided for a $200 million purchase of the outstanding stock of Pergamon and the entire equity of Robert Maxwell LTD.

Upon my return home, I put together a team with members of our finance department to conduct due diligence on Pergamon. The result was totally unexpected and disastrous: We found that Maxwell had taken a large and profitable company and riddled it with deceptive account practices and even outright fraud. Assets had been moved around among members of his family to conceal profitability. Nothing about Pergamon Press was as it seemed; the company's accounting statements were fraudulent.

In order to withdraw our bid, we had to present our findings to the Department of Trade and Industry in London. The DTI's subsequent investigation took nine months to verify our revelations. Maxwell was forced to step down from his chairmanship during that time, and for those nine months, as a member of Pergamon's board of directors, I essentially took the responsibility of running the company.

Our withdrawal from the acquisition deal was not the end of the Maxwell story. This smart, cunning, unscrupulous man went on to build a giant communications empire, but in the end, under increasing investigation by the authorities, it disintegrated. Maxwell drowned while yachting off the Canary Islands. We will never know if it was suicide or some other result of his evildoings.

Robert Maxwell was not an accountant, but he knew more about accounting—especially how to take advantage of it—than anyone I've ever met. He was not a lawyer, but he was the cleverest counsel I had ever met. He would have succeeded in anything he did . . . had he not been a crook.

CHAPTER 9

Buying Loral

All these years later, I remember exactly where I was sitting when I first heard the word "Loral."

I was sitting on top of the world.

Life was good for me at Saul Steinberg's company, The Reliance Group. Not perfect—life is never perfect, and accepting that can save you a lot of emotional energy over the long haul—but, lucky man that I am, I wanted for almost nothing. I had a loving and supportive family, financial security, and the chance to put into practice the principles and techniques I'd been honing my entire career.

The secret of happiness, at least for me, has been to put myself in a position where I'm always either learning something new or overcoming challenges by applying lessons I've learned along the way. I think that's what keeps veteran athletes going, sometimes after they've won everything there is to win or earned enough to live well indefinitely. It's fun to do what you're most interested in—a privilege not everyone gets—and doubly fun when what you're interested in is the thing you do best. For a long time, that described my daily existence at Schnee, Hauer, Schwartz, at APL, and at Leasco and Reliance.

One of the lessons I learned early on was this: You don't have to know everything, but make sure you know what you don't know. When

Saul took over Reliance Insurance Company, we realized we didn't know much about . . . well, insurance. (Before you laugh, remember that the Beatles could not read music!) So we made sure that the previous president, Bill Roberts, stayed on and handled the day-to-day operations. He reported to me, I reported to Saul, and everything worked out very well as we gradually acquainted ourselves with that highly evolved, and at times very arcane, industry.

When we got into leasing shipping containers by acquiring CTI in 1968, we again realized the limits of our knowledge, but in that case it led to a management breakthrough. Saul understood as well as anyone that the two key factors in running a leasing company are raising the cash to buy the equipment and managing the inventory. After that, everything is secondary. The excess cash that came with Reliance allowed us to buy the world's largest shipping container company, but managing those containers wasn't easy.

CTI was a very successful company, but its inventory management was imperfect. If you were a manufacturer in, say, Tokyo, making a shipment to San Francisco, you leased the container one-way. In most cases that left us with an empty container we would have to move out of San Francisco to wherever it was needed next. Meanwhile, a day later we might have a customer in San Francisco looking for a container. It was frustrating and inefficient.

The solution may seem obvious today, but in the late 1960s it took a mind like Saul's to see that this was the sort of problem that computers were made to handle. So he hired a young programmer named David Fox who came up with what became known as the "Kyoto system." By anticipating demand based on history and projections of future needs, we created a plan that dramatically increased our profitability and eventually revolutionized the shipping industry.

Saul knew enough to not get complacent about our main business, leasing IBM computers. Leasco was extremely successful, but the environment was always changing, and you had to stay one step ahead of the game. In 1969 we hired Frank McCracken, who had been a vice president at IBM and was an expert on leasing. He became president of the company, and I moved up to vice chairman.

As soon as McCracken came on board, he stopped by my office and said, "I'd like to start having a staff meeting one morning every week. Is that okay with you?"

That's really not my style. I think staff meetings can be a giant waste of time, especially if the people at the meeting are working together all the time anyway. But I realize that different people have different and sometimes equally valid approaches to business management, so I told him that it was okay to have staff meetings if it suited him.

"Okay," he said. "The meeting will be at nine a.m. on Monday."

I got there at about 9:02, but when I tried to turn the doorknob to the meeting room, it was locked.

"I thought there was a meeting going on in here," I said to a secretary sitting nearby.

"There is," she said. "But Mr. McCracken said he would lock the doors at nine and that anyone who arrived late was out of luck."

I went back to my office, got the conference room key, and went in. I saw that McCracken had been thoughtful enough to leave a seat right next to him, and I sat down in it. He was in the middle of a speech to the fifteen or so people he called to the meeting.

"Everyone in this room represents the company," he said, "and so I expect to see you always looking your best. I expect to see black shoes with a fresh shine on them every day. I expect to see all of the men in white shirts and conservative ties, and there will be no excuses or exceptions!"

I wondered why we needed such a policy at Reliance. Telling people they had to wear certain clothing and colors and behave a certain way was the IBM culture, but it wasn't Saul's or mine. The dress code was a superficial symptom of a larger problem: a basic clash of styles. McCracken was a good man who understood the leasing business as few do, but he was the wrong man for us, and he didn't last with Leasco.

I could have gone on with Saul indefinitely and yet, deep inside, I

realized I probably wouldn't. If there was one thing nagging at me, it
was that for all the success I'd had in the business world, I still hadn't
run my own company. And I'd learned from watching several powerful
personalities and helping them run their companies that, like them, I
thrived on responsibility.

I want to make it clear, however, that I was not mulling a change or
casting about for a company to run when Bob Hodes called me one day
and started talking about a troubled enterprise called Loral. The issue of
running my own company hadn't become an item on what people now
call a bucket list. Loral was not a symptom of a midlife crisis; it was the
opportunity of a lifetime.

No person would have described Loral that way on the day in the fall
of 1971 that Bob first called me, however. This was a company that a lot of
Wall Street analysts thought was on its way to bankruptcy. As I mentioned
in chapter 1, Loral, a manufacturer of electronic weapons detection
systems of very high quality, was managing to do poorly at a time—the
Vietnam War era—when defense concerns could be expected to prosper.
The twenty-three-year-old company was coming off a year in which it had
reported a $2 million loss; its net worth had fallen 20 percent during that
time, to $9.5 million, and its stock price had dropped dramatically.

Even if it had been a healthy company, Loral was in an industry that
is difficult for some investors to get excited about because it makes them
think of government bureaucracy or conflict. I won't say that Bob was
desperate when he called me, but I do think he didn't know what else
to do. He was on the board of Loral, I was his friend, and he probably
thought that as a complete stranger to the defense business, I might be
able to look at the situation unencumbered by past history, prejudices,
and presumptions.

In any case, all he asked me to do was to take a quick look at the
financials and break bread with a few outsider board members who were
understandably concerned about the company's future. "Maybe," he
said, "you can make a few general recommendations." It wasn't a date, in
other words; it was just lunch.

I spent the hour before that lunch looking over the materials Bob had sent me. I saw all the shrinking numbers and noted that after Loral had gone public in 1959, it used the cash it had raised to turn itself into the crazy-quilt conglomerate I described in chapter 1. This was not necessarily a bad idea; the idea of corporate diversification had become popular since the end of World War II, no doubt because it did, in certain circumstances, allow the owner to spread risk. The problem for Loral was that, while it was very adept at its core business, it knew virtually nothing about other businesses it had acquired. And the fatal flaw was that it didn't know how little it knew.

When I talked to the board members, I spoke in terms of broad strokes and first impressions. The flip side of all the problems, I pointed out, was that relatively few adjustments could lead to rapid improvements. "It seems pretty obvious to me that you should sell off these newer divisions and concentrate on what you know best," I told the directors. I didn't expect to hear much about Loral again, but the next day Bob Hodes called to say that the people at the lunch had been impressed with what I said about the company. They had little faith in the current management of Loral, he added, and they had asked him to call me to see if I would perhaps consider coming to the company and leading it away from the edge of the cliff it appeared to be heading toward. Could I see myself as the company president?

I thought that sounded like a perfectly horrible idea. "That's the last thing in the world I'd want to do," I told Bob. I don't mean to disparage Leon Alpert, who was the chairman of the company at the time, but I didn't see myself leaving Reliance to work for him—or anybody else. "Just think about it a while," said Bob. "Maybe you wouldn't have to work for Alpert. Maybe there's a way you could take over the company."

I did think about it, and I came up with a plan. "If I could buy 12 percent of the stock from Lorenz and Alpert but take the company over," I told Bob, "that might interest me. But as part of this scenario, Alpert and Lorenz would have to retire, the board would also retire, and

I would appoint a new board. If that could happen, I'd be willing to investigate this further."

Bob said that sounded reasonable to him, so I began to do my due diligence. This was a responsibility I couldn't delegate. I wanted to sit down with people from inside and outside the company and be able to hear the tone of their voice, observe their body language, and look them in the eye. Sometimes when I spoke to Loral engineers about electronic defense systems, I didn't know what the hell they were talking about, and I realized that if I was going to proceed with this deal I would have to educate myself about the company's core business, and quickly. But at least I knew how much I didn't know.

One of the people I knew during this time was Tom Stanton, president at the First Jersey National Bank of New Jersey. A board member of Loral who was at that initial lunch meeting, Tom had dealt with my brother's firm, APL, so he knew me. I told him I had some real misgivings about taking over Loral because it had been having such trouble getting bank loans owing to the fact that it was showing annual losses. Tom answered me with great assurance, and I'll never forget what he said. "Bernard, you should do this deal. Those other banks are wrong to be denying credit to Loral. They don't understand the company and the particular straits it's in. You should know that there's a lot of collateral in this company that you don't see on the balance sheets." He was referring to the engineering skills of the employees, the reputation for excellence enjoyed by the company's main plant just off Bruckner Boulevard in the South Bronx, the relationships that had been built up with the customers, and other abstract but real assets. "I'm telling you, Bernard, you can turn this company around."

As my investigations progressed, I started to see other reasons to think positively. The defense industry had several unique qualities, the most obvious one being that it had, for all practical purposes, only one customer: the US Department of Defense. Other business opportunities could develop from this primary market, but the principal driver of the industry was the Pentagon. To a lot of people who might be considering an investment in the defense sector, that would be a negative consideration, but it wasn't to me. For one thing, though I may be liberal in my political beliefs, I've always had a basically positive attitude toward the defense industry. A strong military seems vital to me as a way of preserving peace. For another thing, I've never seen the military as some people do: as an arcane and confusing culture that doesn't always answer to the rules of the marketplace. I'd served in the army, after all, and I'd seen a lot of smart people trying to do a good job and generally succeeding. Until the generals in charge of ordering weapons and monitoring production showed me otherwise, I decided, I would keep an open mind and assume they were as worthy as any executives in the private sector.

In 1971 when I was doing my Loral research, defense spending took a marked downturn, even though the Vietnam War was still raging and we had a Republican president, Richard Nixon, whom many still associate with the escalation of the conflict. The slowdown in weapons expenditures not only suppressed profits and expectations throughout the defense industry, it also caused a decline in market values of publicly held defense companies. But that didn't scare me off. I was seeing things that Wall Street didn't.

For me the key to understanding the true state of Loral was learning how Defense Department contracts worked. In those days the process started when one of the branches of the armed forces came to a company like Loral, Boeing, or Lockheed and said, for example, "We need a radar detection system for a fighter plane. Would you like to bid on the contract?" If you said yes, you were charged with coming up with a price for something that did not exist yet. To do that, you had to figure that the product would require a couple of years of research and development (R&D), and that besides that expense, the military would probably want you to absorb the first two or three years of production costs as well. The bid you made was always to some extent an educated guess, and thus a big gamble. The upside, though, was that if you got final approval, you were looking at the likelihood of a long-term, sole-source contract that would be tremendously profitable over quite a few years. In other words, if you accepted the defense industry as a *different* way of doing business, and not an *inferior* way of doing business, it could be a great place to be.

Further, in addition to many smart and loyal employees and a reputation for quality, Loral had four major contracts at the time: two with the air force and two with the navy. Three of these contracts were in the development stage and one was in production. That meant that the latter was producing a profit while the others were a drain on revenue, but probably only in the short term. To me these development contracts weren't weaknesses; I saw them as smart investments.

The most interesting contract of all, I decided, was being executed by a key component of the company called Loral Electronic Systems. LES was developing a passive radar warning receiver system for the F-15, a twin-engine, all-weather tactical fighter plane then itself in development for the air force by McDonnell Douglas. I didn't have significant expertise in military hardware and software, but as I did my research and talked to military officers and engineers, I became convinced that the F-15 was going to be the dominant fighter plane for America and its allies. So, as the holder of a contract for a major internal component of the F-15, Loral was in a terrific position to profit far into the future. Of course, if I was wrong about either the aircraft or Loral's ability to fulfill the contract for the radar warning receiver system, that single misjudgment could deal the company a fatal blow. Was I willing to gamble that contracts like that one made Loral an attractive acquisition? I was.

However, even if Loral's current management realized it was sitting on several large contracts on the verge of moving from the red to the black, they were being distracted and drained by the non-core companies Loral had acquired over the prior ten years. When I walked through the plants and offices of Loral, I heard many employees say they got absolutely no help from management with either their day-to-day or their long-term projects. I knew I could do better than that, and once I got rid of the poorly performing divisions, we'd see dramatic improvement.

As sure as I was about what I wanted to do, the transition from Reliance to Loral was not something I took lightly. I wouldn't be working with Saul on a day-to-day basis anymore; I no doubt would be taking a dramatic cut in compensation, at least initially; and I'd be running a smaller, much less stable company in a sector that some of my friends contemptuously sniffed at. But offsetting all the rest was one all-important factor: Loral would be mine. For the first time in my career, I would truly be the boss.

I was excited, but I didn't want to get so excited that I struck a dumb deal. The poor performance of Loral at that point in time, the mood of the company's founders, the prevailing political climate—all those negatives could give me leverage in a negotiation. With that in mind, I arranged to have a meeting with Leon Alpert and William Lorenz in the fall of 1971. I also thought it would be a good idea to have Bob Hodes there, since both sides liked and trusted him.

We got together at Alpert's home in Florida. After talking to them a while, I could tell that Alpert, who was in his mid-sixties and whose background was in accounting, was a decent man. Lorenz, who was older than his cofounder, was an engineer and an inventor of sophisticated electronic equipment and—that day anyway—not very communicative. At the first meeting, Alpert and I talked in a very general way for an hour or so about my interest in the company and what they thought it was worth, while Lorenz said very little. We agreed to reconvene a couple of days later.

At our second meeting, I came bearing a unique proposition that I made in short order. I knew they owned 12 percent of Loral's outstanding shares and that those shares were at that time worth $2 million. I told them I would buy half of their holdings, or 6 percent of the outstanding shares, immediately for $2 million, and I would also include an option to buy their other 6 percent in four years for an additional $2 million. The advantages to me were that I didn't have to come up with $4 million and that I didn't have to pay for something until I was sure of what I had.

The advantage to them was that if I did exercise the option, they would be making double the amount of money they would get under ordinary circumstances. It was a very good deal for both sides. "I can't say for sure if Loral can deliver on the contracts it has with the navy and the air force," I told them. "But I'm optimistic that it can—and if it does, we'll all do better." Alpert wasn't enthusiastic about my plan; he didn't think I was offering enough and wanted the full purchase price up front. But I told him that my offer was fair and that I would walk away from the deal before I changed my terms.

I should note here that there was another advantage for me in putting up my own money as I took control of the company. The idea that I was buying into Loral for cash would, I knew, be attractive to investors, because it demonstrated that I was not just a professional manager. Nothing was being given to me; I was putting out real cash, and that meant I believed the story I was telling about the company. That also would make it easier to attract the best people to our board.

Alpert and I went back and forth like this for a quite a while, with Lorenz, who was sitting alongside his partner, still saying nothing. Then he finally broke his silence. Turning very slowly and deliberately toward Alpert, he said, "Leon, we are going to do this—and we're going to do it now. Schwartz has a plan to make this company a success. He believes he can pull it off. If he does, we'll still have the balance of our shares, and we can make some money with them, after a while."

"But, Bill . . . ," said Alpert.

"I'm telling you, Leon," said Lorenz, pointing at me, "this man can do what we can't."

After that little exchange, the deal for Loral came together rather easily. My initial investment of $2 million was a tiny amount to leverage into control of what I saw as such a promising company. I was, and still am, very proud of the deal I struck. But it was no small investment for me; $2 million was about all the free capital I had at the time.

Once I made the decision to take over Loral, I had to break the news to three key people (Irene already knew what I was up to). The first two were my daughters, Karen and Francesca. I wasn't going to get into the defense business without first discussing it with them. They were teenagers at the time, about seventeen and fifteen, and very opposed to the

Vietnam War, as were Irene and I, and I didn't want them to be blind-sided by the announcement that I was going into the defense industry.

So we sat down one night after I came home from work, and we had a discussion about it, a frank and free exchange of ideas, as the diplomats say. They already knew I believed in a strong military as a way of minimizing conflicts abroad, and perhaps eliminating future Vietnams. I think they understood that I hadn't changed my beliefs, and by the end of the evening, I felt that I had their full support, just as I had Irene's. I will never take for granted nor forget how my family has always been there for me.

That left Saul Steinberg as the last person to whom I had to break the news that I was becoming CEO and chairman of Loral.

Saul and I had a relationship based on mutual respect, and up till that point we had never had a significant argument. Thanks to him, we'd both had tremendous success, and I think we felt especially close because of the distance we'd traveled and the victories we'd shared. Even so, our professional connection wasn't going to continue forever as it was. I wanted to run my own company, and he was in his prime, with no thoughts of selling his interest or retiring. Still, when I went into his office one morning and told him what I planned on doing, Saul seemed surprised and said he thought it was the stupidest idea he'd ever heard.

He made all the classic arguments against getting into the defense business. "It's a very specialized field . . . You don't know anything about it . . . Defense companies don't make much money . . ."

"Have you ever heard of Lockheed?" I said. "Have you ever heard of Hughes? McDonnell Douglas?"

"Loral is not on that scale," he said.

"You're absolutely right about that," I said, "but it doesn't matter. I want to do my own thing, Saul, and I think I can do it with this company."

He was very persistent. "If you want to do something, to take on a big challenge, do it here. We've got a lot of money. Let's do it together. We'll have some fun." It was flattering to hear him say that, but I was firm. "Saul, this is not a discussion—it's an announcement. I'm going to do this and take my chances, and that's that."

With that I got up and walked out the door. We had cavernous offices, and the hallways seemed as long as the train platforms at Grand Central Terminal. I walked and walked and then walked some more. Then, far behind me, the outer door to Saul's office flew open, and he stuck out his head and hollered down the long corridor, "Schwartz! Schwartz! Should I buy the stock?"

At that moment I didn't want any responsibility to Saul as a shareholder. "No, don't buy the stock!" I yelled back without breaking my stride.

PART III

Not in the Conventional Way

"Bernard Schwartz is one of the legends in our industry.
He brought smart business practices to the defense industry,
which was really lacking in such things. His way of approach-
ing deals and contracts was good for Loral, of course, for its
employees and its shareholders, but it was also good for the
military and, ultimately, the American taxpayer. Bernard
did not do things in the conventional way, at least for a defense
contractor. He would get involved when and where it was
appropriate, but to a great extent he hired smart people and let
them do their own thing. That spirit of entrepreneurship he
brought to Loral was a sign of his wisdom as a
businessman and one secret of the company's success."

—NORMAN AUGUSTINE, FORMER UNDER SECRETARY
OF THE ARMY AND RETIRED CEO
OF LOCKHEED MARTIN CORPORATION

CHAPTER 10

Running "My" Company

When I formally took control of Loral on February 10, 1972, I had a vision for how the company would not just survive but thrive in the dramatic defense-spending cycles that so many people were warning me about—and even for how the company would operate on a day-to-day basis. I had a sense of what it would *feel* like to work at Loral. I hope that doesn't make me sound like a braggadocio. It shouldn't, for by that point I had some hard-won business experience. And besides, any fool can have a vision.

The question is, is your vision any good? Are you Jack Welch rescuing GE or Steve Jobs starting Apple? Or are you the beleaguered brains behind one of the countless washouts? How you manage your vision is also important—you've got to know if and when to modify it or even junk it because it's doing you more harm than good. You can't judge a vision by how strongly you believe in it or how loudly you defend it in front of angry shareholders. You can judge it only by the results it produces. Remember: Performance is the best strategy.

I will admit to one big miscalculation. I didn't think I would be running the company for an especially long time. Rather, I figured I'd move in and weed out all those extraneous divisions that Loral had acquired; make sure that the company was on its way to fulfilling the contracts it had with the navy and the air force; set the course for a more stable and secure future—perhaps by making a few key acquisitions; and then I would sell it all off at a good price and move on. Loral and I would both be better for having spent some time together.

But that part of the vision obviously didn't pan out. Instead, I quickly became much more deeply interested in the company than I ever thought I would. The money was important to me, but it soon became secondary to the satisfactions I got from the job of running the company in a way that dramatically increased shareholder value. Simply put, I fell in love with Loral.

There was a lot about the company to love, starting with the unique compound we had in the South Bronx, where, as I mentioned earlier, products for our core Loral Electronics System division were conceived, developed, and manufactured. What appealed to me about that place was its spirit and personality, which reflected the best aspects of doing business in New York. Though it's not often noted, the city has one of the largest concentrations of technical schools in the country, and good schools too: NYU, Columbia University, Long Island University, Polytechnic, City College, Pratt Institute, Cooper Union, and Manhattan College to name just a few.

The students who graduate from our local schools tend to be New York natives who want to stay in the area after they get their degrees. That they were often middle-class, working class, or even poor kids didn't bother me; that is not surprising, however, given my own background. I saw this continuous stream of talent as a tremendous resource. Loral became one of the largest employers of people graduating from New York City's technical schools because we found these young men and women to be eager for success, passionate about their chosen fields, and, most important, smart as hell.

The employees, from the engineers to the people on the assembly line, were the reason we came up with so many innovative products and enjoyed a reputation for quality unequalled in the defense business. Quite often I heard from groups in places like Tennessee and Kentucky, dangling offers of tax breaks and real estate bargains in an attempt to get Loral to pack up and move down there, as so many other companies had. Although the financial incentives might sound impressive, I never seriously considered those blandishments; I could never turn my back on the Bronx, especially in those days when it was burning down all around us. I'd like to think that the people there appreciated us as much as we appreciated them.

If you're going to succeed, you've got to have the right people in every corner of your operation, whether it be the corporate boardroom or a factory floor. Replacing most of the board was among my highest priorities when I assumed command of Loral. It was obvious we needed stronger leadership, and I wanted to start fresh with people who had expertise that complemented mine: people like Gershon Kekst, who ran one of the top financial public relations firms in the country, a man who was recognized in the investment community as a person of good judgment. He accepted my invitation with enthusiasm. Among the people who stayed on from the previous board were Homer Chapin, an insurance company executive, and Bob Hodes. Yes, Bob was my best friend, but he was also a senior member of one of New York City's biggest law firms, a man known and liked by an awful lot of influential people and thus a valuable contributor to our corporate mission.

I didn't care if a potential board member understood much about the aerospace or defense business as long as he or she was widely perceived to be a reputable and smart person with a record of success. (Mal Ruderman, a physics professor at Columbia, was probably our only board member who could speak the language of the Loral engineers.) All our board members were contributors: Howard Gittis, a leading businessman; Art Simon, a partner in the Touche Ross accounting firm; Sally Minard, a marketing executive; and Allen Shinn, a retired vice admiral who had been commander of the Pacific Fleet in the US Navy. We also had Charles Lazarus, founder and chairman of Toys "R" Us; Daniel Yankelovich, a renowned sociologist; and Donald Shapiro, dean of New York Law School.

I also wanted everyone on the board (except me, of course) to be an outsider, meaning not also a corporate officer at Loral. That was highly unusual, but I felt it was important to bring together people of diverse skills and to show Wall Street and the investment banking community that our board was not just a crew of yes-men, rubber-stamping the boss's decrees. I saw Loral making numerous acquisitions down the line, and when we were raising capital for those deals, it would help if the company did not look like a one-man show. After our first few acquisitions, Loral's reputation started to speak for itself, and I was able to raise many millions of dollars with relative ease. But especially in the beginning, our board was Loral's calling card, and I was proud of the wide-ranging talents of its people.

Although I never for a moment regretted my decision to take over the company, I did realize in those exhilarating first weeks and months that I was in uncharted territory. I never got beyond Physics 102 at City College, and I was running a highly technological company whose product line I didn't really understand and doing business with the US military, a potentially intimidating customer I'd never dealt with before.

We had five divisions in those days, and I would visit each division once a month and sit in on meetings, always accompanied by a man named Bernard Herman, who was the president of Loral at the time. Very often the engineers, designers, and other people would be talking about the basic business of my company, and I couldn't begin to follow what they were saying. Bernie Herman would nod and take notes, and I would sit there, completely lost. This was not a good situation. Not only was it disconcerting to be unable to speak the same language as my employees, but my obvious lack of familiarity with the basics of my business was also something that could undermine my authority and impinge on my ability to lead.

One of the first people I hired part-time was a young PhD candidate from Columbia whose job it was to come to my office at eight in the morning on Tuesdays and Thursdays and give me a tutorial in physics and electronics. I didn't want anyone to know this was happening, so

I kept my door locked and told my secretary that the nature of these meetings was highly confidential and she was the only one who was to know what I was doing.

I won't say that I instantly gained an in-depth knowledge of the business, but after a couple of months of lectures and homework, I did understand the broad outlines much better. I also became able to pepper my conversation with a few technological buzzwords, which both impressed my colleagues and, I could see, surprised them. Exactly how deep my knowledge ran they didn't know, but they did understand they could no longer afford to see me as a rank layman, and between that and their respect for my business and financial skills, I was able fill the role of boss.

Understand, I have no particular interest in cultivating fear among my employees, but recognition of my ultimate authority is key to the way I do business, to what soon became known as the Loral culture that I described in chapter 1. Remember, I'm the guy who would advise you, once I'd heard the arguments and ruled on something, to "just say yes" to the decision that had already been made. Honestly, I place very little value on consensus building. I realize this is contrary to the conventional wisdom about proper corporate behavior, but conventional wisdom and proper corporate behavior are things I've never cared about much.

Consensus building sounds nice, but in my experience it tends to waste time, weaken confidence, and lead to conclusions that are second-rate, or worse. I much prefer strongly held positions that are persuasively argued and based on solid information. The key words here are "strongly held." For me, personal commitment on tough issues always trumps consensus thinking.

Closely related to my ideas about the dangers of consensus building is my belief in a small management staff. Starting on day one of my tenure at Loral and through the thirty-four years I would spend leading the company, we usually had no more than ten people at the highest level of management. I'm sure no other major player in the defense industry had such a small management staff. But having fewer people at the top meant we had better communication among the leaders and personal ties to the operating divisions. But please don't read "better communication" as "more meetings." As I've already said, I've never been a fan of meetings, and from the start we rarely if ever had them.

Instead, communication between the key corporate personnel occurred on a continuous basis: phone calls, office visits, hallway encounters, spontaneous get-togethers in groups of two or three. In that sense, you might say our working lives were one never-ending staff meeting, though it didn't feel that way because of the smallness and the tightness of our decision-making group. Further, though we communicated constantly, we did not talk about situations endlessly. Everyone understood that decisions would be made in relatively short order, and after that it was a closed matter (Just say yes!), and we would move on.

Sometimes people ask me if I think the Loral culture is something that can work in a different environment. I always answer, "All I can tell you is that it worked very well for us."

We never really talked much about honesty and openness at Loral, but those virtues were deeply imbedded in the way we treated each other, our customers, and even our competitors. After one of the first gatherings I attended as the new CEO, I said to the then-president, "You know, we're not asking the right questions at these meetings. We should be asking our operating people relevant questions about performance, budget issues investments, and schedules: 'What is the forward book of business?' 'How much inventory do we need to meet this production goal?' 'What happens if we don't meet the timetable you're talking about?' We've got to get down into the real *essence* of the business."

"We've got specifics—I'll get them for you!" he said. But his responses were too slow and imprecise, and soon I began to speak up more at meetings and ask a lot of questions. I was flexing my growing vocabulary of technical terms and using the years of business experience that I brought to Loral. That company president and I parted ways in less than a year. At around that same time, I hired my first Loral employee, Michael DeBlasio, as CFO. (Mike would remain with the company until his death in 2004.)

In those first few months of my tenure, I wanted to meet our engineers, our R&D people, our manufacturing people, our financial people—everybody. I also wanted to get to know personnel from all the customers with whom Loral had contracts at that time: the air force, McDonnell Douglas, and Lockheed. Before I could set up a meeting with Lockheed, however, their senior vice president, Don Wilder, called *me*. "Congratulations, Mr. Schwartz," he said. "We'd like to sit down with you and have a meeting as soon as possible."

Wilder didn't say what was on his mind, but from talking to our marketing people, I knew what he was worried about, and I understood his concern. Loral was committed to building a cockpit display and countermeasure systems for S-3A Viking antisubmarine aircraft that Lockheed was building for the navy. Without us up and running, Lockheed couldn't fulfill those contracts in a timely manner, and because of some of the things that had happened at and to Loral in the previous year, our continued existence couldn't be taken for granted.

But we weren't just a troubled company—we were a troubled company being led by someone whose long-term plans Wilder could only guess at. He may have wondered if I actually had an interest in the electronic systems and the relationships with the military that had been the core strengths of the company. I'm sure it crossed his mind that I might be more excited about one or more of the newer divisions—the packing, wire, or toy companies—than the LES division. And if that was the case, where would that leave him? Indeed, Don Wilder was hardly the only person thinking like this; the defense industry was rife with rumors about me and my intentions. "Everyone is talking about how you're the new kid on the block, the X factor in the business," one Loral executive told me, "and a lot of people are trying to guess what you're going to do and if you intend to transition out of the defense business."

But the more I learned about the industry, the more I liked our chances. Besides that, while one of the contracts we had with Lockheed was still in the development stage and wasn't yet profitable, the other one was starting to pay off handsomely. I saw the deal to make a tactical display system for navy sub hunters as a beacon leading us to stability and future success. I also saw it as an example of how the investment strategies then available missed the business values of Loral—and what excellent opportunities that knowledge gap provided. In short, there was no way I was going to walk away from our Lockheed contracts. But with only a month of experience under my belt, I wasn't quite prepared to say all that in a public forum.

As soon as I walked into the conference room at Lockheed's facility in Pasadena, California, with my small band of executives, I could see that Wilder viewed our meeting as something important. About a dozen of his engineers, designers, and executives were in attendance, and these people gave a well-prepared and meticulous review of the two contracts that Lockheed and Loral were involved in together. At the end of that presentation, we discussed various aspects of the projects, and then finally Wilder got to the key question of whether we felt we were prepared to fulfill our commitments in a timely manner.

"I'm going to be honest with you," I said. "I've only been doing this job for about a month. I did a lot of research beforehand, and I do know that you are our most important customer. I need you to give me another month. At the end of that time, I'll come back here and answer all your questions." Wilder was amenable to my proposition, and we reconvened one month later in Pasadena.

This time, once the pleasantries were out of the way, I was the one who spoke first. "I want to assure you that I plan to stay in this business. I bought Loral because I liked the company and the industry, and nothing I've seen has changed my mind." I could sense the Lockheed people relaxing a bit. But my next pitch was something of a curve ball.

I assured them of Loral's commitment and particularly our intention and ability to put up the financial resources necessary to complete the development contract on the displays that we were building for them. I explained that we did, however, have a financial concern about the second phase of this program—the production phase. It was conditional upon the contractor completing the development stage in a way that was acceptable to the navy. But Loral had no commitment from Lockheed that it would enter into the production phase. Further, the contract provided that Lockheed's option to acquire equipment from Loral extended for only the first two years of production at a price specified in the contract. In other words, even if we held up our end of the bargain, there was no certainty that Loral would be able to recoup its investment.

I proposed to Don Wilder that we finish the first phase of our commitment as specified in the contract, and I told him I had every confidence that we would meet the navy standards. However, what I wanted from Lockheed was their commitment that if they chose to enter the second phase, they would revise the unit production price for each display purchased so that Loral would be assured an appropriate profit.

I pointed out that my proposal left Lockheed with all the options, and an adjustment of the future price of production was both businesslike and fair. After some discussion, Wilder and I shook hands on the matter, and I thought we had a deal.

CHAPTER 11

Early Hurdles

In a matter of weeks, I'd gone from Reliance to Loral: from an established, thriving company to one that was still more like an *idea* for a successful enterprise.

How busy was my life when I first took over Loral? Let's put it this way: I had a long to-do list, and some days I never even got to it. Some days I never got to what was keeping me *from* the to-do list. I was creating something: a new Loral, built upon the business principles I'd been practicing since the earliest days of my career.

Step one was to get back to basics. It was never my goal to merely shrink or simplify Loral. I wanted ultimately to grow the company far beyond what it was in 1971, and I wanted to shape the new and bigger Loral in a way that would both take advantage of existing synergies in the defense business and buffer the company from the industry's traditional vicissitudes such as cutbacks in defense spending, unforeseeable international conflicts, and the risky and expensive three-stage cycle (development, prototype production, long-range production) that affects the way defense-systems products are produced for the US military.

But as in a garden, the growth of what mattered most depended on a weeding-out process. This meant not just identifying and parting company with certain executives who seemed out of tune with our

emerging culture, but also divesting ourselves of the divisions that no
longer made sense in our overall corporate plan—the toy, wire, and
other companies that represented a failed diversification strategy and
contributed little more than a drain on profit. They had to go, and
quickly, and we had to get back to what Loral was founded to do in the
late 1940s: designing and producing sophisticated electronic defense
systems for military aircraft. Within a year's time I had sold five non-
core divisions.

Saul and I did not part on bad terms. I see my career as a continuum;
I bring the same basic business principles and, when I can, even the same
people, from one job to the next. Thus, the places I've worked became
interconnected. When I went from APL to Leasco, I used the same lawyers and outside accountants. When Leasco became Reliance, and again
when I moved from Reliance to Loral, I kept those longtime advisors.
The friends I made at one job usually stayed my friends as I moved on to
the next job, too, so there was no reason that wouldn't also happen with
Saul. I still served happily on his board, just as I had continued to serve
on APL's board.

To tell the truth, I didn't *know* how to break up with Saul. He
was almost like a family member to me. We'd never had a meaningful
disagreement in all the years I'd known him, and that was odd in a
way because we weren't similar in most respects. I was perhaps a more
disciplined businessman that he was. He tended to operate from instinct,
and that instinct was usually accurate. He was the best seller of assets and
ideas I ever saw: a man who always got his price; a deal maker who was
brave and tough enough to let anyone walk out of the room if they didn't
like his first (and almost always final) offer. I, on the other hand, if I do say
so myself, am a pretty good buyer of properties; I was always fascinated
by the challenge of finding an asset's true worth and communicating just
enough of my interest and enthusiasm to the seller.

Saul and I complemented each other, and for a while made an unbeat-
able team. The two things we shared, I think, were a curiosity about the
world and the ability to learn something from whatever happened to us

along the way, constantly refining our principles and methods. Although Saul wanted to win in business and liked money as much as anyone, he was at bottom a decent guy who didn't want to keep everything for himself. When I first went to work for him, I remember saying, "Well, Saul, I guess we ought to sit down and talk about money," and him saying in response, "How much do you want?" I told him, and he said, "Fine." As the company grew and it came time for adjustments in compensation, stock options, and other perks, there was never a negotiation. "Whatever you want," he would always say. It was a relationship built on the trust and confidence we had in each other. He knew I wouldn't ask for more than was fair, and I knew he believed in my judgment.

But things had changed from that simpler, relatively innocent time when Saul was a happy man hatching brilliant ideas and seeing them pan out. He had much more by the 1970s—he was living in one of the grandest apartments in New York City, eating off china that had belonged to the Rockefellers—but he was no longer happy. He was meeting with the prime minister of England, Edward Heath, and dining with President Richard Nixon, but he had grown apart from his wife, and they had broken up. When we reached the point where I was having a hard time getting through to him on the phone, the same man with whom I had once been in almost constant communication, I knew our relationship had changed.

One day at lunch Saul told me that he wanted to make his brother Bob the president of Reliance Group. I thought that was a very bad idea. I understand wanting to do a favor for someone in the family, but Bob Steinberg not only had no particular expertise in the insurance business, he also didn't realize what he didn't know, which is the most dangerous kind of ignorance. He simply didn't have the experience to be a CEO, to make big decisions, sometimes on the fly, and to shoulder the responsibility. I thought it was a reckless decision on Saul's part.

One ramification of Bob's poor leadership was that the sales and underwriting personnel at Reliance began expanding the liability insurance that Reliance was willing to underwrite, getting into areas that were out of their depth because they were being paid solely on the basis of how many policies they wrote. There was little or no regard for the level of risk the company was insuring against or its ability to calculate that risk. In short order Reliance increased its coverage in the Mediterranean area exponentially but charged premiums inadequate to cover the risk. Disaster was in the cards.

Reliance's financial problems persisted. Saul's work ethic deteriorated, and he all but stopped returning my phone calls. I never thought two guys who, for years, had spent most of their working lives in each other's offices would ever reach this state of affairs. One day when I was traveling in Europe and couldn't get through to Saul, I told Fred Jackson, the company's lawyer, "I'm going to resign from the board of one of the companies successively each time he doesn't return my call until I finally resign from the main company." Not long afterward, Saul finally called me back and said, "Bernard, if you really want to resign, why don't you wait until the annual meeting and resign to the board?"

"No," I said. "I don't want to just disappear. I want to make a statement. If you're not going to return my calls, we can no longer be friends—or business associates."

"Please just come see me as soon as you get off the plane," he said.

When I got back to America, I did see Saul the very next day—in his magnificent apartment in the middle of the afternoon. He looked like he had just gotten out of bed.

"Bernard, why are you resigning?" he said. "Don't do this to me."

"Saul, it's like you're sick right now and I can't make you well," I said. "You have everything anyone could want, but you're not taking care of yourself. You're the wealthiest and the most miserable person I know. But I don't know what to do about it." Obviously, I was very worried about my friend, yet I truly didn't know how to help him.

Thinking about my relationship with Saul puts me in mind of a question I've been asked a few times over the years by students or people in the audience at places where I've spoken about the economy or the infrastructure: Can money buy happiness? I've also heard it cast in a negative way: Does money make you miserable? I think it's best not to overthink these things. If you're unhappy despite having a fortune in the bank, it's probably not because of the money; you probably were going to find a way to be unhappy anyway. Likewise—stop the presses!—it's nice to be rich; much better than the alternative, and I say that as someone who has spent time at both ends of the spectrum. Some people think there's this great leveling force in the universe that ensures that if you have money, you will be miserable (or that if you're beautiful, you will be stupid). But I just don't see that being played out in reality. I know a lot of well-to-do people who seem genuinely happy.

As for me, I've certainly enjoyed my wealth, and though I don't think it has changed me fundamentally, I know it has given me opportunities and therefore made me happier than I would have been without it. Success has allowed me to pay back society for all that it has given me, starting with the GI Bill, which provided me with a free education. That and the system of government under which we live gave me the opportunity to build several companies, to get to know some fascinating people, and to help many others achieve personal fulfillment through the jobs that those companies provided. Not a day goes by that I don't feel like a lucky man, but one of my greatest strokes of luck has been to learn along the way that true happiness comes not from accumulating wealth, but from sharing it.

I'm not a worrier by nature, but even if I were I would not have had the time to fret much over what was happening with Saul at Reliance. I was too busy running Loral and trying to put it on the right course. Our fiscal year ran from April to March, and in my first letter to shareholders as the CEO and chairman of the company, which led off our annual report of 1972, I was able to speak about meaningful progress even as I reported a loss.

"Loral Corporation has emerged from an eventful year in a significantly stronger financial position with a profitable and trimmer operating base and with greater management depth," I wrote. We had sold off several burdensome divisions, repaid our remaining bank debt, and restructured our senior debt in a way that conserved important working capital. I noted that Loral was "vigorously exploring the acquisition of profitable companies which combine growth potential and management skills"—a significant sentence in retrospect—and that we had "started on a challenging and exciting new course aimed at maximizing our potential."

This was more than just annual report–speak, though I still had to prove that to the shareholders and potential shareholders, who were entitled that first year to be skeptical. While the news was basically good if you could read between the lines and see what was really happening at the company, it was not exactly spectacular. What I referred to as our "divestiture program" was an expensive undertaking that offset all our $503,000 in pretax income and left us with a loss of $2,678,000 for fiscal 1972. Clearly, we had work to do—and as people read those numbers, I was already doing it, and our situation was continually improving. "I'm not here to sell you our stock," I told the people at my first shareholders' meeting. "I'm here to tell you the story of a company with tremendous growth potential."

One key to us getting through those rough early days was the contract that we had with Lockheed for the tactical display system for the navy's S-3A Viking. I believed I'd transformed a potentially bad deal for Loral into a valuable one by virtue of my renegotiating the contract with Lockheed vice president Don Wilder, but our handshake agreement all but fell apart a year later when the tactical display system was ready to start coming off the production line.

Under the revised terms of our deal, Lockheed was under no obligation to buy what we produced, but if they did judge the display system to be up to their standards and the navy's and wanted to purchase it, they would guarantee us a profit from the very first unit we produced. We produced units meeting both Lockheed's and the navy's standards, and now it was time, as I understood things, for the Loral engineers and contract lawyers to sit down with their counterparts at Lockheed and come up with a price that would be reasonable but still allow us to profit.

Our team went out to Lockheed's offices in California, and I went with them—not to sit in on the negotiations but to be available for consultation. The Loral team stayed in a miserable little motel out by the airport. Because I wanted to be constantly available to them, I stayed in the room all day to be near the phone . . . for five very tedious days.

The problem was pretty simple: Lockheed was changing its mind on our agreement of several months before, retreating to the position that we had a contract and that the tactical display system for the navy's Viking was going to be an investment for us for at least three years. Every night, after a long day of discussions, our guys would trudge back to the motel and utter the exact same phrase about the Lockheed negotiators: "They're not moving."

Failure to turn this contract into an instant moneymaker might have put Loral out of business. Finally I couldn't face the prospect of another day in that motel room, and I called Don Wilder. "Don, will you meet with me?" I said. "I happen to be not far from you in California."

I could tell he was surprised. "What are you doing here?"

"I'm waiting to resolve our contract."

"Well, okay, I guess," he said. "Where do you want to meet?"

"Let's have breakfast tomorrow morning," I said, and I named a place not far from my motel.

When we sat down at breakfast the next day, I was very direct. "Lockheed is not keeping its promise to me," I said. "A year ago your people assured me that if we finished the production of this display on time, we would begin to make money—not a windfall, but an appropriate amount of money that we would agree on—from the very first unit. Now you're telling me something completely different."

Wilder simply reiterated his position: "My contract people are telling me we have a fixed-price contract," he said. "I can't just rip that up because you ask me to—I mean, this is part of our contract with the navy."

I heard him out, and then I made a proposal.

"Let's say you pay the contract price, but for every unit that I ship to you on time, you give me a bonus, an extra $100,000 per unit."

I knew this would appeal to him because lateness was a problem in the defense industry. Everything always seemed to be running behind schedule, and the military was always threatening to cancel agreements or penalize its suppliers. We had a deal with Lockheed for forty-eight display units—four a month for a year—and if I could guarantee him timely delivery, I knew it would mean a lot to him. Honestly, what I framed as a compromise was quite similar in its net result to the handshake deal I'd made months before. But to Don Wilder this sounded more like a revision to an existing contract than ripping up an agreement and negotiating a new one.

"That's worth it to me!" Wilder said. "I'll pay you a bonus for every one of these units you produce on time."

We had a deal.

I went back to our plant in the Bronx and told my people, "Whatever you have to do to keep to the schedule, do it." Knowing this was the biggest contract Loral had ever had and that it was vital to the survival of the company, the employees there, from the engineers to the assembly-line workers, responded beautifully. *Every one* of the forty-eight units and those that we produced thereafter under further annual contracts was delivered to Lockheed on time. We made *a lot* of extra money as a result.

Some years later, when my team and I paid another visit to Lockheed, Don Wilder stood up at the meeting, pointed in my direction, and said, "You people from Loral have a Machiavellian leader! Bernard Schwartz, I still don't know how you did it, but you bagged me! You knew from the start you could deliver those units on time!" Fortunately he was smiling broadly as he said this, and there was no reason he shouldn't have been, because the outcome was great for Lockheed too.

One thing you learn when you run a company is that problems don't line up and patiently wait for your attention. They don't take a number like customers in a bakery do. They happen whenever they happen, and ultimately it's up to the CEO to determine how and when they'll be addressed. Dealing with the challenges, and the idea that the buck stopped with me, were things I very much liked about the job, but that didn't mean that I sometimes didn't feel like things were happening at exactly the wrong time—not that there's any good time for a strike. The new Loral was just starting to get traction as an important player in the industry when I got a phone call one day telling me that work had essentially stopped and picket lines had gone up at our facility in the South Bronx. That plant—and its more than two thousand employees— was crucial to us, so this was no small matter.

For me, dealing with a strike was a new and somewhat complicated problem. I'm a supporter of organized labor and always have been. So was my brother Harold, and in his capacity as CEO of APL, he dealt with union representatives all the time. He negotiated with several tough unions and tackled all kinds of issues with them over the years, but he never once had a strike in any of his facilities. Why? Because Harold knew how to talk to people, he respected people, and he always lived up to his word, so the union representatives respected him in return. Even though the arbitration could get contentious at times, he accepted the basic idea that people have the right to organize to get what is best for themselves and their families. He always wanted to be fair.

I was not naive about the situation in our Bronx plant. I knew there had been friction between union leaders and the management there, but until just before they went on strike, I had the sense that morale among the rank-and-file workers was reasonably high. Those Loral employees worked, and for the most part lived, in one of the toughest and most economically depressed neighborhoods in America. This wasn't Silicon Valley—it was Fort Apache. There were burnt-out tenements all around the Loral facility. But the absentee rate at the plant was extremely low, all things considered, and people seemed proud to be part of such a successful division. Here's one striking example that illustrates my point.

During the previous winter, New York City got walloped by a bad blizzard. At about ten in the morning, the president of the LES division called me to talk about some business matter, and he went on for a while without ever mentioning the storm.

I couldn't help interrupting him. "Where are you?"

"I'm at the plant," he said matter-of-factly. I was amazed, because schools, banks, and companies were closed throughout the city, and public transportation was virtually nonexistent.

"Is there anyone there with you?" I asked.

"Oh, yeah, I think we've got about 60 percent attendance," he said. "Pretty much anyone who could walk here made it in."

But the mood in the Bronx was very different in the early '70s. The strike was over wages and working conditions, and virtually none of the union members had reported for work on the first day of the job action. Our executives, all of them nonunion, were coming in, but some union leaders who were not Loral employees were giving them a hard time—yelling at them and even threatening to physically bar them from entering. The potential for violence was very real. On about the third day of the strike, the union people blocked the entranceways so cars and trucks could not come and go, and I knew it was time for me to go up there and see if we could defuse the situation.

We went by car, and as soon as we pulled up to the plant—which was actually a compound of three large buildings—the strike leaders spotted me and started to yell some not very nice things. I got out of the car immediately and walked up to them. Chalk it up to me being young and foolish.

We were out in the open and a crowd was forming around us. I could see the police around the outskirts of the group, but they weren't doing anything; just standing by in case violence erupted. "Look," I said to the small group of men who came forward, "I'm going to be straight with you. I've only been in charge of this company a matter of months. I still don't know a lot about it or the issues that have resulted in this strike. But I want you to understand something. I have never crossed a picket line in my life. I come from a middle-class background. I'm pro-union. But if you continue this strike and continue to act this way, I will do everything I can to come out a winner."

At that point one young guy stepped up and said, "So what are you going to do for us?"

I said, "No, that's the wrong question you're asking. That's not how a business works. The right question is, 'What can we do for each other?' We're in this company together. We need to sit down together and figure out what's fair and what's next for us. But in the meantime I'm going to cross a picket line for the first time. I'm going into that plant and seeing my managers, and then I'm going to come back out, and you're not going to bother me. And then we're going to figure this thing out together."

I was trusting them to believe me that I would be fair with them if they were fair with me, and my trust paid off. A short time later we settled the strike, both sides were satisfied with the outcome, and we never had a labor problem at that plant again. I used to go up there frequently and talk to the employees. I once showed up with a four-star general named Colin Powell, who grew up in the Bronx not far from the Loral plant. He has called his visit "inspiring" and has spoken to me about it several times over the years.

In some ways that LES plant was symbolic of the entire Loral culture. As time went on, our business started to change, and there were fewer projects being developed and assembled there. The employees were understandably concerned. "I promise you I will never close this plant!" I told them. "You have my word that as long as I am at Loral you will have jobs to come to here. We will not close this plant." And we didn't, even though there came a time when keeping it did not make a lot of economic sense. The bottom line was important, of course, to the Loral shareholders and me, but so was the promise that we had made. Without trust, there is no relationship.

CHAPTER 12

Problem-Solving

Among CEOs in corporate America it is probably one of the most frequently delegated tasks, but I simply loved writing the letter to shareholders in our annual report. Though I might show it to our corporate staff and consider any suggestions they might have for changes and additions before I sent it off to the printer, I always insisted on drafting it myself. I liked being the one who crafted the description of how we had done.

It was a challenge to convey the excitement I felt for the future of the company while keeping in mind a reader's understandable skepticism. Later, as we had a marathon run of ever-increasing profit, I had the much more pleasant problem of trying to figure out a way to say "It was a very good year for Loral" in new and meaningful ways. The task took a toll on my thesaurus. My absolute favorite shareholders' letter? That would be hard to pick, but the one I wrote in 1973, my second full year at the helm, stands out in my memory, if only because it contained this stirring, albeit number-heavy, passage:

> *Net income for the year ended March 31, 1973, reached $1,039,000 compared with a net loss of $2,678,000 in fiscal 1972. All continuing operations contributed to this year's level of profitability.*

Our largest division, LES, had increases in sales and profits that year, and not only was I able to report our success with contracts for the tactical display system for the navy's S-3A, but we were also developing a control indicator set for an advanced version of the McDonnell Douglas F-4D Wild Weasel, the ALR-56 radar warning system for the air force's F-15 Eagle, and a tactical information processing and display system for the navy's P-3C Orion.

But probably the most significant part of that letter, if you were an investor in Loral or thinking of becoming one, was a short paragraph toward the end that may have slipped by unnoticed because it was about an intention, and not a deed already done, that had resulted in some sparkling numerals:

> *With our base of operations now streamlined, we can more confidently place a higher priority on implementing our external expansion plans. Our criteria for acquisitions include profitable and well-managed companies with emphasis on activities in which Loral is now engaged.*

That was the first draft of a credo that would be central to Loral's culture and key to its unprecedented success.

If you've ever wondered what a CEO does all day long in that big, fancy office, I can tell you now: He or she solves problems. Almost every time someone asks for a "quick meeting" or catches your eye and says, "Have you got a sec?" it's because he wants you to figure something out or render a decision. You can usually assume that the matter is going to be something complicated, crucial, or urgent; otherwise, it would have been addressed before it got as far as your door. And that's fine; that's what you signed up for. But you'd better keep your batting average high, especially if you are running a company, as I was in the early and mid-1970s, with scarce resources and a razor-thin margin for error.

I should have known I was going to be faced with an especially big decision the day our chief lawyer, Al Simon, sat down in front of my desk with a big, Cheshire cat smile on his face. "Bernard," he said, "I've found a way to get us out of our contract with the air force for the ALR-56."

That contract was one of the biggest deals Loral ever had. The ALR-56 was the radar warning system for the air force's F-15. We were producing the passive part (which warns a pilot if he is being "painted," or detected, by enemy radar) while McDonnell Douglas was responsible for the active part (which jams enemy missiles and radar). We had our best designers and engineers on the project, our portion of the ALR-56 system was more than up to snuff, and the air force was pleased with the prototype. The very significant problem was that once we actually started building them, we would be losing money on every unit we produced and would continue to do so until we were able to strike a new deal at a better price.

This was not an unusual situation in the defense industry. Because of the arcane system of contracts, a company would have to come up with a price before it really knew how much a product cost to produce. For a large company, it was part of the cost of doing business. But for a company as small as Loral was at this point, having to endure a year or two of losses on even one major deal could be devastating. Al Simon knew that when he sat down across the desk from me and said, with barely hidden glee, "We have an opportunity to cancel this contract because the air force missed payment of one of its monthly bills."

As Al explained the situation, the language in our agreement gave us a legitimate out. "It's just a bureaucratic oversight on the part of the air force, I'm sure," he said. "It happens all the time. You never hear about it, because usually no one calls them on it. But in this case we might consider doing just that."

He handed me a copy of the contract with the pertinent passages marked. This, I immediately realized, was potentially good news for Loral and bad news for the air force. If we walked away from our deal with them, we would be out from under a costly obligation, and it would take them at least two years to get back to the same point with a new manufacturer. It was an intriguing but delicate situation, so I arranged for a meeting a couple of days later with Jules Frohmann, head of Loral's marketing team at the time, and Admiral Shinn, who in addition to being a new board member was a consultant to our LES division. I especially wanted Allen there to provide the military perspective on the matter.

Al explained the loophole he had found in the contract and the opportunity it gave us. Now the coyness was gone, and he was a strong advocate for abdication. "Bernard, you've *got* to do this," he said. "This is costing your stockholders money every month, and you have a clear path to get out of this contract. You simply *must* cancel!"

Admiral Shinn had a very different opinion, however. "Yes, of course, you can nitpick the legalities of this thing," he said, "but at the end of the day you simply *cannot* cancel a contract with the United States Air Force. You cannot go to this customer and say, 'Sorry, but I'm going to stop producing.' That would throw the F-15 program into chaos, and trust me, they will not take it lightly."

Both arguments, I realized, had their merits. "Allen, I think we need to talk to the air force about this," I said. "This contract didn't start out this way, but it has turned into a very unwholesome deal for us. And what's just as important is that they will soon know, if they don't already, that it's a bad deal for us, and that we just might exercise our right to walk away from it. I think that gives us an opportunity to negotiate. I believe Loral has some leverage here."

Allen simply didn't agree with me. "Bernard, I strongly advise you against raising even the possibility of your pulling out of this deal," he said. "You will be a pariah to the air force."

I had to see about that for myself, so I asked for a meeting with the general officer in charge of the F-15. About a week later, Jules Frohmann and I flew out to Dayton, Ohio, where the program was headquartered. Our meeting was scheduled for eleven in the morning. When we walked into the room, the general was there with his top F-15 advisor. I was ushered to a seat directly in front of the general's desk.

The first thing I did was to hand him a letter. In it we had outlined exactly how the air force had violated our contract, and we cited the clauses of the contract that said we could cancel the agreement under such circumstances. I watched the general's eyes as they slowly scanned the letter from top to bottom. Finally he folded it up and put in on the desk in front of him. Then he picked it up and glanced at it again. "Be here at two-thirty," was all he said. Not "Will you please be here?" or "Can you be here?" Just "Be here at two-thirty." Then he stood up and walked out of the meeting room with his right-hand man close behind him.

Please understand that the Pentagon always treated me fairly. Back when I was thinking about whether to get involved in a business that dealt largely with the military, many people told me, "You're at a serious disadvantage being a Democrat and a New Yorker." Some of my competitors and suppliers *were* downright rude to me because of those things, and if I cared about their opinion, their attitude might have bothered me. But from the representatives of the army, navy, and air force I never got anything but a straight and fair deal.

When we came back after lunch, it was still Jules and me on one side, but the size of the opposing team, if you wanted to call it that, had grown considerably. Now the general was accompanied by his advocate general, several other lawyers, and a fairly large smattering of other brass.

"Thank you for coming back," the general said in a tone that was neither cordial nor hostile. "We discussed this situation during the break, and we agree that technically you are correct. You have every right to cancel this contract. If you do that, Mr. Schwartz, it will have a significant effect upon the F-15 program, as you know. But I want you to understand that I am prepared to do that, I am prepared to let you walk away, and let me tell you why."

At this point he sat up a little straighter and pointed to the decorations on his uniform. "Do you see these two stars, Mr. Schwartz?"

"Yes, I do," I said.

"Well, I'm proud of those stars, and I happen to be up for a third one," he said, "and I mean to get it. *I earned that third star.*" He then paused and took a slightly different tack. "Do you know about Senator Proxmire's awards?" he asked me. I said I did. At the time almost everyone was aware that William Proxmire, the Democratic senator from Wisconsin, gave out what he called the Golden Fleece Award to various government agencies that he thought had been careless with taxpayers' money. The Federal Aviation Administration (FAA) once got one for spending $57,800 on a study of the physical measurements of female flight attendants, with an emphasis on "length of buttocks." The Office of Education earned a Golden Fleece for squandering $219,500 on a program that taught college students how to watch television. The media rushed to publicize these awards, and Proxmire, the chair of the Senate Committee on Banking, Housing, and Urban Affairs, loved giving them out.

"If I were to give you something more to stay involved in this deal, if I had to negotiate a new contract with Loral because the air force screwed up and missed a payment, and if as a result I wind up adding millions to the cost of this radar detection system for the F-15, I think it's quite possible I'll wind up on Senator Proxmire's awards list," the general said. "If that happens, I won't get my star, my career will probably stall, and it will be all because of this mix-up. I'm not going to let that happen, Mr. Schwartz. So I'm not going to accommodate you. If you want to simply walk away from this contract, you are of course free to go ahead."

There was another long pause, and then he continued speaking—and showed me how he got to be a general in charge of important military procurements. He was as good a businessman as you'll find anywhere in civilian life.

"Because I understand the position that you are in, I can offer an alternative to walking away," he said, "something that will not look foolish to Senator Proxmire or anyone else. Something well within the rules.

"If you don't complete this development contract, the air force will not exercise the production contract, and your company will have invested money without any hope of a return. You will, in other words, be in no better position than if we *did* exercise the production contracts and you were obliged to produce this equipment at a loss. However, if you *do* complete the development contract satisfactorily, I promise you that we will renegotiate the production contract along lines that will allow you to obtain what you consider a reasonable price. So if you still want to cancel this contract, I think you'll be missing out on an opportunity, but that's fine with me. Just say the word and this meeting is over."

Then he just stared at me.

Clearly the next move was mine, and as I sat there for a few seconds contemplating what to do, I thought of what Allen Shinn had said—that I could use my advantage against the air force, but they would never forget it. I also thought of what the general had just said.

What I did then was stand up, lean over the general's desk, and pick up the letter of cancellation that I had given him earlier in the day. I then folded it up and put it in my pocket.

"General, Loral is a member of the team," I said. "We're happy to be with you on this project, and we hope to continue on it. Now, is there anything else we have to do today?"

He smiled and shook my hand.

We did of course stay on with the F-15—which is still flying today, by the way, for the United States and several of its allies—and the general got his third star and kept up his end of the bargain in spades. We were awarded a new contract for the manufacturing of the radar system, and it turned out to be the most profitable contract our company had ever had, bringing in several hundred million dollars in revenue over the years. Eventually our radar warning receiver technology became the worldwide standard for the industry. By the time the second iteration of the system came out, we were already working on the third. It just goes to show that if you think in terms of letting the other guy win a little, you can very often both win a lot.

When I took over Loral, I put a high priority on its becoming an international company, but I had my work cut out for me in that regard. We just didn't have a marketing team in place: people who could bridge the gap between the company and its customers and potential customers. My small management staff and I had to pick up the slack. It was during this time, the mid-1970s, that we first started exhibiting our products at the Paris and London air shows, important events for every aerospace company. For me and the other Loral people who went there in those early years, it was an exhausting, nonstop round of breakfasts, lunches, and dinners, with meet-and-greets that went on from dawn till midnight.

Our smallness as a company, however, did allow me the chance to interact with many face to face, talking to them about what they were involved in and what was next on their agendas. As a result, we wound up making profitable deals with the United Kingdom, Israel, France, Saudi Arabia, and many other countries. At one point, nearly 30 percent of our sales came from sources outside the United States. Even after we grew as a company and developed a marketing team, I made a point of making personal contacts whenever I could. When the boss shows he cares, he gives his company an edge. That I was available in key situations, and not some mysterious Oz figure issuing directives from behind his office door, was part of the Loral culture and another key to our success.

When doing business internationally you always have to accommodate yourself to the culture you're dealing with, but our transactions with Israel were sometimes a combination of agility and endurance test. Don't get me wrong: I liked doing business with Israel and, although I am definitely not one of those people who think that as a nation Israel can do no wrong, the people there liked me and my company's products. But working out an agreement with their defense department could be, well, the kind of experience that either keeps you young or ages you quickly.

Israel bought the F-15 in 1975, ordering twenty-five planes from McDonnell Douglas, but they purchased the plane without the standard package of electronics. The Israeli Air Force, or IAF, wanted to design some of their own equipment, and they had some great engineers to do it. They wanted Loral to help by building the electronics for their fleet of F-15s.

The Israeli military was familiar with our work and our standards because we'd had a number of other, smaller contracts with them. The Pentagon had approved our request to work out a deal with Israel on the project (you always need its approval when selling military equipment to a foreign country, even an ally), and we had the knowledge and the production capacity to start supplying them. It looked from every angle like we were good to go.

But nothing was ever simple with the Israeli military. We worked with their engineers eagerly, trying to hammer out a better design for their radar warning receiver and agree on a price, but after almost ten months, we still didn't have a deal. This was especially surprising because the consultant representing Loral in the talks was an extraordinary fellow named David Kolitz, simply the best Israeli business agent you could have. David was a disciple of Ezer Weizman, the seventh president of Israel. Ezer was the minister of defense, an extraordinary, inspirational leader who had been a fighter pilot in the RAF during World War II. I'd become friends with him over the course of several business trips to Israel, and eventually he introduced me to David and his consulting firm, Elul.

As soon as I met David, I was struck by his energy, extraordinary good looks, diplomatic skills, and incisive intelligence. He knew how to navigate the network of procedures and personalities that made up the Israeli military establishment. He knew when to be firm and when to be patient. And it was patience he advised in this instance, when one general whom I can only describe as exceedingly tough kept raising questions and making demands that were preventing our deal from happening. I thought it was a shame, because the Israeli Air Force loved our product and couldn't wait to put it into production, and we were ready and eager to start producing it for them. "I know this is frustrating," David said to me. "But we have to proceed very carefully so the whole deal doesn't fall apart."

We had offered a good, fair price to the IAF, but I was willing to walk away if the Israeli side pushed any further, and I thought it wouldn't hurt if they understood that. My position was that it was time to sign the contract or go our separate ways. David couldn't get the talks past their same old sticking point about price. The IAF representatives wouldn't accept what David kept insisting was Loral's bottom-line offer, and the impasse continued.

Even David sounded a little frustrated when he called me to report the lack of news. "I'm convinced that the only way we're going to get this moving," he said to me, "is if you come here yourself. We've got to shake up the atmosphere here and show you are personally involved. I think you should get on a plane as soon as possible and be prepared to stay as long as it takes."

I didn't like the sound of that. I was having this phone call with Kolitz on a Monday, and Irene had planned a very special dinner party at our apartment in Manhattan the following Saturday evening. I really wanted to be there for that . . . especially since I knew she'd strangle me if I weren't.

"Okay, I'll go," I told David.

I got to Israel on Wednesday, and when I walked into the meeting at which we were negotiating the contract, it seemed like total chaos. There are some real cultural differences between Israel and the United States, and one of them is that when military people sit down to discuss something, rank doesn't seem to matter. You could be a general in the Israeli army and you might say something, but if the guy over here is a colonel and he doesn't like what he heard, he won't hesitate to tell you so, very loudly and very impolitely.

I sat down at the table beside David and another member of our team and immediately an Israeli military man stood up and started attacking Loral. He was waving the proposed contract in the air and acting very agitated.

"We disagree with the numbers you have on page 4!" he said.

There were a lot of numbers on page 4, so I said, "Which ones?"

"Every single one of them," he said.

Our entire negotiations with the Israelis centered on price. We didn't disagree significantly on design, materials, deadline, or anything else. The numbers he was talking about had to do with our costs, which justified and explained our prices, and thus were critical to the discussions. So as soon as he sat back down, we took the time to go through every single number on page 4 with them, explaining where they all came from and why they weren't lower. He mumbled and grumbled through our response. When we had finally finished, he stood up again and said, "We also disagree vehemently with every single number on page 8!"

His demands, and his tone, were a little too much for me. "So far you've had an objection to every single one of our numbers," I said. "How do you feel about the page numbers on the document? Are you okay with *those*?"

At that point David leaned over and quietly said, "Don't talk like that, Bernard. Don't be sarcastic. They're very serious here."

"Well, that's good," I told him, "because I'm very serious too."

We got through Wednesday without a complete breakdown in communications, and somehow we got through Thursday as well. Friday is the beginning of the Israeli weekend holiday, and so on that day no meeting was called. That meant yet another day of no progress. The previous evening I had asked David if he could meet me for breakfast at my hotel. As he sat down at the table Friday morning, he noticed a couple of suitcases sitting near me. "Whose are those?" he asked.

"Mine."

"But you can't leave now!"

"David, I've come to the conclusion that this deal just isn't going to be made. It's not worth it for Loral to make it at the price they're offering. I'm going home."

"No, you simply *can't* go home!"

"Look, some deals are just not meant to happen," I said. "That's just the way that life, and business, goes sometimes. I believe this is one of those deals. It's not the end of the world. We'll still do business with Israel, and so we'll still do business with your firm. We'll all continue to have a good relationship, but we just won't do this one particular deal. I'll leave now before things get any more bitter. I'm okay with that."

David just looked at me. He himself is an Israeli, with all the stubbornness, the passion, and the can-do spirit of those people. For him, this was not how the story of this deal was supposed to end.

"Bernard, you have *months* invested in this thing," he said. "Just give me ten or fifteen minutes."

He left the table, and when he returned he explained to me that he had called General Golan, who was the head of their air force and who'd been front and center at all of our meetings. "I told him 'Schwartz is leaving,'" he told me. "Then I said, 'I know you want this deal to happen, but it's now or never, General.' Golan's response was immediate, Bernard. 'Let's have a meeting right now,' he said." The general knew that if I left without signing a contract, it would delay their F-15 program.

So David and I and his key executive (and my friend), Yalo Shavit, all went back to the same room in the Ministry of Defense building where we'd spent the prior two days going over the numbers and haggling. I was determined that this was going to be a short meeting because there was no way I was going to miss my flight back to New York and the dinner party with Irene. Golan, as it turned out, didn't want to waste any time either. "It's not really a workday and I have to visit my grandchildren," he said. "Mr. Schwartz, what is your problem? Why is it necessary to have a meeting this morning?"

"General, we've been talking for months, and nothing has happened," I said. "I've come to the conclusion that nothing *will* happen in regard to this deal. I think we both agree that Loral has the right equipment for your planes, but we cannot come to financial terms. Not all contracts were meant to be, General, and it looks like this is one program that will not happen. I think the relationship between Loral and the Israel Defense Ministry is more important than this one contract. And so I thank you for your courtesy and your consideration, and I'm prepared to leave for home today."

There was a moment of silence, and then the general turned to his staff and said something in Hebrew—they, David, and Yalo Shavit burst out laughing.

Since I don't understand Hebrew, I asked to be let in on the joke.

The Schwartz brothers, Jules, Bernard, and Harold *(left to right)*, circa 1936.

My brother Harold in full gear as a radar officer on B-24s. He survived being shot down behind enemy lines in 1945.

In 1944 I joined the US Army Air Corps where I was accepted into the air cadet program.

I never forget my roots. This vintage 1930s photograph by Berenice Abbott, which hangs in my office, pictures a milk cart like the one my father drove as a young man.
Berenice Abbott/Masters Collection, Getty Images

Harold *(left)* and me in uniform, with our mother, Hannah, in 1945. Harold had just gotten home from the hospital after his release as a prisoner of war. I was granted a furlough to go home and visit him.

With my parents, Hannah and Harry, at Irene's and my June 17, 1950, wedding.

Irene and me in the early days of our marriage. The marriage lasted longer than the beard.

Irene — young, beautiful, smart, and active.

Ditto.

Saul Steinberg (center left) and me with the chairman and vice chairman of the New York Stock Exchange on the day Leasco was listed.

My office didn't change much through the years: same art, same lamps—same Mickey Mouse tie clip. Jimmy Carter was president when his photo graced the wall behind me; after a few years, I moved him to the conference room.

Loral Corporation
1975 Annual Report

For the fiscal years ended March 31,

	1972	1973	1974	1975
Sales	$27,416,000	$34,763,000	$39,685,000	$54,819,000
Earnings From Operations	18,000	717,000	1,049,000	2,812,000
Net	(3,001,000)	1,244,000	1,978,000	3,554,000
Earnings Per Share From Operations	.01	.27	.40	1.08
Net	(1.10)	.46	.76	1.37
Backlog	30,300,000	34,900,000	42,800,000	94,700,000

LORAL CORPORATION

Loral's 1975 annual report cover said it all: In the three years since I took the helm, sales doubled and net income swung from a negative $3 million to a positive $3.5 million. It was the beginning of a string of ninety-six consecutive quarters of earnings increases for Loral. *Photo by Adrian Kinloch*

How is it possible that Frank Lanza placed first and I took second in our company tennis tournament at the 1978 management meeting? Surely our employee-opponents didn't let us win . . .

Governor Hugh Carey *(right)* gave us crucial encouragement and cooperation in our 1979 purchase of the Ridge Hill facility in Yonkers, which allowed for the expansion of our defense electronics development and design operations. Though aggressively courted by other states, we were determined to stay in New York.

It looks like we had a Western theme at the gathering where I addressed the attendees of our President's Meeting in Scottsdale, Arizona, in 1981.

Ambushed at Karen's 1982 wedding by the bride *(left)* and Francesca, her maid of honor.

BERNARD L. SCHWARTZ
CHAIRMAN, CEO
LORAL CORPORATION

"I wanted to be governor of New York"

In 1990 *Avenue* magazine included a profile of me along with other New Yorkers in an article that asked the question "What did you want to be when you grew up?" Apparently I wanted to be governor of New York!

Duane Michaels, Bernard Schwartz, 1990. Courtesy of the artist and DC Moore Gallery, New York.

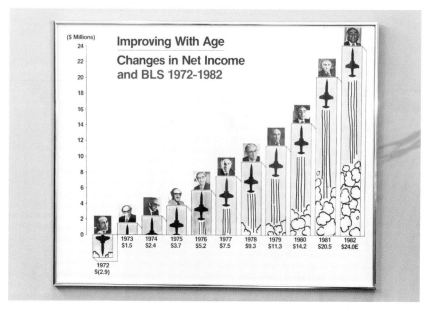

On my tenth anniversary as chairman and CEO of Loral, the team put together this poster, which still hangs in my conference room at BLS Investments. It marks the progress of our steadily improving net income and my steadily graying hair. *Photo by Adrian Kinloch*

General Colin Powell honored us with a visit to our Loral Electronic Systems division in Yonkers in 1991, just after the conclusion of Desert Storm, where many of our counter-measure systems were used by our armed forces.

Our hangar in Akron, Ohio, acquired as part of our purchase of Goodyear Aerospace, was the setting for a 1992 rally for presidential candidate William Jefferson Clinton.

Bill Clinton speaks to the rally attendees.

At work—Loral's New York City headquarters.

This five-foot-tall, hand-carved wooden Mickey Mouse statue, wearing my father's Bushwick baseball cap, has followed me from Loral to my current office. Each year I presented the Mickey Mouse Good Guy Award, represented by a statuette of the cherished cartoon character, who was both honest *and* a winner, to one of my employees in recognition of his or her contribution not to our bottom line but to our culture.

Photo by Adrian Kinloch

Loral technicians prepare to ship Spainsat, a military communications satellite designed and built for the Spanish Ministry of Defense and launched 22,000 miles into space in 2006. There were always six or seven customer satellites on the floor of our Palo Alto plant in various forms of completion.

I placed the first ever telephone call from the bottom of the Grand Canyon using our Globalstar satellite phone.

Four Globalstar satellites are enclosed in the nose cone of this Boeing Delta rocket, lifting off from the Kennedy Space Center in the late 1990s.

Conferring with President Clinton at a 1999 conference in Little Rock.

Irene and I receiving the Millennium 2000 medallion at the White House.

Rather than making a speech when I was honored in 2005 for my support of New York University's Langone Medical Center, I was treated to an off-the-cuff interview by Charlie Rose and then-Senator Hillary Rodham Clinton.

All-American food and music are featured at the nonpartisan election night parties Irene and I have hosted since 1968 at such iconic Manhattan venues as a Horn & Hardart Automat, the Rainbow Room (pictured here from our 1992 party), and, most recently, the New-York Historical Society.

The invitation to our 2012 election night party. *Photo by Adrian Kinloch*

I am likely pressing for action on my infrastructure initiative here with President Obama.

My brothers and best friends, Jules *(left)* and Harold *(right)*, with me around 1997.

The ocean has always been a draw for us, and our Southampton home a frequent gathering place for family and friends.

The entire family gathered for a recent trip to Africa.

Photo by Adrian Kinloch

"Permission to translate?" David said to General Golan. The general nodded.

"What the general just told his staff," said David, "is that this is obviously not the first time Mr. Schwartz has negotiated a contract!"

Everyone laughed again, and then the general looked me in the eye and said, "What is your bottom line that you need to make this work?"

I had been telling him all week, of course, but I told him again. This time he nodded, turned to the head of his air force, and said, "These are terms we can live with. Will you please finish the negotiations with Mr. Schwartz?" Then he left the room, going off to visit his grandchildren. By now I barely had enough time to get to the airport and catch my plane, and I told that to the remaining Israelis. We left the meeting room as a group and got on the elevator, continuing to talk specifics all the while. Down in the parking lot, after a few more minutes of discussion, we finally shook hands on a deal, and I jumped in my car and held on tight as Yalo, a former air force general, took off at hair-raising speed for the Tel Aviv airport. Once you shake hands with an Israeli, the deal is done. They may be tough to the point of being utterly exasperating at times, but they are as good as their word.

One lesson to be learned from this is that while it can help to have the CEO show up to do the deal himself, it might be just as impressive when the head guy says that in all honesty, he is okay with going home without an agreement. One side's willingness to walk away from the table is often what leads to getting the deal done.

Another lesson is that when trying to get through famously diligent Israeli airport security in a hurry, it is good to have friends in high places. I made it onto the plane and, yes, I made the dinner party back in New York. Champagne, that night, was my cocktail of choice.

That wasn't the only interesting encounter I had with the IAF. Some time later we worked with them on the Rapport system for their F-16 aircraft. The Rapport was a technological breakthrough designed by Frank Lanza, then the president of our LES division. For the first time ever, it combined in one system the passive portion—the radar warning receiver—with the active portion—the jammer. Combining these elements created a system that was significantly cheaper, and even more important, was smaller and lighter.

We worked diligently with the IAF to design and build the Rapport technology required for its special military needs, but when it came to striking a deal with the Israeli government, we had our usual difficulties with the financial terms.

It looked as if negotiations were breaking down, but then I received a telephone call at my home one Thursday afternoon in November—right at the start of the Schwartzes' Thanksgiving Day dinner. The caller was Yitzhak Rabin, at the time the Israeli minister of defense. Rabin explained he did not want to get into financial contract negotiations, but he also stated repeatedly that he wanted Loral to stay involved with this program. "We need this equipment," he said, "and so one way or the other, we're going to make this work. Bernard, please do not walk away from this contract."

Even though it came on a day filled with deep personal meaning for me, I was deeply gratified by the call. Loral and the Israeli Air Force continued to discuss the program, and over time we addressed our issues and completed the contract for the Rapport. Many people in the IAF told me how much they depended on the system we provided. It turned out to be hugely successful for Loral as well, and we sold many Rapport products to many other allies through the years.

As time went on, my professional relationship with the Israelis only grew stronger. I had noticed not long after I started doing business with them that they were far ahead of the United States in some areas of R&D for military electronics, and they shared this advanced knowledge with the US military. This led me to suggest that Loral might be able to help certain private Israeli companies sell their equipment to the Pentagon for use on American aircraft. The Israeli companies naturally liked this idea. The US Army, Navy, and Air Force loved their products, and Loral forged partnerships with these suppliers that proved to be highly profitable both for Americans and for the Israelis. That we had helped these companies also pleased the government of Israel, and that only made it easier for us to do business with their military in the future.

CHAPTER 13

Good News . . . and Better News

Loral was growing, and fast. My third annual letter to shareholders began like this:

> *The consistently increasing trend which has characterized Loral's performance during the two prior years continued throughout fiscal 1974—and has extended into fiscal 1975.*
>
> *Net income for the year ended March 31, 1974, reached $1,812,000, equal to $.70 per share. This compares with net income of $1,039,000, or $.39 per share, in fiscal 1973.*
>
> *This substantial year-to-year improvement is the result of steadily rising business levels at all Loral divisions, and it has been achieved concurrently with the considerable strengthening of our financial condition.*

Sportswriter Red Smith said in 1946 that writing was about as much fun as sitting down and opening a vein, but maybe he didn't have my kind of good news to report. The next year the news got even better, and I devoted the cover of the annual report to a stark, handwritten accounting of just how far Loral had come since 1972. Our sales had increased from $27.4 million to $54.8 million during those four reporting periods. Net earnings from operations went from $18,000 to $2.8 million. Net earnings per share from operations went from $0.01 to $1.08. Our backlog of orders, $30.3 million in 1972, now stood at $94.7 million. The Loral I had taken over—on the verge of going out of business, whose common stock almost saw a government-mandated halt in its trading—was a rapidly fading memory. I was enjoying myself. The news I had to report to shareholders was not just good from a financial perspective; it was also personally gratifying. I had gone into Loral without any previous experience in the aerospace business, but I did have a three-part thesis that I thought I could employ to turn the company around, and it was working.

The first part of my thesis had to do with the company being undervalued by Wall Street analysts and even veterans of the industry who either didn't understand or fully appreciate the true worth of a well-managed defense company. I had seen much hidden value on Loral's asset sheet. The second part of my thesis had to do with synergy benefits, that is, using our successful management and technology skills to consolidate the industry. The third part was to apply Loral's culture—our small but engaged corporate management team, our belief in promoting from within and encouraging an entrepreneurial spirit, and the bold decisiveness with which we made business moves—to smaller companies that we knew would benefit from it.

I have often been asked—by industry analysts, bankers, and business professors familiar with the Loral story—how I knew what I knew about the company going in, especially since I was such an outsider. The true answer is that the culture predated Loral; it was present in all my prior business experience. I fine-tuned it along the way, but if you look at the record, you can see me operating basically the same way years earlier at APL and even before that. I've always had the confidence to feel that I could trust my gut in a new situation while I was still learning the specifics. That's why I could move from accounting to plastics to computer leasing to insurance to aerospace without missing a beat or changing my basic approach.

One of the ramifications of our rapid growth at Loral was that we came to need more manufacturing space, especially for our LES division. Although we had a three-building compound in the South Bronx that was, by any measure, one of the most successful factories in the aerospace industry, by the mid-1970s that space just wasn't big enough for our growing business. As I've mentioned, people representing other states, like Kentucky and Tennessee, were always trying to entice us to move into their beautiful mountain settings. And those offers weren't bad: cheap space, favorable tax rates. But I simply refused to move this plant from New York City. I thought highly of the local technical and engineering schools and the talent they produced, and I wanted to create as many jobs as possible in the metropolitan area. I suppose you could say I valued my relationship with the city.

One day we had a meeting to discuss our need for more space for R&D. There was a big map of the northeastern United States on the wall. I took some string, measured out twenty-five miles to scale, and with a thumbtack secured one end to the South Bronx. Then I stretched out the string, measured out several points along the map and drew a circle connecting them. "This circle encompasses everything within a forty-five-minute trip from our LES plant," I said. "I want you to find me a facility within this circle. Forty-five minutes is the biggest gap I'll tolerate between the engineering people and the manufacturing people. They should be close together so they can get together regularly and talk in person."

Soon after my staff at Loral put out inquiries about manufacturing space in the New York City area, I got a call from the governor, Hugh Carey. I didn't know Carey very well at the time, but I knew he was the first Democratic New York governor in sixteen years, an office he won after serving seven terms as a US congressman. In the best sense, Carey was an old-fashioned politician who knew how to cut through the baloney and get things done for the people he represented. He was a real New York guy, raised working class in Brooklyn and educated locally at St. John's University. He understood what had to be done to get a struggling city back on its feet. By spearheading projects like the

Jacob Javitz Convention Center, Battery Park City, and the South Street Seaport, he was largely responsible for helping New York City survive the economic crisis of the late 1970s. (He also stopped Republican legislators from reinstating the death penalty and antiabortion laws.)

Governor Carey was one of the good guys, in my opinion, and though I hadn't spent much time in his company, I was delighted and honored to take his call. I immediately liked his style. He didn't say, "Please come to see me in Albany" or even "I'd like to come see you." He said, "Can you spare an afternoon?" I thought that was a classy way to pose the question.

I didn't know what he was getting at, but I said, "Sure."

"Good," he said. "I'll come in my car and pick you up, and we'll take a ride. I want to show you something."

Carey obviously shared my view about the importance of the top guy getting personally involved. He also believed as I did in the power of face-to-face communications.

A couple of days later, the governor's car pulled up at Loral's South Bronx plant, and we rode for about twenty minutes to a spot in Yonkers called Ridge Hill, just off the New York State Thruway. It was a strange place: beautiful, in its way, but devoid of people. Enclosed within a big wall were a couple of fairly large buildings and about twenty smaller ones. The governor explained to me that until recently the compound had been a minimum-security detention facility devoted to young drug addicts who had been convicted of crimes and needed rehab as well as confinement. The smaller buildings had been the dorms where the inmates lived.

We drove around a bit then got out of the car and walked the grounds together.

"Can Loral use a space like this?" Governor Carey asked me.

"You mean just the way it is?" I said. I knew what he was getting at, but the first thing I thought of was the distinct possibility of a long, complicated battle with state bureaucracies and then the legislature before we were even allowed to *start* putting in the kind of buildings we would need.

"No, I mean if you had the space and the right to build on it, could it satisfy what you need?" he said.

I looked around. It was a magnificent plot of land. "Sure," I said. "It just depends on the economics."

"I can't sell it to you," he said, "but I can rent it to you for ninety-nine years."

That sounded all right to me, so I started to talk about price. But he cut me short, saying, "Bernard, that's not what I'm here today to discuss. If you can get together with my people, I'll get it done for you."

I was still worried about dealing with the state government. "What about the problems of getting it through the legislature?" I said. "We don't have a lot of time."

He stopped walking and looked me in the eye. "Let me worry about that. I can get it done in sixty days."

You don't hear too many politicians talk like that anymore, but this was a leader at work. There was certainly nothing in this for Carey personally, and I don't even think that the bragging rights for getting a piece of unused real estate on the tax rolls and creating jobs were foremost on his mind. He just wanted to do the right thing for the people of lower New York State. Over the course of the next several weeks, we struck a deal. We would tear down everything at Ridge Hill except the gymnasium and put in a fantastic facility.

Getting the permissions through in sixty days sounded like a tall order, especially in a state where the legislature has often been a laughingstock for its corruption and inefficiency, but Carey wound up pushing them through in exactly that amount of time. In the end it became not only an engineering facility but a manufacturing plant as well, so the employees— and there were about two thousand of them once we got revved up—were not forty-five minutes away from each other, or even twenty, but together on the same congenial campus. New York State won and Loral won, and all because of a Democratic politician who knew what it meant to take charge.

It's great to trumpet good news when you're coming off a profitable year, but usually it's better not to boast about what you're planning to do in the future. Performance is the best strategy, and as the head of the company you gain a lot more from fulfilling and exceeding expectations than from describing them. Thus it was that our well-thought-out program of outside acquisitions began somewhat quietly, with the announcement that we had reached an agreement in principle to acquire the Conic Corporation of San Diego tucked rather deeply into the shareholders' letter of 1974.

Conic was a small company that specialized in solid-state communications systems and equipment for satellites, CATV, aerospace, and marine applications. It also owned a six-and-a-half-acre site that housed its engineering and production facilities. It was a modest beginning for Loral's expansion program, but Conic was a good fit for us, acquired on favorable terms.

"Good fit"—synergy—was the key. I wanted to own companies that fit with Loral in ways that would make the marriage greater than the sum of its individual parts. Looking for companies that promised these synergies—and taking advantage of the low valuations that existed in the industry—became my consuming passion and a major component of Loral's long-term success. This policy resulted in *ninety-six* successive quarters of increased net earnings over the same period of the prior year.

I didn't rely on bankers or brokers to tell me what companies were out there and available. I knew the landscape of the industry and what I wanted. And when I found what I wanted, I wasn't afraid to take a chance. Sometimes I would simply go to the Loral board and say, "We're going to make a purchase, and this is the price. It's going to cost us a little in our earnings per share this year, and maybe the next, but after that it will make a significant contribution." The record will show that I was a pretty good buyer of such complementary properties.

As I put together a string of successes and went from being an outsider to an insider, deal-making became easier. For one thing, people would always take my calls. But by the time they heard from me, I already had a good idea what their company was worth; very often—though I certainly didn't tell them this—it was worth more than they thought it was. Before I made an offer for a company, I might go to the air force, army, or navy and say, "What do you think about these guys?" Or I might talk about a product that a potential acquisition manufactured, but which one or the other branch of the military was not yet buying. I'd say, "Does something like this interest you?" and then I'd listen to how receptive or resistant they were. I tried to put the odds in my favor as much as possible, and in the end we did okay. All our acquisitions turned out to be profitable investments, and most of the companies we bought contributed to our bottom line—not in a year or two but from the day we took them over.

I sought out two kinds of companies in particular. One kind was smaller firms like Conic that had reached the limit of their technical capabilities or marketing resources—and thus needed to broaden their product lines—or believed it was time to sell and monetize the firm's investments. The other kind was bigger businesses whose main assets were not in the defense area, but they had secondary product lines there and divisions they wanted to sell. I'm talking here about giants like IBM, Goodyear, and Ford. Many of those kinds of blue-chip firms felt that further investment in the defense sector would be counterproductive to their market valuations. After all, Wall Street did not look kindly, or in some cases with very much wisdom, on companies in our industry, so the parent firms wanted to get out of the defense business.

Does this mean that these major corporations were shortsighted to sell us these divisions? No, it just means that those divisions no longer fit with their former owners' long-term strategies. Meanwhile, they were just what Loral wanted and needed, and they could help us grow exponentially, if we managed them right.

I had tremendous success with these kinds of acquisitions, but doesn't that mean that IBM, Goodyear, and Ford were stupid to sell to me, or that Loral single-handedly outfoxed all these huge conglomerates? No. These companies were looking to increase their value in the stock market, but not necessarily the value of the side businesses they were in.

The divisions I was interested in were no longer part of their long-term plan, so they were bad for them but good for us. But remember: We wouldn't buy just anything that came on the market. As with the smaller companies we acquired, the key factor was synergy, and the question always, "How can this acquisition help both Loral and the company we are buying to *get* bigger and stronger than before?"

None of our acquisitions were hostile takeovers. When we first approached a company in which we had an interest, we would tell them that we had an unusual plan. "If we acquire your company, no one is going to get laid off," we'd say. "No plants will be shut down. Instead, we're going to bring you more business than you ever had before. You're going to bring us more business that we ever had before. Both of us will *grow*." Sometimes I had to say that two or three times because their top management didn't believe it or they thought they must have misunderstood. No one else was doing business the way we were. Most people we talked to this way found the idea of being acquired by Loral to be very attractive. But if they didn't and they persisted in their resistance, we would ultimately walk away. Taking over a company against its leader's wishes just never sounded like a good idea to me.

I was always motivated by business reasons when I thought about acquisitions, but I have to confess that I absolutely loved making deals. Quite a few of my former colleagues who were interviewed for this book said, "Bernard lived for those acquisitions!" and it is true: The art of buying is something that genuinely excites me. I could be a tough negotiator, but ultimately I sincerely wanted everyone involved to be glad they had participated in one of my deals. If it felt like I was trying to force things, if the other side just didn't understand the benefits of partnering with me, I took that as I sign that I should walk away.

The synergy I was looking for could come any number of ways. In some cases the companies I was interested in made unique products that I thought would work well on, say, the F-15, but they had no contractual connection with that program. If Loral acquired such a company, we could be the bridge between it and the air force, creating a demand for its one-of-a-kind product and expanding Loral's role in the F-15 even as we upgraded America's arsenal of fighting jets.

The benefits flowed in the other direction too. Sometimes we acquired a company not only because it did unique things and made great products but also because it offered a connection *we* didn't yet have. For example, we had a strong relationship with the air force and a solid one with the navy, but in the beginning of my tenure, for some reason, we couldn't make much headway with the army. By acquiring companies we liked that also did business with the other services, we were able to grow our core business. During my years at Loral, we went from being known as an "air force house" to serving all branches of the military. No matter what the circumstances, however, acquisition was always a matter of addition or multiplication—never subtraction.

This illustrates the difference between a company like Loral and a venture capital firm like Bain Capital or KKR, which buys a company and then immediately begins to consolidate and close down functions. When we acquired a company, we wanted it for the long haul, not for a one-time expense reduction that came from eliminating so-called redundant activities or from the ability to strip out and sell off assets, close plants, and fire people. Sure, I believed in being efficient, keeping close tabs on every dollar and eliminating true redundancies, but I didn't believe in being shortsighted or pound-foolish. I've spoken to groups of entrepreneurs about my way of doing business, and when I got to the part about how and why we acquired companies, some just stared at me blankly. But that's okay. I wasn't trying to make any converts; I was just explaining what had worked for us.

I should make it clear that while integrity was very important to us as a company, I wasn't acting out of altruism or kindheartedness when I rejected the ways of the venture capitalist; it was strictly a business decision. Figuring out how two companies fit together was more challenging for us than just tossing away big parts of each, but I thought the extra effort was in our best interest because it increased the marketing, technical, and R&D activities of both Loral and the company we were acquiring. These great advantages were not generally priced into the cost of the acquisition, but in time they were fully realized by Loral. We made a total of sixteen acquisitions between 1972 and 1996, and each improved our capabilities, our reputation, and our profitability. Our expanding web of strategic relationships allowed us to go from strength to strength.

This acquisition policy was part of the Loral culture, and it helped make Loral a special place to work. Because I could honestly talk to the employees of each acquired company about new opportunities while assuring them that there would be no downsizing or loss of jobs, we were able to build a network of successful and loyal management teams across the company's many divisions. Only once in thirty-four years did I close a plant because of an acquisition, and that was because we wound up with two similar plants in close geographic proximity. But in that case it was only the building that went away; I continued to employ all the workers from the affected plant.

After we made an acquisition, my corporate staff and I would have a kind of "Welcome Aboard" meeting with the management and employees of the new division. These meetings were upbeat and energetic, but they could also be rigorous. We would go over their financials and our notes, questioning our new people closely about their methods and strategies. We would also spend a good deal of time explaining how we felt about their business and the industry in general, describing the potential synergies we saw with them and telling them about the Loral culture— our belief in fairness, quality, open communication, entrepreneurial thinking . . . and the "Just say yes" concept, of course, when it came to dealing with the boss. We told them we were not big on memos, fancy multimedia presentations, or formal staff meetings. We tended to just stop each other in the hallway and say what was on our minds about issues large and small—to forgo formalities in favor of simply getting things done.

In all but one case in my thirty-four years of running the company, the people at our divisions bought into the idea that they were better off working in this kind of atmosphere than they had been before. Part of the magic of the Loral culture was that it was consensual; it lived on and spread into the companies we acquired because people liked it and wanted to keep it going.

Of course, the education process worked both ways. Sometimes I had something to learn about the new division's culture. I remember one such time during a visit at the headquarters of a recent acquisition. I said my piece about Loral and then decided to take an impromptu tour of the plant and talk to some of the assembly-line workers. I walked around introducing myself, saying how happy I was that they were part of the company, predicting good times ahead, and asking if they had any questions. But the response I got was weird: a few quick, sidelong glances and a couple of grunts, but mostly just silence as they continued to work away intensely at their stations. I was baffled, so I went into the general manager's office and asked if something was the matter. "Have I offended your people somehow?" I asked.

"Uh, no, Bernard," he said. "But this really isn't the best time to try to start up a conversation. These people get paid by the piece, and every second counts for them."

I had to laugh at myself. "As long as they stay as productive as they have been," I said, "they can be as rude to me as they want."

There was one other unique aspect of the Loral culture regarding acquisitions: Instead of their top guy coming to meet with the corporate staff, we—not just the CFO or the COO but all eight of us—would fly out in our corporate jet once a month to sit down with the newly acquired division's management to review performance and to talk about what was on their minds. If there was a problem in a division, its president could get direct and immediate access to our small corporate staff, and we would immediately take action.

I've never heard of a CEO and management team who visited their divisions half as much as we did (according to some people, we weren't supposed to do this because if the plane went down, *all* of Loral's leadership would be wiped out), but from my perspective it was an indispensable part of the business—perhaps the single most important aspect of the Loral culture.

Usually, part of our visit was structured and part was not. In the structured part, there would be a technical report, a financial report, a development report, and so on, and people could ask questions of my staff and me. Employees from virtually all levels of the hierarchy were present, and I think they felt safe enough to say anything they wanted. And I wanted to hear what a lot of different people from each division, in different departments, had to say, to show that we were interested in them and to stay up to date on the particular frustrations they faced.

In the unstructured part, either before or after the reports were given, I might take a stroll around the plant with the division president and talk to him, without an agenda, about the issues of the moment. This was a great way to find out about little problems before they became big ones.

Visiting the divisions once a month wasn't an easy thing to do in the early years. It meant we were on the road quite a bit. I look back at my diaries, and I get exhausted just seeing how many business trips I made. But traveling to the divisions was the most useful thing I could do as chairman and CEO, as well as probably the single most enjoyable part of my job. When the management team would head back to the airport, all of us would be discussing what we'd just learned and what it all meant. On the plane ride home, we might squeeze in a little backgammon, but our business talk never ceased.

The upshot of all this traveling and talking was that the people who worked for us felt listened to, cared about, and like they were truly a part of the process, which in fact they were. Loral employees were happier, more loyal, and less likely to leave than other groups in our industry.

CHAPTER 14

Mickey Mouse and Good Management

Barbra Streisand famously sang about people needing people, but no one needs them more than the CEO of a company that's growing exponentially and surging forward toward new and once-unimaginable horizons. Which pretty much describes me in the late 1970s and early '80s, when Loral was setting all sorts of records practically every quarter, as I acknowledged in this letter to shareholders:

> Of necessity, annual reports principally focus on statistics. This often masks the human dimension of a company's accomplishments. At Loral we have a particularly dedicated and committed group of people whose efforts are responsible for our success. This fact is underscored by our productivity—sales per employee at Loral total $42,000 annually—among the highest in our industry. This tangible human contribution forms the basis of our performance to date and our optimism for the future.

I've been asked if I had a policy in regard to managing people. I didn't; I had very many policies. Just as we would never treat our divisions as if they were interchangeable, we would never imagine we could deal with any two employees the same way.

As the boss of bosses at Loral, though, I always tried to combine toughness with compassion. The trick is getting the proportions right.

I learned a lot about dealing with people from being the father of Karen and Francesca. As the head of a successful company, you act the part of a leader all day, and if things are clicking, as was the case at Loral, you may start to believe that your agenda is the only agenda, or at least the only one that matters. That's where children can be helpful.

I'll never forget the Thanksgiving when Karen announced that she wasn't going to be part of the family dinner, a longtime tradition. She was studying psychology at the time, in the doctoral program at Emory University in Atlanta. It was a few days before the holiday, and she was at our home in Manhattan when she told us that she would be spending Thanksgiving with the family of her fiancé, John Paddock, in Cleveland.

I liked John very much, but I was very upset by her declaration. I cherish our Thanksgiving get-togethers, and neither she nor Fran had ever missed one before. I tried hard to get her to change her mind and bring John to our house. I was mad at her for "ruining" our tradition, and she was angry with me for not understanding.

On the day before Thanksgiving, I drove her to the airport, but we both made the trip in total silence. When we got to JFK, I took her bag out of the backseat, carried it in, and put it down by the entrance to the gate. I was about to turn and leave when Karen put her hand on my arm and said, "You know, Dad, growing up is very hard to do."

I melted, and those words have stuck with me. *Growing up is very hard to do.* To me, that means we all have our challenges, our particular collection of things that life asks us to be especially brave about. Sometimes we just have to do what we have to do. And we all need to empathize with one another.

I always felt that the people of Loral were part of my extended family, and I tried to respect their feelings and be sensitive to their needs. Just how did I find out what those feelings and needs actually were? One way was our chairman's meeting. This was an annual event at some fun site—often a resort in the Caribbean, the Princess Hotel in Scottsdale, La Quinta in Palm Springs, and Rancho Bernardo, near San Diego, among others—where the heads of all our divisions and ten or so people who reported to each of them gathered to discuss how things were going at the company.

The chairman's meetings evolved to the point where a couple hundred people would attend. The format was always a dialogue, with both management and troops getting an equal share of the spotlight to talk about what was working and what could have been going better. We'd have some frank and useful discussions in the morning. In the afternoon everyone would play tennis or golf or swim. We'd also book some stimulating guest speakers. One year we had political advisor Richard Perle; another time we had Dick Cheney, former secretary of defense and future vice president. It was a superb way of keeping open the lines of communication.

If you come to my office on Fifth Avenue, you will notice several statues and pictures of Mickey Mouse. I've always admired and felt a kinship with Mickey; we are, after all, from the same generation, born just a couple of years apart. I think he's a superior role model. He could have been a rat, but he wasn't. He had a sense of justice. If you were one of the bad guys in his little universe, he could be very tough on you. Remember Pete, the villain, who looked like a big bulldog? He often wound up drenched with water, blown to smithereens, or otherwise defeated and humiliated. But mostly Mickey was quite nice. He treated Minnie Mouse well, and he stood by his friends, Donald Duck, Horace Horsecollar, Goofy, and Pluto. I thought Mickey Mouse belonged to everybody; he showed that you could be honest *and* a winner.

One year early in my tenure at Loral, I ad-libbed a reference to my favorite cartoon character in a talk I was giving at our annual management meeting. I wanted to make the point that the company didn't have to cheat or cut corners to succeed, and that as managers and keepers of the company flame, they should be as clean as Mickey Mouse. It got a chuckle—and I guess struck a chord. At first there were ten or fifteen people at those meetings, but eventually the number grew to two or three hundred, and everyone waited for my annual reference to you-know-who. After a while I started giving out the Mickey Mouse Good Guy Award to one employee who made an important contribution to Loral—not to the bottom line but to the culture. I'd buy a Mickey statuette for about $85, we'd put a little plaque on it with the winner's name, and we'd bestow it with proper ceremony. Employees treasured those things. Eventually people started sending *me* Mickey Mouse things—hats and pens and, once, a Lalique glass figurine that must have cost at least a few hundred dollars. Those are the items I proudly display in my office today. Mickey is still my hero: the good guy who was a winner.

But don't get the impression from what I've just said that the other Loral leaders and I were a bunch of softies. I can direct you to some generals from both the US Air Force and the Israeli Air Force who will testify to my ability to drive a rather hard bargain. No less an alpha male than Rahm Emanuel, the mayor of Chicago, has described me to an interviewer as "surpassingly tough."

Over the years, whenever journalists have asked me if I would rather be feared or loved, I have always chosen the former. It all comes back to my style of management: I believe it should be clear to everyone that I am the boss and that succeeding is extremely important to me. At the same time—and here's where Mickey Mouse comes in—I have absolutely no desire to succeed at any cost.

When I explain this to people, they sometimes ask where my belief in the power of ethical behavior comes from. Do I think in terms of karma? Is my attitude perhaps rooted my Jewish faith? No, I'm not an observant Hindu, Buddhist, *or* Jew. I do what I do because to me being fair just feels like the right thing to do. It also makes good practical sense.

To return a moment to the discussion of Loral's acquisitions and our empathy toward acquired personnel, you'll recall that I saw the people I worked with as an extension of my family. The Loral culture was predicated on everyone looking out for one another and treating one another with integrity. The company was all but devoid of office politics. When we acquired a new division, we did not behave like private equity investors. We did not say, "Now that we own you, we'll just merge your legal or your accounting or your finance department with ours." If we did that, we'd be firing a lot of good employees that we'd paid money to acquire. Our purpose, rather, was to help each division *grow*, just as we hoped that they would help the core company prosper. It was a more challenging way of doing business, to be sure, and it left us open to queries from stockholders and others, but ultimately it suited us *and* them.

We offered an entrepreneurial approach to our divisions. Once we acquired an outside firm like Goodyear Aerospace, IBM Federal Systems, LTV, or Ford Aerospace, each division also became an independent profit center—infused with the Loral culture. We wanted to give our acquisitions the freedom to succeed, which they did in all cases.

We likewise gave our division presidents plenty of leeway. Mistakes were permitted, up to a point. Remember what I said about our bias for action? Probably the worst mistake you could make as an executive at Loral was to be like George B. McClellan, the Civil War general who famously prepared and prepared but never thought the time was quite right to act. I once heard Jack Welch say, "I never remember thinking that I'd wished I'd taken six more months to make a decision," and I've always felt the same way. In the Loral culture, we favored action over endless study and consensus.

Because we wanted to be fast on our feet, we had virtually no bureaucracy at Loral, no middle layer of management. We tried to keep things simple and not stand on ceremony. I was talking to our former treasurer Nick Moren recently, and he said, "When I worked at Loral, I don't think I wrote two memos in ten years." We didn't need memos.

Process and the proper channels, so very important in most large corporations, meant nothing to me; I cared only about results and had no patience for fancy PowerPoint presentations or any kind of unnecessary discussion. I think we sometimes confused people by being too terse. Occasionally I would call someone to my office and say, "I'm giving you a raise," and if the person asked for a "360-degree performance review" or whatever it's called, or if he or she said, "Well, Bernard, how do you think I'm doing?" I would say, "What's the problem? You're doing fine. That's why I'm giving you a raise. Let's not overcomplicate this."

I gave a lot of raises, good ones too. A large part of my empathizing with others is that I wanted people to prosper and be happy. I believed in providing people with a generous salary, a stock-option plan, and health benefits—not just "competitive" compensation, in other words, but something better than that. In the 1990s, when a change in corporate accounting practices made it very expensive for employers to continue giving full medical coverage, we kept our rank-and-file employees on the plan, completely at the company's expense. I was doing quite well for myself, after all, and these people were an integral part of the company.

On October 19, 1987, I was at our annual management meeting in Scottsdale, Arizona, when my assistant came in and handed me a note saying that the stock market was falling rapidly. The Dow would drop 508 points by the end of what soon became known as Black Monday. I wasn't worried about my board members or myself; I knew we'd be all right because the conditions that caused the crash were transitory. But I realized that my employees holding stock options—and there were quite few of them, up and down the ranks—would be hurt. And that bothered me, because I knew those people counted on those options to pay for their kids' college tuition or to buy a house. So at the next board meeting we canceled all outstanding options and issued new ones with a strike price that was closer to the current market value. Did that cost Loral some money? Yes, of course, but the relationships with our people were worth it.

I also know that money isn't the only thing that matters when dealing with employees. In the late 1970s, after we had started to acquire new companies, I decided to change the name of all our operating companies to include "Loral." Thus, Conic became Loral Conic and American Beryllium became Loral American Beryllium. It was in this way that we built a brand and reinforced the synergistic relationship among the divisions, but it was a big sociological change for many of those divisions, especially those that had forged strong identities as independent companies before we acquired them.

After I announced the policy, the president of just such a division asked to visit me. William F. Gates, from our California subsidiary Randtron, explained that changing the name of his company was troubling for him. He had started the company not long before, following the death of his young son, Randy, and in fact had named Randtron after him. He viewed that name, understandably, as sacred. I told him without hesitation that I understood his problem and that we would not change the name from Randtron until he was ready to do so, and if that day never came, that was all right too. He thanked me sincerely and said goodbye. About a year and a half later—during which time we hadn't spoken about the matter—he came to see me again and told me that after thinking it over, the new name we had originally proposed, Loral Randtron, was fine with him. And so with his approval that became the division's title.

Over the years I have developed three basic beliefs when it comes to dealing with employees.

The first of those ideas is the importance of promoting from within. This is something everyone likes to do in theory, but some don't try hard enough to make it actually happen. Sometimes, I realize, it's simply not possible to promote from within, especially when you're overseeing a fast-growing company and your corporate organization chart is constantly changing. But anytime I could let someone rise through the ranks, I did. In the first place, it made *me* feel better to see my people growing and moving up. But I also found that when I promoted from within, I didn't just please myself and the person who got a raise and a new title; I gave an injection of hope and encouragement to everyone on the staff, letting them know that I had no special fascination with outsiders and that good work and diligence would be noticed and rewarded. When I elevated one employee, I was letting all the others know they had a future with Loral. And that encouraged people to be loyal, to work harder, and to stay with us longer.

The second thing I believed about managing employees was that I should build the organization from the people up, as opposed to starting with an organization chart and filling in the blanks. We looked at the talent we had and created job descriptions to fit the individuals. This may not be what they teach in business school, but it's always seemed wasteful to me to have a rigidly defined position and then spend a lot of time, energy, and money searching for a perfect fit. The Loral culture was all about human values.

My third belief about employees is that they should be encouraged to think and speak freely. At its essence, Loral was an entrepreneurial company that fostered the creativity and technical skills of its people. If an employee at any level had an idea for a new product, an enhancement of an existing product, or a new way to do something, he or she was rewarded for speaking up. And the more passionate someone was, the better. I didn't want people to censor themselves, and I never cared if, in the course of one of our thousands of informal meetings, anyone's ideas or opinions were in conflict with mine. Yes, believe it or not, the "Just say yes" man disdained yes-men and thought they were not good for the company. You could definitely win an argument with me. In fact, if you were motivated by what you truly believed, I *preferred* that you push back. You just had to realize that when the final bell had rung, the fight was over and you either had or hadn't prevailed—and we moved on.

What good people-management came down to for me in many cases was fostering a feeling of security. I wanted Loral's employees to feel comfortable enough in their work environment to say virtually anything, especially, "I need your help." Running a business is mostly an exercise in solving problems, and when a problem of a certain magnitude came along, as soon as it cropped up, I wanted to hear about it from the person who oversaw whatever it was that needed fixing so we could start addressing it together. I can tolerate and forgive almost any kind of dilemma or setback as long as I know someone hasn't tried to hide it, minimize it, palm it off on someone else, or let it fester until it gets much worse.

As I think back on the people I hired over the years at Loral, a few stand out—for various reasons.

When I interviewed Rich Townsend for the job of chief financial officer of Loral in 1998, the company was already big and rapidly getting bigger. Mike DeBlasio, our great CFO, was moving up the management chain, and we had no logical in-house successor. Rich, an outsider, wasn't exactly an obvious candidate. A forty-eight-year-old accountant who had worked at IBM and then ITT Industries, he seemed, on paper, about two or three steps distant from the top financial job at a fast-moving company like Loral. But I had heard good things about him. In other words, a fancy-looking résumé doesn't necessarily mean much. Also, he had initially said, "No, I'm not interested," and since I couldn't understand why anyone wouldn't be eager to work for Loral, that kind of intrigued me.

Rich was then working in White Plains. Because I planned to be at my house in Southampton, I asked him if he wouldn't mind making the drive there. Rich wasn't sure how to dress for the occasion. He had left his office in Westchester wearing casual attire, but then, on the drive out to the Hamptons, he had second thoughts and went into a gas station men's room to change into a suit and tie. That's how he was dressed when he rang my doorbell, and I greeted him wearing tennis clothes, dripping sweat. "Sit down, please," I said, motioning to a chair on the patio. We talked over coffee, and in a very short time I got a sense of what kind of guy he was and how much he really knew. After less than an hour had passed, I had offered him the CFO job, and he had accepted it.

Later he told me that he wondered if he hadn't been set up for an elaborate practical joke. "For a job like that I expected multiple interviews with you and others, maybe psychology tests, and I don't know what else," he said. "I didn't expect to hear a man with a towel on his head say, 'Well, would you like this job?'" But that's the way we often did things at Loral, and we must have been onto something, because our batting average with important hires like Rich was quite high. Later, when I asked him why he had changed his mind and agreed to be interviewed, he said, "I'd asked around and everyone I spoke to told me you were a man with a vision. I liked the idea of working for a guy like that."

Another important lesson I've learned is that it's not always a mistake to talk frankly to a potential boss. Let me tell you about a job interview that did not go so smoothly, at least a first.

In 1981 Loral had reached the point where we needed to hire a corporate director of communications. The first place I turned to for recommendations was the great external resource available to us in the form of Kekst & Company, a world leader in the field of financial communications headed by Gershon Kekst. When I made my decision to acquire Loral, I called on Gershon to discuss how to communicate my plan and how to handle my transition into Loral. We needed to reach out to the press, shareholders, and the analyst community. Gershon's company had (and still has) the credentials to do that for us. A young man named Jim Fingeroth was the member of Gershon's team designated as the liaison between Loral and Kekst & Company. He worked shoulder to shoulder with us over my entire tenure at Loral, formulating messages about our acquisitions, our progress, and our vision for Loral; introducing us to important members of the press; attending analyst and shareholder meetings; and, perhaps most important, providing me with an objective perspective on our activities.

Gershon was a Loral board member, an insider from the very beginning., but Jim was no outsider. He was a trusted and valuable member of the Loral family. (Incidentally, Jim rose to the position of CEO of Kekst & Company in early 2013, a well-deserved recognition of his substantial accomplishments.) So, when Jim put forth a recommendation for filling the corporate communications position at Loral, I acted on it and called a woman named Jeanette Clonan, who was then working at a large packaging company in Stamford, Connecticut.

She had a fairly high-level job in communications, but she wasn't running the department, so the Loral job was a step up for her. Both Gershon and Jim had interviewed her already on my behalf and given her high marks. Now it was up to me to see for myself if she knew how to communicate in a way that was consistent with the Loral culture.

Her appointment was for five in the afternoon. By that point in the day, things had backed up and I was running behind—farther than I realized. Because it was summertime, the sky was still bright, and the office was humming along at full speed. It didn't feel like six in the evening, but when I was finally ready to see Jeanette that's what time it was.

As Jeanette walked into my office, I heard my assistant say, "Sorry to have kept you waiting," so I made an executive decision to not say anything more on that subject. Instead, I launched into a brief history of Loral, which had been under my stewardship nine years at the time. I also talked in a general way about what the job might entail and asked her how she would handle certain kinds of problems and situations. Her comebacks and questions were all very sharp and smart, she was poised and more than presentable—important with a communications person—and I was very favorably impressed. She was really acing the interview.

Things got even more interesting when I asked her one of the classic wrapping-up questions. "Is there anything you feel that I should know about you?"

"Well," said Jeanette, "you should know that I smoke."

I didn't like that, particularly, but I did admire her straightforwardness. Because I wanted my employees to be healthy, I told her that if she came to work for Loral, I'd do my best to encourage her to stop. In the meantime, I suggested that she reach for a piece of chocolate every time she craved a cigarette. Chocolate was my solution to a lot of life's problems, then and now.

She smiled pleasantly and I felt the interview was all but done, so I said, "Is there anything else you'd like to say to me?"

Once again, Jeanette didn't hesitate. "Yes, there *is* one thing I'd like to say. You kept me waiting for an hour in a small, windowless office. What that tells me, before we'd even met, is that you think your time is more valuable than my time, and I didn't consider that a very nice or appropriate message. Besides, that's not a terribly inviting room you have for people to wait in, and there's nothing to read in there. If I hadn't brought my briefcase and gotten some work done, it would have been like being a prisoner in solitary confinement. I enjoyed our talk and you were very cordial, but, Mr. Schwartz, you *really* need to work on your schedule!"

"Okay, I'll do that," I said, trying not to seem nonplussed. "And if you come to work here, maybe you can help me."

A couple of days later, I asked her to come in again, and it was during that conversation that I offered her the job. I liked the skills she had to offer, but I especially liked the intangibles she brought to the position—her style. As far as I was concerned, her parting outburst had sealed the deal. She would be the first female department head in what I have to admit had been an all-too-macho company, but I was sure that she could handle that. We agreed to a start date of September 1.

But in the middle of August, I got a phone call from Jeanette telling me that she had become pregnant with her third child. She didn't know this at the time of our interview, she explained, but she and her husband were delighted. The only problem, she acknowledged, might be mine, since she would be giving birth the following March and needing to take maternity leave. She apologized for putting me in a potentially awkward situation and, though she'd already given notice at her previous job, graciously offered to let me out of my commitment.

"Let me sleep on it," I said.

When I called her back, I said, "I've spoken with my top advisors in these kinds of matters—my wife and two daughters—and they have given me the rather astonishing news that pregnancy does not affect a woman's brain. So I expect you in the office on September first at nine a.m."

Jeanette Clonan, I could see from just two brief meetings, was a Loral kind of person, which is to say a bold thinker who follows through with honesty and fairness. She was a great hire and a tremendous employee, especially after she gave up smoking. I still appreciate and admire the way she handles communications and other matters for me today, more than thirty years later, at BLS Investments.

Just as in life outside the office, you can't always trust your first impression when assessing an employee. In fact, the recruitment process can be full of surprises. When I first met Lisa Stein, she was very young—and very shy. Or so it seemed. Lisa was hired in 1979 by Loral's vice president of administration, Steve Jackson, to work as an assistant to Ed Wilson, Loral's general counsel. When Steve told me about Lisa, practically the first thing he said was, "Wait till you see her, Bernard— she's a real looker."

Later that afternoon I was introduced to Lisa, and I started off with a dumb joke. "Oh, you're the one who can't type," I said. She was a little too retiring, it seemed, for me to kid like that, and she blushed crimson as we both endured an awkward moment that came courtesy of me.

Within a short time, though, Lisa had a reputation as a true up-and-comer, one of the best hires Loral ever made. Eventually she became my assistant, which many people said made her the real boss of the company—and it was true; she can handle any problem that comes up. She was the perfect representative of the Loral family and its culture. Lisa was not always as docile as she seemed, and in times of adversity she was a rock, available 24/7 to provide wisdom, a can-do attitude, and whatever else was needed. I was delighted when she chose to come along to my office overlooking Central Park when I started BLS Investments and be an important member of my almost all-Loral staff.

For better or worse, putting together a team like we had at Loral wasn't just a matter of finding great employees. It was, as it always is in such situations, about saying goodbye to some people, too.

Not long after we acquired the San Diego–based company Conic Corporation in the early 1970s, the Loral management team went out for our regular monthly visit. I spent time with the division manager, whom I'll call Ed Stern, who had been with Conic at the time of the acquisition. He was an Israeli native—smart, ambitious, energetic, a good businessman who had built a strong division. There was no reason for me to think we'd have any problems.

At one of our subsequent monthly visits to the facility, the Conic executives presented us with something, and when I looked a bit closer at the numbers they were providing, I saw a lot about it that I didn't like. "Ed, we can't do this," I said. And then I gave him an alternative way that I'd like to see the project go. "Fine," he said.

When we came back one month later, though, Ed Stern hadn't implemented my suggestion. I was more than a little annoyed.

"Ed, you haven't done what I asked," I said. "I'm telling you, we are going to implement this procedure. I know you don't agree with it, but this is what we are going to do."

"Yep, right," he said.

But the next month there we were again, face to face in the meeting room, and the situation was exactly the same. "You know, Bernard," he said to me a short way into the conversation, "I'm just not going to do that. I don't believe it's the right thing."

I looked around at the group and said, "I wonder if you'll excuse us for a moment. I'd like to talk to Ed alone. This will just take five minutes."

He and I walked a short way down the hallway to an empty office. We were there half an hour, during which I gave him every chance to say why he still hadn't followed my direct orders. He simply disagreed with me, and furthermore, he was testing the boss. Finally, I said, "Ed, you're fired. I want you to go and clean out your desk and leave the premises. I'll help you in any way, but not at Loral."

He took the news calmly—he must have known termination was a distinct possibility—but said, "I'll just go back in the meeting first and say goodbye to everyone."

"No, Ed, you won't go into the meeting," I said. "You'll just leave."

And with that he was gone from the company forever.

He had given me no alternative.

CHAPTER 15

A Good Man

If you had been in the corridors of Loral in the days when I ran it, you would have seen that the culture made for a very free-form work environment. We had well-thought-out plans for expansion, for securing new contracts and completing them on time, and for managing the people in our various divisions. But the daily schedule of activities came together as we went along, improvising in response to challenges and opportunities. My management staff rarely resorted to memos, formal meetings, or multimedia presentations because we were always in and out of one another's offices, talking about whatever was on our minds.

I'll never forget the day I walked into Frank Lanza's office to talk about a contract and saw him with his head down over his desk, furiously sketching on a pad. If he was aware that I'd come in, he did absolutely nothing to acknowledge me.

"What are you doing, Frank?" I asked.

"Oh, nothing," he said, without looking up.

"No, really, what are you up to?"

"Just something."

"Oh, I see."

Frank was one of our corporate vice presidents and president of Loral Electronic Systems. He was an unusual guy. He wasn't at all corporate, polished, or bland. He had a heavy, dark moustache and sometimes a gruff manner, and when he had a cigarette between his lips, which was pretty much always, he gave off a kind of gangsterish air that you don't see in too many conference rooms.

Frank was an engineer by training—a brilliant one—with a creative mind that ranked with the best thinkers in defense electronics. He absolutely loved working on the electronic equipment in which Loral specialized, and in addition to being able to create wonderful technology, he was a genius at coming up with design and manufacturing solutions that kept our products profitable. But because of his look and his manner, he was not exactly Jeanette Clonan's go-to guy when we needed someone to appear on television. Frank spoke only when he felt like it, which wasn't often, and even then he didn't say much. Some people who didn't know him were intimidated by him. But I really liked Frank. He was an okay guy who told it like it was.

He would often do drawings on scraps of paper or yellow legal pads, but on the occasion that I mentioned above, he was working with extra purpose and intensity. In fact, every time I visited his office during that period, he was thoroughly absorbed in his sketches.

"Still drawing I see, Frank."

"Yes."

"Well, you have all these reports stacked up on your desk, but you're not getting to them."

"I'll look at them."

"Okay," I said.

Frank's "just something" turned out to be what we called Rapport, the first successful attempt to integrate the active and passive functions of radar detection into a single system. (You might recall I introduced Frank and the Rapport in chapter 12.) At the time the US Navy and Air Force were buying the active and passive units from two different manufacturers, and as soon as Frank told me what he was working on, I realized it had several advantages for our customers.

The first was that a customer would be dealing with one company instead of two, which greatly simplified the transaction. The second advantage Rapport provided was that it eliminated the technological redundancies that are inevitable when you have two closely related but different systems. That meant a simpler system, one that was a lot easier to manufacture and maintain. The third advantage was that it was smaller and lighter than any two complementary systems wired together. This was key because space and weight were extremely important considerations in electronic weapons design. The constant challenge for our engineers and designers was to not just invent brilliant products but to make their state-of-the-art technology fit on a compact, modern fighter plane as well.

The Rapport system turned out to be one of Loral's most important and profitable products. But the odd and somewhat frustrating thing about it was that we could never sell it to the US Navy, which had suppliers that they liked in this area as well as established patterns for filling their needs. They were, in other words, comfortable, and when a customer is comfortable, it can be very difficult to talk it into a new product and a new approach. None of the excellent arguments we could make for the Rapport system's superiority could make our navy budge. That's just the way it is sometimes when you deal with the military. So instead of sitting around bemoaning the craziness and unfairness of it all, Loral went out and, with the permission of the US government, sold the Rapport system to the Israeli and the Belgian air forces for their F-16s. It worked beautifully for them. Frank's "nothing, really" expanded the boundaries of what Loral could do in the marketplace.

Frank, as you'll appreciate from that anecdote, was a one-of-a-kind guy. And he and I had a most unusual courtship. From the day I'd taken over Loral, I had been serving as both CEO and COO. I needed someone to handle our largest division, and since there were no likely in-house candidates, I started to look and ask around the industry in 1974. One name I kept hearing was Frank's. I did some background checking and found that people whose opinions I respected thought of him as a great electronics engineer and that he had been responsible for some very successful products. I thought we might complement each other well, and I decided to give him a call and invite him in for a conversation.

Frank at that time worked for Dalmo Victor, a subsidiary of Litton Industries, which was based in California and was one of our competitors. I thought Frank wouldn't mind hearing from me because I would be talking to him about a better situation than he was in: not just more money and a bigger title but also an opportunity to work within the Loral culture. I'd found that Loral was an easy sell to prospective hires because of our reputation for quality and fairness and because we were successful and growing, no matter what the overall conditions in the industry. At Loral, you could do your job with an absolute minimum of office politics—and there was always free chocolate lying around on the conference tables. Pretty good deal.

I met Frank at one of the restaurants at the Los Angeles airport, which I chose because I was getting on a plane soon after our meeting. We talked about many things—the industry, his view of the direction that the technology was taking. He asked many questions about Loral, the way we operated, our investments in R&D, and what our future plans were. I explained to him why the job I was looking to fill was so important, that it was the operating head of our largest division. I told him I could only offer him three things: One, we would build a big company; two, he would get rich; and three, we would have a lot of fun.

Frank said he had a lot to think about and that he would be in touch.

About a month later, after not hearing from him at all, I called him back. "Frank, I'm going to be in California," I said, although that was a slight fabrication. "I'll just be passing through; perhaps we can meet at the airport."

At the end of that discussion, Frank told me that he was interested and had done a little homework but needed to do some more before he made a commitment. We ended our meeting and I expected to hear from him shortly. But after a few days, I again called Frank and asked if he had made up his mind. He told me yes, he had decided to join Loral, but he'd have to come to New York to explore housing opportunities, schools for his children, and a few other things.

"What I thought I'd do is come there, visit your plant, then spend a little time looking for a place. Thanksgiving weekend is coming up. Does that work for you?"

"Certainly," I said. "And since you won't know anyone and it's Thanksgiving, why don't you come and have dinner at our house? It's a tradition for us to go all out and have family and friends come. It'll be great."

"Sure," he said.

Frank arrived and walked into the usual Schwartz family scene. Irene that year had made two turkeys, and we must have had three or four different kinds of vegetables and at least four kinds of dessert. The kids were seated at one big table and the adults were seated at an even bigger one. And everyone was talking loudly and excitedly: arguing about the Vietnam War, and about sports, movies, everything. Frank, meanwhile, was sitting there saying virtually nothing. It was, as always, impossible to tell what he was thinking.

That year we had a unique addition to the Thanksgiving agenda. Our longtime housekeeper had asked Irene if her son, who was taking a cinematography course in high school, could show us a "little movie" he'd made. "It would be very important to him," she said. Irene agreed, so after dinner the boy appeared and set up a screen and projector, we pulled up our chairs—and he showed us an utterly incomprehensible and mind-numbing experimental film that lasted for a little over one hour. I thought to myself, "Frank must have decided we're all absolutely crazy."

We had agreed to a start date of January 1, but December wore on and, as I probably don't have to tell you, I didn't hear from Frank. So I called.

"Are we still good for the first of the year?"

"Oh, I've been meaning to call you," Frank said. "I can't make it by the first. I have some things I have to finish up here."

We agreed to move his start date to February 1. "By the way, Bernard, the chairman of Litton has asked to see me."

"Oh? About what?"

"I'm not sure."

Frank and I didn't have a contract at that point, but we had an understanding: a handshake agreement that I think both of us considered binding. Still, when I heard about his meeting with his boss, I told Frank, "I want you to know that as of this moment you are relieved of any responsibilities to our agreement. You owe it to yourself and your family to listen to what this guy has to say. He's going to make you an offer. For your own sake, you should listen to his offer free and clear of any obligation to me. I want only one thing from you in exchange. I want you to promise me that if in the course of your conversation you hear something you like, and you want to change your mind, that you call me and give me the opportunity of talking to you about it."

Of course he didn't, and when I called him back and said, "What happened with your boss?" he just said, "We had a meeting, but everything is all right. I'll see you February 1."

When Frank finally reported for duty on February 1, I was sure that I'd hired a stand-up guy. He'd had every opportunity to say to me, "Actually, Litton offered me a deal" or "I changed my mind." But he didn't, and I think, in his own way, he appreciated the patience I showed. Like me, I think he believed that money was important but not *the* most important thing. The whole time that he worked for me, he never once opened a discussion about a raise. I gave him plenty of raises, bonuses, and stock options, but he always took what I offered with a simple "thank you."

In virtually every way, as it turned out, Frank Lanza was a first-rate guy to work with. He was a first-class manager. Not all his people liked him, but everyone respected him. When he had a problem, he was up front in expressing it. He fought hard for his convictions but was willing to go along with decisions he didn't wholly agree with. Once when he was resisting my direction, I had to give him an ultimatum: "I'll be sorry to see you leave and we'll miss you, but I've made a decision and we're going to carry it out." Frank made the decision to stay on board.

I'm glad he did, because after he was president of the LES division for several years, I thought Frank was ready to become president of the entire company. Whoever took it would report to me but to no one else at Loral.

I decided to talk to Frank about this possible promotion during a cross-country flight. Shortly after takeoff I took a piece of paper from my briefcase and began sketching a crude corporate chart. I drew a relatively large box and labeled it "Board of Directors" and below that I put a smaller box called "Chairman of the Board." The box after that I left empty, and below that I put a series of boxes named for each Loral senior vice president. Further below were still more boxes representing all our divisions.

"So, here's our company," I said when I was done, holding the chart in the space between us. "Here is where you are right now, and if you look closely at it, you'll see there is an empty box, where the president and COO of the company should be. Loral needs a president and COO, and it should be you. I'd like very much to put your name in that box, Frank, but I won't until you tell me that's what you want me to do. If you don't say yes, I'll go out and get someone else."

"Let me ask you a question," Frank said. "If I take this job, can I fire one of these executives who report to me without getting you involved? Or if someone under me does something that I don't like, can I fire him or her?"

"Yes, you can," I said. "Those positions are all under you, and you can hire and fire at will. I would hope that if we're talking about one of our bigger divisions and someone in a senior-level job, you would come to me first so we could talk about it. But you definitely have that power, and I will back your decisions one hundred percent."

"I'll take the job," Frank said.

Frank really showed me something that day. We didn't talk about money, stock options, or office size. He only asked me one question, but he knew *exactly* which question to ask.

CHAPTER 16

Exceptional Growth in the 1980s

By the end of the 1970s we had, for all practical purposes, created our own niche in the defense business: defense electronics. As I phrased it in the 1980 annual report, my strategy had transformed Loral from "a one service, 'black box' subcontractor into a multi-service, multinational developer and manufacturer of full electronic systems with scientific capabilities that are in the forefront of advanced technology." We were really going places.

Here are the opening lines from my shareholders' letters as we moved into the 1980s:

1979

Fiscal 1979 was another outstanding year for Loral. The company's financial performance once again set new records.

That year we increased our annual dividend to $1 per share of common stock, booked more than $100 million in orders from NATO countries, and added the US Army and Navy as customers.

1980

Several significant events in fiscal 1980—ranging from Belgium's selection of Loral's Rapport III self-protection system for its F-16 aircraft, to the successful public offering of

$50 million worth of additional common stock—have dramatically expanded Loral's role as an international high technology company.

We also announced a two-for-one stock split, and had acquired, in exchange for stock, a Massachusetts company called Frequency Sources, a manufacturer of microwave components and assemblies vital to the electronic warfare and telecommunications industries.

1981

Fiscal 1981 was another year of notable financial and technical achievement for Loral.

That was our ninth consecutive year of improved sales, profits, and earnings per share. We booked orders of the ALR-56 system, the first software-programmable radar warning receiver, in use on the F-15, with an aggregate value of $327 million. We also increased our cash dividend for the fifth consecutive year, to an annual rate of $.72.

1982

In fiscal 1982 we made significant strides toward our objective of broadening Loral's role in its principal market—electronic warfare—thereby reinforcing our leadership position.

We expanded further by acquiring Randtron Systems, a manufacturer of antenna systems, and Aercom, which specialized in microwave packages for the defense industry, both based in California.

1983

1983 saw a significant advance in Loral's targeted strategy to enlarge its role in the defense electronics market.

We acquired Narda Microwave Corporation in exchange for Loral stock valued at about $46 million and established a technology think tank for developing advanced microwave integrated circuitry.

1984

Fiscal 1984 saw the expansion of our role within the defense electronics market . . . We won important initial production awards and turned in another year of record financial performance—net income increased 28 percent, backlog grew 51 percent—our twelfth straight year of improved results.

That year we announced another two-for-one stock split, and for about $40 million in cash, we acquired from Xerox its Electro-Optical Systems company, which brought us three critical technologies: infrared countermeasures, laser-based simulation systems for training, and advanced electro-optics.

1985

Fiscal 1985 was another milestone year. We became a complete electronic defense systems supplier, broadened our technology and product base, and won important contracts—all while achieving record financial results.

That year we acquired Hycor, a Woburn, Massachusetts–based company that made expendable chaff and flare systems for shipboard applications. We also announced our plan to purchase from IBM the Rolm Mil-Spec Computer Division, a leading producer of high-performance militarized computers for electronic warfare.

What I hope all these excerpts convey, apart from the particular successes we were enjoying, is the sense of momentum that had become palpable within Loral. At times I felt as if I was holding the reins of a galloping thoroughbred.

In 1986 it came to my attention that Goodyear was putting its military division, Goodyear Aerospace, up for sale. The corporate raider Sir James Goldsmith was attempting a hostile takeover of Goodyear, and the company was raising cash to help fight off his bid. This was the biggest acquisition I'd ever considered, but I liked the idea because it fit all the major criteria of my master plan for Loral's expansion:

Goodyear Aerospace had potential synergies with Loral that would help both companies grow, and because Wall Street was overly pessimistic about the defense industry at that time, it would probably be something of a bargain.

My chief problem was that someone at Goodyear had drawn up a list of people the company was inviting to make a bid on the division, and Loral wasn't on it. The sale, I knew, was being handled by a senior investment banker at Drexel Burnham named Michael Milken. I decided to call him up.

"Mike, I would very much like to buy this company," I told him.

"I'm sorry, Bernard. They gave me names of who to go to and Loral isn't one of them. But let me see what I can find out." A short while later he called back and said, "They don't think you have the resources to put up the price they're asking"—which was about $600 million.

I thought Goodyear's assessment of us was kind of strange. Loral was already a Fortune 500 company, and we would become a Fortune 200 company in 1992; we ranked eleventh in the United States in total return to shareholders over the last ten years and tenth in earnings-per-share growth over the same period. I had never had any sort of problem raising money, and I had good relationships with a large number of big banks. Could it be that I wasn't a member of the "club" of companies and executives that Goodyear, an Ohio-based company, was used to dealing with? I didn't know and I didn't care. I just wanted to be considered as a serious bidder, and I told Mike Milken that.

I'd known Milken for quite a while, although not terribly well. The press often referred to him as the "junk bond king." The term was originally meant as an insult, but he didn't take it that way. He was as smart as anyone I knew, and he worked hard for that title. He read every word on every bond instrument and decided which bonds selling at thirty, forty, or fifty cents on the dollar were the equivalent of blue-chip investments.

At the height of his success, when a new stock or bond was issued, he would call up the wealthiest and most powerful people in America and say, "I want you to buy this," and strictly on the basis of his recommendation, they would invest millions. Everyone made money with him, and when people wanted to sell their bonds, Milken would make the market for them. In the process he created a massive company and became extremely wealthy.

I first met Milken through Saul Steinberg, while I was at Leasco. He was a friend of Saul's and they did business together. I would get invited to Mike's legendary meetings in Los Angeles at which there were business presentations as well as first-class entertainment, such as Diana Ross, and he always solicited business from me—he never stopped working. I enjoyed Milken's company. Once I called him and said I was going to be in Los Angeles, where his main office was, and asked if we might get together to talk about a potential financing. "Sounds great, let me check my book," he said. "Can you come in on Thursday at five-thirty?"

"That's a little tight for me," I said. "I have a meeting before that at one of our plants, in Pasadena. But I'll make it work."

"Good," he said. "It's really the only opening I've got—and you won't have any traffic at that hour."

"What do you mean?" I said. "There will be plenty of traffic."

"No, not at that hour of the morning."

"Mike, five-thirty in the *morning*?"

"Yeah."

"I'm sorry," I said. "I don't work at that hour. I'm not going to make this meeting." Still, we remained friendly.

Milken and I had never worked on a deal—I had my own bankers, for one thing—but a couple of days after I had called him about Goodyear Aerospace, I got a call from someone else at Drexel Burnham who said, "It's all set. You're on the list for Goodyear." In the end we made a bid of $588 million for the division, and we won. At the closing dinner to celebrate the deal, the chairman of Goodyear came up to me and said, "Do you know why you were able to buy this business? Because Mike Milken called me and said, 'If Bernard Schwartz makes a commitment to you, you can bank on it. If he says he can bankroll the divesture price, he can do it.'"

After our initial conversation concerning Goodyear, however, I had never heard from Milken again about that matter. A lot of other people would have called to say, "I hope you liked what I did for you with that deal," but not him. To me, that showed class. I felt I owed him one.

Sometime later I got an opportunity to pay him back. A lot had happened to Milken in the interim and almost all of it wasn't good. He was under investigation at the time for insider trading, and the rumor was that he was going to be indicted. If he had done something wrong, I certainly didn't condone it, but I felt for him as a human being, and I was still very grateful for the favor he had done for me in the Goodyear acquisition, which by then was panning out beautifully. We were planning an underwriting at the time, and I got a call from Milken. "You run an important company, and this is an important underwriting," he said. "I'd like to get in on the deal. This is very important to me." Although Mike wasn't one of our bankers—we were working, as usual, with Lazard Frères and Lehman Brothers—I said, "Sure, but you will not handle the book," by which I meant he wouldn't be the lead banker on the deal.

When I met with the representatives of those other banks and told them what I wanted to do, I could sense they were somewhat surprised. A few days later I got a call from Felix Rohatyn, a longtime personal friend and the head of Lazard Frères. "Listen, you're the customer," he said. "If you want Drexel Burnham in on this deal, they are in. But frankly, I don't know why you'd do that. No one on the Street will understand why you're doing business with Milken. If in the middle of this he gets indicted, it could scuttle the whole underwriting. People will wonder what's going on—they already are."

"Felix, there should be no mystery about this," I said. "I have a debt to pay to Mike Milken and I'm going to pay it. It's as simple as that."

Not too many months after we conducted a successful underwriting, Milken pled guilty to reduced charges of securities and reporting violations and was sentenced to ten years in prison. He was also permanently barred from the securities industry; my deal was one of the last ones he did. But he didn't just sit back and collect his fee. Once he got on board with the underwriting, he gave it his full attention and worked very hard to help make it the success it turned out to be. Every couple of days he was on the phone, asking me to try this or that innovative thing. He'd make suggestions about repackaging the deal and changing the interest formula. He truly earned whatever money and other benefits he got for the underwriting.

In the end Milken managed to have his sentence reduced to less than two years, and ever since he got out, he's become a leader in raising funds for fighting cancer and other life-threatening diseases. I get the impression that he's happier now than he ever was.

The acquisition of Goodyear Aerospace—which soon was renamed Loral Aerospace—was important in so many ways that it fundamentally changed the nature of the company. Until that point we basically had been a components business. Now, because our large-scale new division was in the business of supplying highly technical systems for the US military, we would be a big systems business, competing against Hughes, Lockheed Martin, and the other industry leaders. It was a tremendously important step for us, and I'm proud to say we accomplished it in a fairly creative way.

Tucked into the portfolio of subdivisions and other assets that Goodyear Aerospace comprised was a company called Aircraft Braking Systems Corporation. As its name suggests, ABSC designed and manufactured brakes for a variety of small- and medium-sized commercial and military aircraft. It was a healthy, growing business—the third-largest company of its kind in the world, in fact—but it didn't fit into Loral's portfolio. It was a relatively low-tech "metal bending" business that had nothing in common with the sophisticated electronic devices we were designing and producing. As a result, it was a condition of the loan Loral received from Lehman Brothers to purchase Goodyear Aerospace that ABSC would be sold and the proceeds used to pay down the financing.

Once the deal went through, however, and we learned more about ABSC by managing it for a while, I started to see some opportunities. One thing I noticed was that the company hadn't had a clear idea of where it fit into the industry. Honeywell and Goodrich had pretty much wrapped up the brakes market for bigger planes in the United States, and another European company dominated in the area of large Airbus planes. But I realized that if ABSC concentrated on fostering relationships with companies like McDonnell Douglas, Bombardier, and Embraer, it could build a much stronger business model based on servicing regional aircraft. I still didn't think ABSC was synergistic with Loral, but I was seeing it not so much as a poor fit but as a *very* interesting company.

The aircraft braking business works on the same principle as the razor blade business: If the customer can be convinced to use a certain kind of fixed tool (the razor), he will keep coming back to you to replace the part that wears out (the blade). With aircraft brakes the razor is the wheel and the blades are the brakes, which need to be replaced every eight or nine months. If you can make that initial sale when a manufacturer is introducing a new model of aircraft, you're likely locked in solidly for as long as twenty-five or thirty years. In short, there was a lot to like about ABSC, and so every time Lehman would report to me that they were still looking for the right buyer for the company, I'd say, "That's okay. No rush. Things are going well."

Eventually, though, Lehman arranged for an open bidding contest, as called for in our borrowing agreement. The best bid we got for ABSC was an offer of $225 million. That was a lot of money, but from what I had determined, not enough. At our next board meeting, I reported the offer to the members and said, "I know we told the banks we're going to sell this to the highest bidder to reduce our debt, but I'm not going to let this company go for $225 million. I would pay more than that for ABSC myself!"

After the meeting, Bob Hodes said to me, "Were you serious that you would pay more money than our top bidder?"

"I sure was," I said.

"So why don't you buy it?"

"How could I possibly do that? I'm chairman of Loral."

"How much would you pay?"

"I'd easily pay $300 or $400 million. They make good products; it's a great company. I really love it."

"Listen, Bernard, for Loral to lose maybe $200 million just because you're in an unusual position to make a bid—there's something wrong with that. In fairness to the shareholders, I think you ought to be allowed to make a bid."

"Let me think about it," I said.

When I did think about it, I decided I wanted the braking company, but I didn't want to do what some people have done in similar situations, which is to ask for bids and then top the final bid by a nominal amount. Instead, because I wanted to be more transparent than I had to be, I disclosed that I was making a bid and what the bid was. This put me at a marked disadvantage, I realized, but I wanted my interest and participation to be entirely above board.

My bid was $425 million in cash. I remember at the time my CFO, Mike DeBlasio, said, "I think you're paying too much for this. If you're overpaying, that's good for Loral, but I do think you're overvaluing the company." Other people told me similar things. But I thought I was paying an appropriate multiple of earnings. My $425 million was not only far above the previous high bid, it also meant that for the sale of what had been a relatively low-profile asset, Loral would be receiving a large percentage of what it had spent to purchase all of Goodyear Aerospace.

To help finance my bid I went to Lehman Brothers, my bankers for many years, with a proposition. I suggested that we each put up 50 percent of the amount in cash, and that I would receive 65 percent of the equity and they would get the remaining 35 percent. I defended this split by saying that this was a deal I was bringing to Lehman as a complete package, and thus I deserved the bigger share. The meeting I proposed this at was conducted by David Brand and attended by Bob Towbin, both investment bankers who worked for Lehman. David objected strongly to my 65-35 split, and after we tried to hash things out for an hour and a half, I was seeing no progress and decided we weren't going to be able to make a deal. As I started to put my papers in my briefcase, Bob Towbin said, "Where are you going?"

"Back to my office. It doesn't look like we're going to come to terms."

"Bernard, would you mind just waiting a minute? I want to get someone."

"You have as long as it takes me to pack up my papers and get to the elevator."

"I'll be right back."

About two minutes later, he returned to the room, accompanied by Dick Fuld, the CEO of Lehman. "Bernard, what's happening here?" Dick said.

I told him we couldn't make any progress in our talks and I was moving on. "Can you step into the next room with me?" he said.

That room was a conference room with several Lehman people seated around a large table. Dick pointed to me and then said to the head guy, "Whatever this man wants, give him!" And then he walked out of the room.

The Loral board was happy with my $425 million bid, but three days before the end of the sixty-day period allowed for due diligence, takeover artist Jeffrey Steiner swooped in and bid $430 million. "What are you doing?" people in the industry and in the business media asked him. "Have you investigated this company?" In fact, he admitted, he had done absolutely no research. His position was, "If it's worth $425 million to Bernard Schwartz, it's worth $5 million more to me."

The problem with Steiner's bid was that the $430 million was not all cash. When the board considered both bids, the members said they favored my cash bid over Steiner's slightly larger but more debt-based one. Still, I wanted to be absolutely fair to the Loral shareholders, so I suggested we have a run-off auction between Steiner and me, with the final bids due in fifteen days. He made a bid of $440 million, still mostly in the form of financing. I bid $460 million, almost all in cash, and won the company.

My first action as the CEO was to rename ABSC after my daughters. When I told them what I had done, Fran, the younger one, complained loudly that she always came second whenever her sister, Karen, was involved. I was sympathetic and told her that I would have liked to put her first for a change, but I didn't think naming a company F & K would be appropriate.

In the end when the bids were raised and the amount of cash needed increased, I went back to Lehman and asked them to put up additional funds; we shared equally in the equity, although I would run the company. I had to be up to speed from the start when it came to managing K & F. One of the first decisions I faced involved the McDonnell Douglas MD-90, a new plane that was just coming out at the time. The way it worked in the aircraft brake business—consistent with the razor blade analogy—was to pay the manufacturer cash up front to own the design of the brake component for the life of the model. The amount you paid was determined by bidding.

Many of my competitors were assuming that I wouldn't be spending serious money as head of K & F because I had just spent so much to take it over. They also thought I would be conservative and cautious because I was new to their game, and that it would be a long time, if ever, before K & F would be a major factor in the industry again. But I knew the MD-90 was one bid we just had to win, because it would not only lead to a great piece of business but also send a strong signal to airplane manufacturers and our competitors that we intended to do business without missing a beat. We bid around $20 million to win the contract, and the MD-90 became part of the K & F success story.

Ken Schwartz is the son of my older brother Jules. When my nephew graduated from college as an accountant, he came looking for a job, and I sent him to our largest division, LES, to be interviewed. They decided to hire him for a low-level financial job, and through the years he worked up to a position of greater responsibility and authority. One of LES's executives said to me once, "You know, Kenny is an okay guy and smart. He would do better if his name were not Schwartz." This bothered me, but I didn't do anything to interfere or support Ken's career at LES. I didn't have to: He was smart and engaging, and everybody liked him.

When I bought the aircraft braking business, I asked Ken if he would come over as the chief financial officer. Happily for my partner, Lehman Brothers, and me, Ken accepted the job. When we sold K & F to Aurora Capital Group, Ken became the CEO of the business. He was important to its continued success and also for reinforcing the Loral culture in the Akron, Ohio, company. Under Ken's leadership, the company continued to grow. When Aurora sold K & F to Meggitt PLC, Ken continued as chairman and was an outstanding executive. He continued to produce record performances until he chose to retire in 2012. When he's ready, I'm sure he will take on an important corporate responsibility and will continue to live a good life with his wife, Beth, and two children, Jonathan and Ilana. Of course, this is perfect from my viewpoint, as long as I can still beat Ken at backgammon.

The purchase of K & F probably turned out to be one of the best deals Lehman or I ever made. The people who told me I was overpaying were proven wrong, because the company was tremendously profitable and its value dramatically increased. Throughout their twelve years of part ownership, Lehman realized about $300 million. They had two men on the board, Alan Washkowitz and David Brand, who completely supported me. Even though it wasn't a Loral company, the Loral culture and its values permeated K & F and helped it succeed.

As I alluded to above, K & F was sold in 2004 to Aurora Capital, a private equity group that invests in mid-sized industrial companies. It was just time for me to move on, I felt, and because Lehman's part ownership of the company was in a trust that expired at the end of ten years, a sale was in their best interest. When Larry Bossidy, a strategic advisor to Aurora, called and told me he was interested in buying K & F, I told him straight away that the price would be nine times earnings before interest, taxes, depreciation, and amortization (EBITDA), based on the trailing twelve months prior to closing, and I was not going to negotiate. At the time of that discussion, the sale price was $1 billion.

Aurora took a long time to close, and as the months went by, K & F made more money and the purchase price rose. I was especially proud that after they spent a year in due diligence and looking into our financials, not one number changed. That says something about K & F and our style of doing business.

By the time Aurora was ready to close, the price had reached $1.1 billion. Gerald Parsky, the chairman of Aurora Capital, and Larry Bossidy visited me in New York to say they would have to walk away from it because the company couldn't get enough financing. I paused a moment and said, "You want to walk away? That's too bad, but okay."

I knew what the company was worth and so did Parsky and Bossidy. In due time they yielded, and I got my price.

And that turned out to be a fair price because under Aurora, and with Kenneth Schwartz in the CEO's chair, the company just kept making more money. In 2007 Aurora sold K & F to Meggitt-USA, Inc. for $1.8 billion. Everyone got a good deal.

CHAPTER 17

Operation Ill Wind

Goodyear Aerospace consisted of several tremendous assets that we knew about going into the deal, and a few pleasant surprises like K & F. Unfortunately, it also came with a man named Bill Galvin, who, though never a direct employee of Loral, constituted our connection to the FBI's investigation named Operation Ill Wind, which uncovered a major scandal involving corruption among Defense Department contractors.

William M. Galvin, a big, barrel-chested guy who was in his late fifties at the time, was an independent marketing consultant with all sorts of connections in the defense industry. He was also, though we had to find it out the hard way, big trouble. At the time we made our acquisition, he had been working with Goodyear on procuring a reorder contract with the navy that involved lighter-than-air vehicles—dirigibles. We took over the project when we bought the division, but things weren't going particularly well with the endeavor. The procurement was taking longer than expected, and the R&D and marketing costs were starting to get prohibitive.

Galvin had a reputation in the defense business as a guy who got things done, and after the Loral takeover, he got assignments from a number of Loral divisions, including our biggest one, LES, where he worked for Frank Lanza. I met Galvin during my regular periodic review of Loral

Defense Systems and let him know early in our conversations that the amount of money I was willing to invest in the development of dirigibles was not unlimited. Our chances for success were hardly assured, and I wanted to be cautious in terms of our financial commitment and sales effort. At the same time, the division manager was deeply committed to the project and to Galvin. I realized they were both unhappy with my stance on the matter, but I couldn't help that.

One day I got a call from Galvin. "Bernard," he said, "Loral cannot let this navy deal slip through its fingers. It's something that will be very important for the company's future, and I feel it is my obligation to advise you to stay committed to it. I really think we can get this deal done."

I told him that while I agreed it was potentially a good opportunity for Loral, I had to set limits. I gave him until January 1, about ninety days, which I thought was realistic and even generous. "At the end of that period, if we don't have a contract for the dirigibles, we will terminate the program," I said. "Do what you have to do, Bill, but I want to be clear that I will not go beyond that limit."

Galvin's relationship with our LES division was managed by a mid-level marketing executive there whom I'll call Les Johnson. Together they were working to land a contract with the air force for the kind of electronic warfare equipment that was Loral's bread and butter. Our main competition in the deal was Litton Industries, a firm we competed with on a regular basis. It was, in other words, a non-extraordinary situation, except for one thing—the amount of attention and favors that Galvin was lavishing on our man. Unbeknownst to me, he had invited Johnson out for lavish parties at his seventeen-acre estate in Front Royal, Virginia, where they schmoozed and mingled with prominent figures in the defense industry. This itself was not illegal or unethical, but at some point during their joint marketing effort, as I found out later, they crossed a line. Galvin asked Johnson if he would like to see Litton's proposal for the deal—a document that contained prices, specifications, deadlines, and all sorts of other highly confidential information that would be extremely useful for a competitor to have. "I can't let you keep it," Galvin said, "but I can let you read it if you'd like." To his discredit, Johnson said yes. At the same time, without our knowledge, our proposal wound up in the hands of Litton. This was how Galvin operated, and how for a while he thrived as a defense industry consultant. He gave you what you couldn't get elsewhere—sometimes what you knew you shouldn't have—but there was always a quid pro quo.

When we reached the deadline and there was no contract for the dirigibles, I terminated the marketing effort. With that project now over, I didn't think we needed Galvin's services anymore either, and I fired him personally. This was unusual, but since the division manager was disturbed by my decision and Loral had a long-term contract with Galvin, I wanted to make sure it would get done. When I told him that we'd be parting company, I said it was simply because we weren't going to pursue the projects he'd been working on, and that perhaps in the future we would work together again. "What goes around comes around," I said, trying to soften the blow.

A few months later the Operation Ill Wind scandal erupted. The name may draw blank looks today, but at the time it was front-page stuff. As it turned out, the FBI had been investigating white-collar crime in the Pentagon for several years, and it had found plenty. Galvin was among the leading criminals—a thief and a giver and receiver of all kinds of illegal favors. He had a secret Swiss bank account where he hid his ill-gotten income, and he was caught red-handed in so many different cases that all he could do in the end was admit his involvement, cooperate with the authorities, and make a deal.

In March 1990 he pled guilty to bribing a former navy undersecretary to help an Israeli company obtain a contract and also to working with Loral's man Johnson to bribe a former air force official to get a deal for Loral. He could have been sentenced to forty years in prison, but because he'd struck a bargain with the investigators, he got only thirty-two months and some large fines. Loral itself had to pay fines totaling about $5.7 million, and the deal in which Johnson had access to Litton's proposal was declared void. Several other large defense contractors, most notably

Hughes and Lockheed, were found to be involved in the corruption, and their penalties were considerably more severe than Loral's.

It wasn't that easy to be done with the Ill Wind scandal, though. Johnson himself was never convicted of or even charged with anything, but after the investigation brought his transgressions to light, the Defense Department asked that he be barred forever by Loral from all future transactions having to do with the military. That still left me with the problem of what to do with him. I simply could not believe that a mid-level executive could do something like that on his own; I did not feel comfortable putting all the blame on him. At the same time, I had to take some action. I decided I would suspend Johnson for one year without pay, but during that time he would be required to perform some public service, and if he came back, he'd have no involvement in military matters. I thought it was a good solution to the problem, but when I reported to our board of directors about the events of Ill Wind, described our independent investigation of the Loral-Litton affair, and announced what I'd decided to do with Johnson, one of our directors, the retired US Navy admiral Allen Shinn, spoke up immediately. "Fire him!"

I told him and the other board members why I was uncomfortable doing that and that I didn't feel it was fair to terminate one person when logic and my instincts told me others shared the blame. Allen politely waited for me to finish speaking, and then repeated, "Fire him!"

It was unusual for a director to give such a clear-cut directive. I said I completely understood the way he felt and noted that I had felt the same way, too, at first.

"Fire him!" Allen said yet again.

I didn't, though. This was one of the few instances in which I did not follow the strong advice of one of my board members. I believed my course of action was correct, even if it was difficult to justify. The issue resolved itself, as it turned out. After Les Johnson took a year off to work with his church, he stayed in that position and never came back to Loral or any other company in the industry.

But the Operation Ill Wind story didn't end there. I believe it was in early 1988 that I received a call from the Justice Department, asking if I would consent to be interviewed in connection with their still-ongoing investigation of defense industry corruption. I said I would and, at the suggestion of Bob Hodes, I retained Elkan Abramowitz, a prominent New York criminal lawyer. I wasn't a criminal, but Bob thought it would be a good idea if Elkan came along with me to provide his counsel if necessary.

After we arrived at the Justice Department, he and I were ushered into a depressing little room with gray walls and grayer furniture. Seated at a table were a Justice Department attorney, a court stenographer, and a rather large man who immediately got up and took off his jacket, revealing a gun in a holster. They were not friendly. Needless to say, this was not the atmosphere I was used to when I came down to Washington to meet with our customers in the army, navy, and air force.

The attorney explained to me that the FBI had made recordings of Bill Galvin's telephone conversations as part of its Ill Wind investigation. They had tapped Galvin's phone—not mine—and had two tapes that involved me. The first one was a recording of the call that Galvin had made to me urging me to stay committed to the navy deal, the one in which I told Galvin that I was setting a ninety-day deadline and that he should "do what you have to do." They played this tape over and over.

Finally the lawyer spoke. "Mr. Schwartz," he said, "what did you mean exactly, when you said, 'Do what you have to do?'"

I told him that Galvin was leading our efforts to land the contract for the dirigibles and that I was trying to convey that he should do what he thought was appropriate, but that we were putting a limit of time and money on the entire initiative.

The lawyer paused.

"Mr. Schwartz," he said, "let me play this again for you."

He played it several times.

"'Do what you have to do,'" he repeated. "What were you trying to tell him?"

"I just told you," I said. "I don't know what more I can say."

"Yes, Mr. Schwartz. Let me play it again."

Finally we moved on to the other tape from Galvin's phone tap, the one in which I'd fired Galvin. I was glad for the change and pleased that they had a record of me giving the boot to this guy.

Of course, they played it several times.

"Mr. Schwartz," the lawyer said, cocking an eyebrow, "what did you mean when you told Mr. Galvin, 'What goes around comes around'?"

At this point I noticed that the assistant attorney general had quietly slipped into the room and was observing the proceedings with a serious expression. The presence of such a distinguished visitor made me wish I had a better answer than what I told the Justice Department attorney.

"To tell you the truth, I have absolutely no idea what I meant by that," I said. "I was just trying to let him down easy, to suggest that we might someday work again, to say *something*."

"Mr. Schwartz, let me play the tape again for you."

And so the questioning went, with him playing the tape over and over. My answer was always the same, because I was telling the truth.

On the way home on the train, Elkan, whom I didn't know very well yet at the time, said he expected I would be called before the grand jury. He said that my prominent position in the defense industry as CEO of Loral, as well as my active participation in Democratic politics, made me a very attractive witness in the Justice Department's case. "They need big names to justify the existence of Operation Ill Wind and to keep it going," he explained. "If you get called," he said, "I would recommend that you take the Fifth Amendment."

I leaned toward him and I said, "Elkan, I will *never* take the Fifth in this case. I am completely innocent. I have done not the slightest thing wrong, and most people will see taking the Fifth as nothing more than an admission of guilt."

I was angry—not at my new lawyer, but at the unfairness of the situation. Elkan took my response with equanimity. "Let me tell you what will happen," he said. "One day in his jail cell, Galvin will receive a visit from someone in the Justice Department, and he will be interviewed. This person will suggest to Galvin that they review certain items in the file, one of which will be his various conversations, on and off the phone, with Bernard Schwartz. Galvin is a smart man, so he will see what they are trying to do—namely, get you involved. You are innocent. But he is also a dishonest and desperate man, so he will try to please them by reporting exchanges between you and him that never occurred or giving an untruthful interpretation of others. It doesn't matter that you've done nothing wrong, Bernard. You would never be found guilty. But you will endure a year or so of Justice Department harassment. So that's why I'm telling you to plead the Fifth Amendment. And I'm also advising you that if you *don't* take the Fifth, you will have to get yourself another lawyer."

As things turned out, I was never called back by the grand jury and therefore never had to choose between Elkan's sage advice and my gut instincts. However, something good did come out of that miserable morning in the all-gray room: my personal and professional relationship with Elkan, which enriches my life to this day.

About a year after the Operation Ill Wind investigation was declared over, an assistant attorney general called Elkan and asked very nicely if he would bring me down to Washington for an informal discussion. I was eager to go, and soon afterward, Elkan and I returned to the Justice Department. This time the office we were ushered into was large, bright, and airy—it had not a hint of gray—and everyone was being pleasant. The first thing the assistant attorney general did was to advise me, with a smile, that I was under absolutely no cloud of suspicion or in any way involved in any investigation being conducted by his department. He just wanted to find out some things, if he could, that might help everyone at Justice do a better job in the future.

"Your termination of Bill Galvin happened some months before any news about the Ill Wind scandal broke," he said. "What I'm wondering is, had you received some information . . . had anyone tipped you off to the fact that he was under suspicion in a corruption investigation?"

"I had absolutely no information like that," I told him. "Nor did

I know at the time that Galvin was doing anything illegal or even improper. That all came out later, after your investigation was made public and people were accused of crimes. I fired Galvin in the normal course of business and frankly thought nothing more of it until I heard about Ill Wind."

The assistant attorney general seemed more than satisfied with my answer this time. "The timing of Galvin's termination by Loral," he said, "made us wonder if there might be a leak in the Justice Department."

"Not as far as I know," I said. "But can I now ask *you* a question?"

"Certainly, Mr. Schwartz."

"I had the advantage of not just being innocent, but of being in a financial situation where I could fight back for as long as I needed to, and I know people in high places who would pay attention to the matter. What about someone else, who might also be innocent, but who doesn't have money to hire a top-notch lawyer for advice while he testifies before the grand jury? That guy might get railroaded just because he doesn't have the means to stand up before the government. That doesn't sound to me like the way a free society should treat its citizens."

The assistant attorney general looked down at his papers for a moment and then up at me. "Mr. Schwartz," he said, "there are good guys out there, and there are bad guys. My job is to catch the bad guys. Sometimes, in the process, an innocent person gets hurt, and that's just the way it is."

He was only being honest, of course, and I appreciated that. Still, what he said was a sad commentary on our system.

PART IV

Choices and Decisions

"If you had to give one single reason for Loral's success, if you had to reduce the culture of that company to its very essence, it would be that Bernard Schwartz was never afraid to make a decision. Other CEOs, when faced with critical choices, start having meetings and calling in consultants. Not Bernard. That's not his style. And incidentally: His lack of fear may be the reason he made the right decision the vast majority of the time. Bernard is proof that success breeds confidence and confidence breeds further success."

—HARVEY MILLER, SENIOR PARTNER, WEIL,
GOTSHAL & MANGES, LLP

CHAPTER 18

China Opening

In the late 1980s and early '90s, Loral was making a heck of a lot of money. "There is now an aura of success about this company," I told our shareholders in my 1987 letter. The year before, the company's net income had increased 26 percent, to $53 million, or $2.21 a share, compared with $42.1 million, or $1.79 a share, in 1985. We made two important acquisitions in 1986: Hycor, a manufacturer of radar and other electronic defense systems, and Rolm Mil-Spec, which designed and manufactured militarized computers for the army Black Hawk helicopter, among other products. These helped our bookings and backlog rise by 19 and 21 percent, respectively, over the prior year. By any standard, those were breathtaking advances.

I further wrote in my shareholders' letter:

> *Our strategy is uncomplicated. It is to add continuously to our already broad base of defense electronics technologies in order to reinforce or widen our market penetration. Thus, we add value to our products and gain a larger slice of the pie.*

In that same letter I also expressed confidence in our core industry's prospects, despite a dramatic cutback in defense spending that had rattled others and led some large corporations to divest themselves of defense-related divisions. I wrote:

> We live in an imperfect world. Our nation's global interests will expose our citizens and military to organized and sometimes indiscriminate terror. Our dependence on conventional weapons is hardly likely to diminish. Thus, appropriations will accelerate to fill the gap in deployed equipment.

We were right about that—all too right about some of it—eventually. But even though defense spending remained constricted, in 1988 I reported our sixteenth consecutive year and sixty-fourth consecutive quarter of growth. For the first time, Loral's sales exceeded $1 billion, as net income rose 29 percent to $74.3 million. Our success was so obvious that there was no way I could couch it in cold corporate terms. I wrote to shareholders, "Fiscal 1988 was a terrific year for Loral . . . The integration of Goodyear Aerospace was speedily and smoothly accomplished."

But if profit was a big part of the Loral culture, so was R&D spending. Keeping our technological edge and our reputation for quality and creativity were key to our continued growth. I was always willing to plow back a healthy part of our earnings into quality control and R&D. In 1988 alone Loral invested and expended more than $70 million in company-funded R&D, as part of a total R&D budget of $200 million, to maintain our technical lead. "We're spending as much or more on these areas than any company in the industry," I told our board. "But I think that's smart."

Anyone who didn't believe me could look at the record. Although 1989 was another year of Defense Department budget contractions, Loral continued to report earnings records: Net income jumped to $87.6 million.

How could we continue to prosper and grow while others in our industry suffered? I'll give you three reasons.

The first reason is that we were in tune with the times and our customers' requirements. During that period of cutbacks, 80 percent of our company's revenue stream came from follow-ons and upgrades to existing platforms. We understood that our customers had to think more conservatively during lean times.

The second reason is that we kept to our knitting. We did what we were good at—and we were good at quite a bit. In December 1989 Loral won a $94-million follow-on award for the ALQ-178 Rapport III self-protection system for Israeli F-16s. The company also received $13 million in development funding for the $150-million Vertical Launch ASROC program to defend navy cruisers and destroyers from undersea attack. Our single most significant development in the late 1980s, however, was winning the competition to place our ALR-56M radar warning systems on F-16 fighters. After a three-year competition, the contract was awarded to Loral on the basis of superior technology, lower price, and past performance. For the parent company, it was a blockbuster achievement that represented a collaboration between older and newer Loral divisions and confirmed our strategy in electronic combat. When considered with Loral's similar system for the F-15 and our Rapport system that was being used by the air forces of both Belgium and Israel, it meant that we expected to install our leading-edge technology on more than four thousand aircraft worldwide.

The third reason for our success is that we continued with our acquisitions program. It was a good time to be doing that; companies were eager to monetize their investments or divest themselves of divisions whose fortunes seemed to depend on Defense Department spending, and so the prices were right. Good management and creative deal-making could make those bargains even better. We acquired the mainstream defense electronic activities of Goodyear Aerospace Corporation for $133 million (the $588 million originally paid for Goodyear Aerospace minus the $455 million proceeds from the sale of two of its divisions, Aircraft Braking Systems and Engineered Fabrics): a cost equal to about 28 percent of its 1989 revenue base. We also acquired Fairchild Weston Systems' defense division—a business with annual revenues of $270 million, a backlog of $260 million, and an operating profit of about $22 million—at the very reasonable price of $180 million.

In my shareholders' letter I referred to Fairchild Weston Systems as a "non-dilutive purchase," which means we made that acquisition without diluting the value of the stock. We expected the annualized operating profit from the Goodyear and Fairchild Weston businesses to be $26 million in the year ahead, and it was in fact more than that.

In 1990 I made a bold move in designing the cover of the annual report, but one I've never regretted. I used a picture of the pro-democracy demonstrations in Beijing's Tiananmen Square. The dramatic photo showed demonstrators carrying what looked like the Statue of Liberty through the centuries-old square. I said in my letter to shareholders:

> Sometimes a single picture tells a full story. The cover of this annual report simultaneously depicts the hunger for justice and democracy around the world, and the speed of the changes that are taking place. We should be proud that the universal response to these events is to turn to America's brand of free-market democracy. Even in remote corners of the globe people are adopting a replica of our Statue of Liberty as their freedom symbol.
>
> At the same time, the picture reminds us of the tragic and bloody repression which followed, demonstrating that progress is not linear. Although we rejoice in the movement toward democratic institutions, we cannot believe that we have witnessed the last of repression, nationalism, terrorism, and military aggression. Thus, the cover picture also reminds us that strength and vigilance remain the price of freedom.

There was an obvious connection between these developments and Loral's strategy, which reflected my belief that while America must be compassionate, it must also be strong. Loral was a leader in electronic combat, reconnaissance and surveillance, simulations and training, and telemetry-command-control, and we had an important niche in antisubmarine warfare. The company by that time was also an incumbent supplier of significant hardware on more than 60 percent of the air force's tactical fleet. My letter continued:

> *These dramatic changes in China are reflected in Loral's strategy. Our business premise recognizes our nation's continuing need to maintain a vital U.S. defense presence to protect our national security and global interests. Although the nature of the threat may change, the American people must and will maintain a strong military capability supported by the modern industrial base.*
>
> *Further, our nation's defense capability will be driven by technology. Therefore, even as overall budgets decline, certain segments, particularly those at the leading technological edge, will receive continued resources for development and deployment.*

Because Asia was on the rise as a potential market and competitor, I had already traveled to Beijing by the time Tiananmen Square became an important chapter in the struggle for democracy. My first visit to China occurred just a few months before the demonstrations in the spring of 1989. I wanted to see the country and, if possible, sell their army a military communications system. I had the full approval of the US government in trying to make this deal. But because I wanted to spend some time there and get a sense of the culture, the business climate, and the people, I went with my wife, Irene, and two of our closest friends, Sir Fred Warner and his wife, Lady Simone. Fred had been the British ambassador to Japan and was later a charter member of Loral's international board, established in 1980. In those days when it was still difficult for Westerners to travel within China, and government officials were very wary of Americans of any sort, it was advantageous to be in the company of a full-fledged ambassador. Fred died in 1995 and I miss him terribly; as a traveling companion he was extremely knowledgeable, always gracious, and great fun. His wife continues to be a very special friend of Irene's and mine.

Tiananmen Square at that time was a perpetual sea of bicycles. The hotel I stayed in on the first trip overlooked the square, and if you looked out the window at two or three in the morning you'd see nothing but thousands of people riding bikes, in the middle of the night. Today you'll see relatively few bicycles there, replaced by thousands of cars, most careening around in a way that would get their drivers pulled over in America.

I wanted to see a number of cities on my first trip to China, and I made it a point to go to Beijing, where my customer was, last. I knew that if I went there first, the people I was meeting would insist that I have a guide, and I'd wind up being ushered around by someone who worked for the government. I preferred to make my own way, with Irene and Fred and Simone Warner, and to see things for myself.

There were relatively few first-rate hotels in China in 1989 and only a handful in Beijing. You couldn't even get bread and butter put on the table before your meal, and even if you asked for chocolate in Chinese, nobody knew what you were talking about. It wasn't just because bread and chocolate were not part of the culture there; it was because there were so few foreign visitors to ask for them. Irene and I went one night to a theater in a working-class part of Beijing. The place was packed, we had a great time, and we were the only Westerners we saw.

Dealing with the Chinese army was easy in some respects. I was selling them a military communications system that was good but not state of the art. It was the first generation of a product for which the US military was then purchasing the third generation. The Chinese government officials, however, were very happy to be dealing with Loral and acquiring an American-made product, even if it was somewhat outdated. So in some ways our relationship couldn't have been better. Still, because of the ever-present cultural differences, things could at times get a bit strained.

For example, when we arrived in Beijing, we learned that our hosts had arranged for us to stay not in one of the better hotels but in a kind of government housing complex. We were told that Henry Kissinger and his entourage had stayed there just a couple of months before and that we'd be right in the middle of a lovely park. Well, the park *was* lovely, but when we got there, at about eight on a winter's evening, it was pitch dark, and the building we were ushered into looked cavernous and forbidding. Once inside, we found the place to be sprawling: something between a guest house and a warehouse—you could have easily seated thirty-five or forty people around the dining room table—but also dreary and dilapidated. The four of us felt like we were rattling around inside the Addams Family mansion.

"You folks can do what you want, of course," I said to Fred and Simone, "but I'm not going to stay here. Irene and I are going find a hotel."

"Bernard, you can't do that," Fred said. "I know it's bad, but you can't reject what they're giving you, you can't say it's not good enough. They will consider it a loss of face."

"Fred," I said and then gestured toward the moldy walls and the dusty furniture. No other words were necessary.

"Okay," he said, and the four of us checked into a hotel.

There were no repercussions.

The culture clashes weren't over, though. A couple of days later, we learned that our Chinese hosts were planning a banquet in our honor. It was a lovely, friendly gesture, to be sure—but only men were invited.

This was something I just couldn't go along with. Yes, I had come a long way to make a deal, that deal was important to me, and I didn't want to offend my potential customers. Nevertheless, I wasn't going to leave Irene and Simone back at the hotel while Fred and I went to a gala dinner in Beijing. I said exactly that to the man acting as the liaison between the Chinese army and us. I could tell he was surprised, but in the end they accommodated our request and opened the banquet to men and women, which I was told was highly unusual then.

At the dinner I wound up seated next to the wife of the head of the Chinese army. As members of the Red Army, she and her husband had participated in the Long March of 1934–1935, which marked the ascent of Mao Zedong. The two of them were the only people there that night wearing traditional Chinese clothing, and I learned later that because they had been on that historic march, they were revered by their countrymen as something like living saints. I found them both very down-to-earth and charming. Before the dinner, during the cocktail hour, I had sat talking to her husband, the general, through an interpreter. He was quite old but very sharp and focused on the future. Every once in a while, he'd kind of whack me on the knee and say, "You know, we should not be enemies. We should be friends. We're the most important government in Asia, and you have to deal with us. You're the most important country in the West, and we have to deal with you. What's the point of fighting?"

During the dinner I was expected to stand up and make a toast to the general and his wife, our official hosts. I didn't have anything rehearsed, but I wanted to pay him a compliment and be personal. I had noticed that his hair was still jet black, and so I said, "I have met many great men in my travels, but rarely do I hear so much wisdom from a man who still has black hair." As soon as my remark was translated, a stunned silence fell. I hadn't realized that the general was known to dye his hair. Everyone knew it, but nobody dared say it aloud. I'll never forget raising that glass of champagne and looking out on a room full of frozen smiles.

I thought for sure that I'd blown the deal, but everything turned out all right.

A few years later, in August 1994, I returned to China as part of a delegation of eighteen American CEOs invited by Secretary of Commerce Ron Brown to explore new business opportunities. On the long flight over, Brown, sitting with several of his staff in a forward cabin of the plane, invited each member of the mission to come up and discuss how best Commerce could help US companies connect with China.

Previous to this I'd had several informal dinners with the secretary (who died in a plane crash in Croatia less than two years later), and we'd become friendly, but in this case he was all business. When he and his staff talked to me about Loral, I told him that we had an idea for some communications equipment—some of it satellite dependent—that might be of interest to the Chinese government. Brown said he thought that was an interesting possibility and volunteered to arrange for me to meet with one of the Chinese ministers.

I was pleased to be introduced by the secretary to a potential customer, but on the morning of the meeting, when the car came to pick me up, there was already someone in the backseat: one of my competitors, who was hoping to sell the same kind of equipment to the Chinese. It was an awkward moment for both of us, to say the least. I don't know if the other guy got the deal, but I know I didn't.

Whenever I recall that incident, I think of Ronald Reagan's famous line about the nine most terrifying words in the English language: "I'm with the government, and I'm here to help."

CHAPTER 19

Satellites, Continued Growth, and Profitability

In August 1990 Iraq invaded and annexed its neighbor Kuwait, setting in motion a series of diplomatic maneuvers that led inexorably to the start of armed conflict in mid-January 1991. This war, in which the United States led a UN-approved coalition of thirty-four nations against the forces of Saddam Hussein, lasted only about six weeks. But it demonstrated once again that a technically advanced military capability is an essential ingredient to an effective foreign policy. I wrote in my shareholders' letter in the 1991 annual report:

> *The apparent ease of victory should not beguile America into the belief that our preparedness can be casual. In fact, our victory, with minimal casualties, was a tribute to the effectiveness of our country's high-tech weaponry, brilliant planning, excellent training, and, of course, the courage and motivation of our forces.*

As CEO of Loral I was grateful for the opportunity to have contributed to our nation's success. Many of Loral's systems were engaged in Desert Storm—and they all worked. We were not at all surprised by that, but we were proud and thankful, and we saw the entire experience as a validation of our company's global strategy. Loral's emphasis on products and tech-nologies that served tactical defense requirements for regional conflicts was particularly relevant. Our state-of-the-art electronic weapons and systems not only proved to be a force multiplier but also were cost-effective and saved lives. Since I believe that a strong America is the best way to ensure a peaceful world, that pleased me immensely on a personal level.

The early 1990s were a challenging but fascinating time to be at the controls of Loral. So much was happening in the company and in the world. Despite four years of no-growth Department of Defense budgets, the momentum of our company had accelerated. Here are some things I was able to tell our shareholders in 1990:

> *Good performance turns out to be the best strategy.*
>
> Our backlog rose by 56 percent, to $2 billion, partly through acquisitions, but an impressive 20 percent was from internal growth. Our margins had improved, and we looked forward to continued improvement.
>
> *Our acquisitions of Fairchild Weston Systems and Honeywell Electro-Optics in fiscal 1990 were models of our approach.*
>
> Each was a leader in one of our core businesses, and their pur-chase prices were very attractive.
>
> *Our confidence in our strategy and our industry continues unabated.*
>
> We continued to strengthen our financial condition. Cash totaled $105 million at year-end and our debt-to-equity ratio improved to .75:1 from 1.1:1. Cash dividends increased for the eighth consecutive year. Income from continuing operations rose to $77.5 million. We also invested over $70 million in internal R&D and over $60 million in new a plant and equipment.

In 1991 as our rapid growth continued—despite the dramatic downsizing of our nation's defense forces—I had even more good news to convey in my shareholders' letter:

The success of Loral's strategy has been confirmed by our consistent performance, which has been outstanding by any standard but particularly when measured by our industry.

Loral's compound rate of growth in operating income and earnings per share over the previous ten years was 21 percent and 13 percent, respectively. In fiscal 1991, operating income rose 45 percent to $215.5 million, and earnings per share rose 15 percent to $3.55.

Loral is the largest training company in the US.

Our integrated C-3—space communications, surveillance, and reconnaissance capabilities—covered a broad spectrum of high-priority programs and applications, and our sensor and guidance systems were a key ingredient of precision weapons.

More earnings records. A rising stock price. Expansion through strategic acquisitions. In some ways it sounded like a typically great year for Loral, one of those years when our biggest challenge in putting together the annual report was finding fresh ways to describe our success. But for us, 1991 was hardly a time of business as usual. Here, in one more excerpt from my annual letter, is why: "Foremost among our 1991 achievements was the acquisition of Ford Aerospace—renamed Loral Aerospace Holdings." With those words I announced one of the major milestones in Loral's history.

For the most part, I felt as if the new division connected to pre-1991 Loral. Ford Aerospace had been in the defense business, just as Loral was: It made missiles and similar military products. It was in many ways a highly successful company, with annual revenues of about $2 billion and a high backlog of orders. What's more, it was thriving in an industry that we understood as well as any company in the world. There was no reason to think we wouldn't both grow as a result of the acquisition, becoming greater than the sum of our combined parts.

But this wasn't just a classic case of synergy. Besides its electronic warfare, intelligence, and command and control operations, Ford Aerospace also manufactured satellites, and while satellites could have important military

applications—reconnaissance and intelligence gathering, for example—
and be sold to the Pentagon like other Loral products, the market for
them went far beyond that. Depending on what kind of payloads their
owners equipped them with, satellites could be used for air traffic control,
data transmission, weather forecasting, telephone communication and
television signals, and a host of other purposes.

It was an exciting business on the cutting edge of technology, and
still a fast-growing one in the early 1990s. But it wasn't an easy business
to succeed in, as Ford's own experience indicated. At the time of our
acquisition, their satellite division was languishing; for all practical
purposes, it had only one customer, a satellite communications company
called Intelsat. Ford had built most of Intelsat's satellites over a period of
more than thirty years, and that business accounted for about 10 or 15
percent of Ford Aerospace's annual revenue. Intelsat was a great customer,
but I had to ask myself, as anyone who was on the outside of the satellite
business looking in would have to ask, why was it the only customer?

There was never any question about whether I wanted to acquire
Ford Aerospace at the right price. But once we owned it, did I want to
hold on to the satellite part of the division? For the previous twenty
years, we had done very well by sticking to our knitting. Since branching
out would mean a significant financial commitment, I had to think hard
about whether this wasn't too much of a departure for Loral.

There were four questions we had to ask ourselves to determine
whether Loral could succeed in the satellite business. The first was this:
Will we have the expertise to compete on a high level in this different
field? This was an easy yes, because in fact we already had outstanding
engineers and designers who were skilled in sophisticated electronics, and
much of the weapons technology we were already producing was not
all that different from satellite technology. For us, the satellite business
was not "diversification" in the sense that the term was employed by
companies in the 1950s. Rather, it would be more a matter of extending
the spectrum of our considerable talents.

The second question facing us was whether we could deal with the many new and different kinds of customers we hoped would come. This was actually a trickier consideration than the technological one was. For twenty years we had sold our products either directly to the military or, when we served as subcontractors, to military suppliers. We knew the protocols and the codes of conduct, written and tacitly understood, that came with dealing with the various branches of the service. We knew and admired the military mind, and we had worked hard to forge and maintain good relationships with the people in the Pentagon whom we dealt with regularly. Would our marketing side be able to adapt, servicing a diverse customer base in which the military played only a minor part?

This was a key question. It wasn't just a matter of some customers wearing a uniform and some not. Basic attitudes were different inside and outside the military. For example, in a large portion of the satellite business, price was not just paramount—it was sometimes the one and only thing that mattered to a customer. We could talk all day with some customers about Loral's long-standing reputation for quality and timely delivery; we could tell them, "You don't really want the *cheapest* satellite. You want a satellite that *works and gets delivered to you on time.*" Our military customers, who were almost always disinclined to sacrifice quality and reliability to save a few dollars, would be open to that kind of argument. But most of the civilian satellite buyers would inevitably bring the discussion back to price.

That was a less than ideal situation, to be sure, but I thought we could handle it because one basic tenet of the Loral culture was to always understand the other side's needs, which was something our people were skilled at doing on a case-by-case basis. Sometimes, in fact, we understood the customers' needs better than the customers themselves did, and when they realized that, they appreciated it and rewarded us with their loyalty. Because we would bring this same sense of empathy to nonmilitary customers, we would do okay. And if we made one sale, I knew we could likely make more with the same customer. I especially liked that the satellite business had a strong tendency toward repeat business.

The third question I had to ask myself as I considered Ford Aerospace was this: Could we handle the unusual rhythms—or the lack of rhythm—that characterized the satellite business? Even a major manufacturer of satellites usually sold only five or six units a year, and that could mean the work flow on the manufacturing side was not steady. It took a certain size company, simultaneously involved in other businesses, to handle this mix of slack and busy periods inherent in the manufacturing of satellites. I thought Loral had become that kind of company by 1990.

My fourth question had to do with financial commitment. If we kept the satellite business, the acquisition of Ford Aerospace would mean Loral was doubling in size. Apart from those employees we inherited from Ford, we would need to hire a significant number of new people at virtually every level, from engineers to assembly workers. We would also need to add plants and office space. This was wonderful in the sense that we were preserving thousands of jobs and creating many new ones as well. But it would also lead to the largest expenditure in Loral's history. If I sold off the satellite division and played it safer in terms of Loral's parameters and mission, I could significantly reduce the cost of the Ford acquisition.

But as CEO I didn't want to just steer a conservative course for the sake of maintaining the status quo, as good as the status quo was; I wanted to grow Loral by taking advantage of extraordinary opportunities. The more I learned about satellites, the more I was excited by their business potential and the more I wanted to be involved with them. I thought they could ultimately give us success on a whole different scale. By the time we got down to the nitty-gritty of the Ford Aerospace acquisition, the only issue that remained for me was how to structure the deal for the acquisition.

In late October 1990, Loral, in partnership with Lehman Brothers, purchased Ford Aerospace for a price that netted out to $540 million in cash. A short time after that, we sold a small minority interest in the division—at that time officially designated Space Systems/Loral (SS/L)—to three European aerospace companies that I believed could help us learn the business. But by 1996 Loral had bought back the European partners' interests as well as Lehman's shares, and we were the sole owners of SS/L. Our faith in the satellite business was that strong.

We based that faith on performance. This was the deal of a lifetime. Not only were the financial aspects of the Ford Aerospace transaction very favorable, it also added immediately to our earnings per share, doubled the size of Loral, and broadened our presence in the industry with formidable skills and technologies. In 1991 sales and bookings at Loral reached $2.1 billion and $1.8 billion, respectively, reflecting the activities of Loral Aerospace Holdings; backlog totaled $3.1. In addition, for the same period, SS/L, an unconsolidated affiliate, reported sales of $181 million, bookings of $378 million, and backlog of $549 million.

Yes, satellites were something new to Loral in the early 1990s, but this was synergy as its best. The expertise in our Loral Aerospace Holdings division complemented and broadened each of our core business areas. We would soon realize the substantial marketing and development advantages that come when a company is not hampered by size, resource, or leadership restraints. We had come a long way from those days in the early 1970s when one bad contract could have dealt us a deadly blow. But through it all we had remained a company where the individual voice could speak up and be heard. As big as we had become, and as quickly as we had done it, we were still entrepreneurial at heart.

At a *Business Week* symposium of CEOs held in October 1992, I gave a speech in which I described how we maintained this spirit at Loral. Our company, I explained, had structured its entire organization on the precept of emphasizing individual rewards for individual performance:

> *In our multi-divisional structure, each division exercises a fair degree of authority; each is nevertheless bound into a central corporate responsibility which is deeply engaged in all activities . . . The objective is to create an atmosphere in which corporate entrepreneurialism will flourish and not be oppressed.*

The key, I continued, was

> *to treat employees as long-term assets, not chattel or*
> *commodities to be traded at will . . . We have never sold a*
> *division in an auction to the highest bidder; we have only*
> *sold to management, thereby protecting their stake in the*
> *company. I think this makes good business sense.*
>
> *Acquisitions are not financial transactions, but are*
> *part of a strategy to build the business . . . Loral has*
> *acquired several small companies run by the founders*
> *who have stayed at Loral because, no matter how big the*
> *company gets, our culture caters to small, independent*
> *entrepreneurs.*

So far, I concluded, it had all worked.

CHAPTER 20

Tough Questions and Short Answers

Once, fairly early in my career at Loral, I got an unexpected call from John Young, the CEO of Hewlett-Packard, whom I did not know. "I am going to be in New York next week," he said. "Can I come to see you?" We were a good customer of Hewlett-Packard, but I could not imagine what his agenda was; our relationship with Hewlett-Packard was just fine.

When Young arrived, he was accompanied by the company's chief of marketing for the New York region. This was a customer call. Young had been visiting customers to learn about the market, to find out if there were any complaints, and to see if there were new opportunities. "Is there something more we can be doing to help you?" he said. "I'm here to listen."

I was deeply impressed by his visit. It showed me something that I've never forgotten: No matter how many employees a customer has, the head man or woman is always the face of the company and is in fact the salesperson in chief. From that time on, I incorporated the strategy of directly calling on our customers, making it an important part of my personal business strategy.

I called upon our customers or potential customers not just to see how we were doing but because I was truly interested in their views on emerging technologies, new business opportunities, the political environment, globalization, and a host of other significant matters. I always hoped that my visits to Loral customers impressed them as much as John Young's visit impressed me.

In 1991 we sold a satellite to Mitsubishi Electric Corporation. On this occasion the satellite malfunctioned and was lost in orbit.

One fundamental truth of the satellite business is that about 8 percent of satellites malfunction or get lost after launch. Significant engineering skills and provisions for redundancy—and sometimes double redundancy—go into the building of any satellite so that from the harsh environment of space, the satellite can provide the ground control center with alternatives in the event of a mishap. But sometimes a malfunction is beyond the corrective capacity of the engineers at ground control. It is part of the cost of doing business, but sometimes a painful part. Satellites take two years to build and cost about $250 million apiece, or more, and that was a lot of money in the 1990s.

As soon as I heard about what had happened with Mitsubishi, I called Bob Berry, who was the president of our satellite division, SS/L. Bob was a good engineer, an inspiring leader, and a terrific salesman. He had made many trips to Japan and established relationships with all our current and potential customers there.

I asked him what we should be doing about this piece of bad news. "Well, I'm going to Japan, and I'll sit down with our customer and explain the circumstances of this loss."

"I think I'll go with you," I said.

"Bernard, I don't think that will be a good idea. If you go, it will elevate the issue and make it appear we had responsibility when, in fact, we did not. For the chairman of our company to make this visit would be an admission of guilt, and that would make it more difficult to regain our former good relationship with Mitsubishi."

I remembered that not long before this happened, a Japanese airline had lost one of its passenger jets in the Bay of Tokyo, and twenty-four passengers had died. The chairman of the company had gone to the home of every one of the victims to apologize. I was very impressed by that.

"I understand what you're saying, Bob, but I think going over would give a message to the chairman of Mitsubishi that we care about what happened." The personal apology of Loral's chairman seemed the least we could do for an important customer.

So Bob and I went to Tokyo and met with the Mitsubishi CEO and six or seven of his colleagues at an eleven a.m. meeting. We entered a small conference room where the Mitsubishi group was sitting on one side of the room and Bob and I were to be seated on the other. They did not speak English and we did not speak Japanese, so everything we said was through an interpreter. The Mitsubishi executive spoke first.

"Thank you for coming, Mr. Schwartz and Mr. Berry," he said. "Allow me to explain something. Mitsubishi is a uniquely constructed company. The Mitsubishi Corporation is the head of many far-ranging and unrelated companies. These companies are related to each other through corporate ownership. But each operating company has its own budget.

"And now we have lost a satellite," he continued. "When something like that happens and $250 million needs to be provided that is not included in the corporate budget, it is necessary for us to tax every operating company to provide this new requirement. That is to say, the steel division, the automobile division, the tire company, and so on have to pay for the loss of the satellite. Although they understand this requirement and that it could not be planned for, what they don't understand is why Mitsubishi should choose to do any further business with the company responsible for the problem." He then stopped talking, and he and his colleagues stared at Bob and me and waited for a response.

My response was simple but sincere. I explained that we had been a good supplier to Mitsubishi for some years and that our products had worked well to make Mitsubishi a leader in satellite communications. I explained that a satellite loss in orbit was part of the cost of doing business and should be evaluated as a part of Loral's performance. I expressed my sincere sympathy for their loss and then pledged, "I give you my personal assurance that if you continue to do business with Loral, I will be personally involved with the design, construction, and performance of your next satellite and will make certain it adheres to the highest standards."

The chairman nodded and ended the meeting. There was a certain frostiness in the air, confirmed by the fact that ordinarily an eleven a.m. meeting in Tokyo would lead to lunch—and we had received no such invitation.

But then the chairman walked over to me and apologized for not inviting us to lunch. "It's too late to make such arrangements now, but perhaps you'd join me for a drink." He said something to an assistant to bring the drinks. When the bottle arrived, he looked at it for a few minutes. "That's the wrong bottle," he said. "Come with me to my office; that's where I keep the good stuff."

He said this in perfect English! We went back to his office and had a drink of some very fine scotch. When I walked out of his office, I saw Bob and told him, "I think we're going to get the next order," and we did. Mitsubishi wasn't happy about losing the $250 million satellite, but its CEO appreciated our sense of responsibility and believed that, in fact, we were good people to do business with.

That was not the only occasion on which I chose to get personally involved with a difficult customer. In 1995 Loral had proposed taking over a contract with the FAA for an air traffic control computer system that had been in design and construction for a number of years. This important project was being carried out on a cost-plus contract by one of our competitors. Unfortunately, the program was behind schedule and failed to meet the requirements of the FAA. The air traffic control system used in the United States was technically in the dark ages; it was very important that the FAA upgrade this system as soon as it could.

We met with the FAA at its invitation and introduced a different approach. We offered a fixed-price contract that included the most modern technology. This arrangement placed the responsibility for performance on the supplier rather than on the government, and we thought it represented a real advantage for the FAA. I personally led the sales effort for Loral. The person representing the government was Linda Daschle, the wife of Tom Daschle, then a senator from South Dakota.

Daschle, the deputy administrator for the agency, was very demanding during our negotiations and pointed out the failure of our competitor to do the job for which it was paid. She was down on the entire industry. "Why should we believe that Loral would be any different, that in the end you will perform as you promise you will for this very important system?"

These were not easy meetings, as you can tell, and finally I said to Daschle and her colleagues, "You have never done business with Loral before. I assure you that if you look at our history, you will see that we have an outstanding record of performance and, further, by entering into a fixed-price contract, we are taking the financial responsibility. I am confident our performance will prove that we are the type of company you should be dealing with." We got the contract, and although some years later the program lost its major funding from the government, the performance of Loral was consistent with all our promises, and we had the best of relationships with the FAA.

As tough as Daschle was, dealing with her was fun compared to some of my other adventures in customer relations. One of the strangest experiences I had was making a customer call in Saudi Arabia. In 1992 the Saudis had an F-15 program and, with the permission of the State and Defense departments, Loral entered into a contract with the Saudi government for the electronics that went on their F-15s.

The Saudi prince who was in charge of military contracts, Prince Fahd, had invited my Loral colleagues and me to have dinner at his estate near Riyadh. His palace was contained within a walled compound, some miles into the desert in the most barren of landscapes.

The prince served a very hospitable dinner, and it was my privilege to sit at his right—a place of honor. Fortunately, though Prince Fahd and the Saudi guests were in traditional Saudi dress, the table arrangements were Western, and we were seated on chairs rather than having to sit cross-legged on the floor. The food and the service were outstanding, and the conversation was relaxed and enjoyable. But then something strange happened.

The prince, speaking perfect English, leaned forward and said out loud, "Mr. Schwartz, you are not eating enough," and with that he reached with his hand into a large plate of food, grabbed a fistful of lamb, and placed it on my plate. "I want you to enjoy yourself," he said with a laugh. I knew that this was not the first time Prince Fahd had done this, and he was leaning forward to see what my reaction would be. I was a good soldier. I smiled at the prince and said, "This is the best lamb I have ever eaten," and emptied my plate. The Saudis eventually became good customers of Loral.

When marketing your products, it is always best to keep things simple. I once appeared before a Senate Commerce Committee hearing on the purchase of satellites for the Atlantic Coast of the United States. Senator Ernest "Fritz" Hollings, a tall, distinguished, handsome gentleman from the state of South Carolina, was the head of the committee. He had a particular interest in obtaining an advanced weather satellite that would offer the people of South Carolina the most advanced and accurate hurricane warnings. This was not a casual subject for Senator Hollings, who represented a coastal state.

Under consideration was the purchase of four weather satellites from SS/L. Usually this kind of project was done on the basis of a cost-plus contract for development. But we proposed a fixed-price contract instead. During his interrogation, Senator Hollings said in his deep southern drawl, "Do you mean to tell this committee, Mr. Schwartz, that your company is proposing that you will take on the design and manufacture of these four weather satellites on a fixed-price basis and that you will assume responsibility for timely delivery and performance?"

"Yes, sir."

There was a long delay of almost a minute. Everyone in the Senate room was swiveling their heads and looking around at me and then back at Senator Hollings.

At last he said, "Mr. Schwartz, in this town we are not used to short answers."

We got the contract and delivered the satellites on time. The senator must have liked my answer because for many years afterward, whenever I encountered him, he would say out loud for all to hear, "Bernard Schwartz—the man who is all action and very little talk."

I took that as a compliment.

CHAPTER 21

The Win-Win-Win and Launching Globalstar

A deal is not a zero-sum game. The best and most satisfying deals I've ever made are those in which both sides benefited, the win-win situations that I've written about several times in this book already. But, as I explained in chapter 5, there is also the rare win-win-win situation. Multiple parties can emerge from a deal as winners—even without a formal contract.

In 1992 the LTV Corporation was emerging from what had been the second-largest bankruptcy in our nation's history. LTV was a huge conglomerate that owned steel mills and coalfields and also made airplanes and missiles. At its height, it had reached $8 billion in annual sales, but it got caught in a recessionary period and could no longer service its debt. As a result, it ended up in Chapter 11. As part of the process of emerging from bankruptcy, a court in Manhattan arranged for the sale of the company's assets. One of these was its aerospace division, which was involved in aircraft and missile manufacture. Since Loral was always keeping an eye out for possible acquisitions, it was only natural for me to be at least initially interested in them.

I thought the missile unit might be an especially good fit for our company, but I also saw some things that I didn't think were advantageous for Loral. Lockheed was also interested in LTV Aerospace and so was Martin Marietta (they hadn't merged to become Lockheed Martin yet).

And there were other potential bidders. A man I truly admired and respected, Norm Augustine, was the CEO of Martin Marietta at the time, and he forged a partnership with Lockheed for the purpose of acquiring the aerospace companies of LTV—Norm really wanted those businesses. But I prided myself in knowing the true value of a company and, feeling there would be no bargains in regard to LTV, I turned my attention elsewhere.

Sure enough, before long the Lockheed Martin partnership got into a heated bidding war with Thomson-CSF for the divisions. Thomson-CSF was a company that was 75 percent owned by the French government. They went through five rounds of bidding in four days, battling like gladiators. Lockheed Martin argued to the bankruptcy court that a for-eign-owned company would never be granted permission to acquire an American company involved in the defense industry, so it shouldn't have even been allowed to bid. But when Thomson-CSF bid $450 million, topping Lockheed Martin by a wide margin, the judge nevertheless said, "I am going to approve this offer." Norm Augustine was frustrated, but what could he do but let the situation play itself out.

Not surprisingly, the US Senate Committee on Foreign Investments refused to approve the sale of LTV Aerospace to the French concern, which lost the $20 million they'd had to post with the court, and the deal was off. When the bankruptcy court asked if he was still interested, Norm, who was now, thanks to an ensuing merger, the head of Lockheed Martin, said yes he was—but he didn't want to be involved in any more bidding wars. He made a bid of $440 million and said he would not exceed it under any circumstances.

While all this was going on, I had been talking to a man named David Rubenstein about LTV Aerospace. Dave is a smart and fascinating guy. The son of a postal worker, he went to Duke and the University of Chicago Law School and became a brilliant lawyer, a domestic policy advisor for Jimmy Carter, and the founder of a very successful private equity firm, the Carlyle Group. Dave had called and asked me if I wanted to join with his group (which had partnered with Thomson-CSF in its failed bid) in making a bid for LTV Aerospace, the idea being that he would take over the units that manufactured aircraft components while I would retain the missile manufacturing unit. Although I told him I thought the division was likely to be sold at a price above what it was actually worth, I also invited him and his partner, Bill Conway, to New York to discuss the matter further.

When we sat down together in my office at Loral, they told me they were bringing in the Northrop Corporation as a partner in purchasing the aircraft unit from LTV and asked me to propose the terms under which I might be interested in joining their consortium. I told them what my price was for the missile part. In the meantime the drama between Lockheed and Thomson-CSF was playing out in the court, and when the US Senate nullified the sale of LTV Aerospace, we saw a great opportunity.

At a subsequent meeting at my office with Dave, Bill, and Ken Kresa, the chairman of Northrop, we agreed on a plan to proceed, and since Lockheed's bid was a matter of public record, we also agreed on what our offer would be and how we would later handle the assets if we were successful. As part of our strategy, I would represent our partnership before the bankruptcy judge. It was a very creative deal that we concocted, but the most remarkable thing was that it was sealed with a handshake. We had to move too quickly to stop and get it all down on paper, and we trusted each other.

On the day of the bidding, Lockheed's lawyers were in court, swiveling their heads around every time the door opened to see if someone was going to come in and bid against them. That's how it works in bankruptcy court; as long as someone has the money, he can show up at the last minute and walk out with the spoils. Norm Augustine was not with his legal team that morning; true to his word about offering only one bid, he was at his corporate headquarters in Bethesda, Maryland, running his company and awaiting a phone call to see if his offer of $440 million had carried the day. His absence and his unwavering position were both good news for our side. As much as I always enjoy seeing Norm, I was pleased that he was not there that morning.

When I walked into the courtroom with my attorney just after nine in the morning, Lockheed's lawyers seemed stunned for a moment. Then they got up and ran for the pay phones. Harvey Miller, a wonderful lawyer who worked for Lockheed at the time and later worked for me and became a good friend, told me that he would never forget the sight of five attorneys squeezing into one hallway phone booth, all trying to talk at once to their boss. "Mr. Augustine, you don't understand," one said. "Bernard Schwartz is here. He's a tough businessman. How much do you really want LTV Aerospace? Because Schwartz comes to play, and he wouldn't waste his time if he wasn't going to top our bid."

They were right about that. With only hours to go before the deadline, I formally submitted a bid of $475 million for my group.

Then the judge turned to Harvey. "Mr. Miller?" he said.

"Your Honor," Harvey said, looking downcast, "we are not increasing our bid."

Back in my office a few days later, Dave, Bill, Ken, and I met and concluded the transaction based on our original handshake deal. Acquiring the LTV Aerospace units turned out extremely well for the three interests involved—win-win-win.

When I look back on that time now, I realize how much the world has changed, and not for the better. If you don't believe me, try to do a deal like the one I've just described, based solely on a handshake.

The mid-1990s continued to be a time of declining defense budgets and industry doldrums, but you'd never know that by looking at the performance of Loral. In fact, by most measures, that was the period of our greatest success.

In 1993 I wrote to our shareholders that our results were "stunning," and I wasn't exaggerating. Our income that year, $178 million, represented a 46 percent increase over fiscal 1992, which itself was an improvement of 35 percent over the prior year. Our compound annual growth rate over the previous twenty-one years was 35 percent. Fiscal 1993 sales and backlog increased to $3.335 billion and $3.851 billion, respectively, up by 16 and 32 percent.

Our ability to grow in tough times depended on making smart acquisitions: finding the right companies to begin with, paying the right price for them, and then blending them into the Loral family in a way that kept their momentum going, preserved jobs, and boosted morale.

In 1993 our primary acquisition was the missile branch of LTV Aerospace that I described above. Loral paid $261 million for what became Loral Vought, completing the transaction without the need for new outside financing, which gave us flexibility in creating the most desirable structure for the transaction. The merger reinforced each organization's position in the tactical weapons market. It added $1 billion to our backlog and also added immediately to our earnings.

The cover of the 1994 annual report showed the launch of one of our satellites and featured what you know by now as my favorite phrase: "Performance is the best strategy." Here are some headlines from my shareholders' letter to convey a sense of how we were doing.

Fiscal 1994 was another spectacular year for Loral.

Income of $228 million represented a 44 percent increase over fiscal 1993. Overall bookings were robust, reaching $3.5 billion, and funded backlog and total backlog rose to $6.5 billion and $10 billion, respectively.

The acquisition of Federal Systems adds earnings power, new technology, and leadership in systems integration.

Our purchase of this division from IBM for $1.5 billion put us in the new core growth business of software development for radar warning systems, antisubmarine warfare, satellites, and air traffic control. It also continued our unblemished record of substantially increasing the profit margins of every company we acquired.

When I sat down to write my 1995 chairman's letter, I remember I had to really think about how best to describe Loral's performance. My problem wasn't that I had some mistake or setback to explain; my problem was that I'd already used "stunning" and "spectacular" to describe the last two years. Finally, I just threw up my hands and wrote "Fiscal 1995 was *another* spectacular year for Loral." A CEO can have much worse problems.

That year—particularly bad for the defense industry due to budget cutbacks—our income increased over 1994 by 26 percent to $288 million. This extended to twenty-three years our record of successive earnings improvements. Loral's bookings increased by 13 percent—and even more important, we continued to win our share of the big contracts, particularly for the PAC-3 missile; the ATACMS long-range surface-to-surface fire support missile; the Predator, our next-generation, low-cost, man-portable antitank weapon; and the Multiple Launch Rocket System, a major weapon for the army. The potential value to Loral from those products alone exceeded $8.5 billion.

The turnaround of the $3.6 billion air traffic control contract, inherited in the acquisition of Federal Systems, was an example of Loral's management focus. At the time of the acquisition, this was a high-profile but troubled program. We immediately brought in software engineering specialists from other Loral divisions to redefine the program and get it back on course. The result was a new $955 million contract from the FAA to modernize the US air traffic management system. That once-losing program would now be profitable.

The acquisition of Unisys Defense Systems, Loral's fifteenth acquisition since 1974, was another excellent example of our strategy. We paid $862 million for the aerospace and defense holdings of Unisys, based outside of Philadelphia. Together with Federal Systems, the company we had acquired in early 1994, it added in excess of the originally projected $0.60 per share to Loral's annual earnings and brought substantial added value to key businesses such as air traffic control, systems integration, radar, shipboard and underwater defense, helicopter avionics, C3I, and space. The integration of those companies was smooth and swift, and we soon began to realize the considerable operating, development, and marketing benefits that were the primary objects of Loral's acquisition strategy.

Even though things at Loral were flying high and we continued to make exciting plans for the future, my life during this time was not without its heavy moments. It was particularly difficult for me to observe the continuing downward spiral of Reliance Holdings, the company where I had worked with Saul Steinberg years before.

Reliance's business had, through the years, worsened steadily until that once-great company finally filed for bankruptcy in 2001 and entered into a process of liquidation. By that time Saul had suffered a stroke and had had a falling out with Bob, his brother. It was a sad ending for a once-great company.

But, thankfully, that wasn't the end of the story. Eventually Saul was able to recover from his stroke to the point where he regained all his mental ability. He had also found happiness through his marriage in 1983 to Gayfryd, a beautiful, bright, communicative, and no-nonsense woman. She took control of Saul's household and of Saul, and only good things came from that relationship. The Steinbergs nurtured a brood of six wonderful children, and, so far, three loving and beautiful daughters-in-law and five grandchildren. Saul's son Jonathan and his wife, Maria Bartiromo, have each lived their own lives in the public arena and have enjoyed much success. I could never be around the Steinbergs without noticing the extraordinary affection and respect between the children and the parents; it is the principal characteristic of this loving family. I'm glad our friendship survived. The true test of friendship is not the good times but the tough times, and I can honestly say that Saul and I were friends.

Saul died in his sleep in December 2012. I miss him. He had brilliant successes, and he had his setbacks, too, as we all do. But I know that, thanks to his family, the last chapters of his life were grand.

Certainly you need to be smart to be successful in business, but it's just as important to be bold. That's why at Loral we didn't make decisions by consensus, why we encouraged an entrepreneurial spirit that allowed virtually any employee to pick up an idea and run with it—at least for a while—and why we always looked for reasons to say yes to a potential acquisition. It's been said since the time of the ancient Romans: "Fortune favors the bold." You won't be right all the time, but if you do your homework and have good instincts, you'll keep your batting average very high, and that's the best you can reasonably hope for over the course of a business career.

In 1991 we started a company called Globalstar. The driving idea behind it was the great potential we saw for satellite telephones. Mobile telephones were still relatively recent innovations in those days, but the way the market was trending, it was obvious they would be the phone of the future. The type of mobile communications that we know best today is cellular, which works off a base station located somewhere on the ground; the user needs to be within a certain proximity of the station for the phone to function properly. In cities and towns, cell phone technology works well, but what about the less densely populated but massive areas of the planet that have no base stations? That's where satellite phones come in.

Satellite phones operate on a signal relayed by one or more low-earth-orbiting satellites. They can connect a user to another phone—satellite, cellular, or landline—anywhere in the world, be it the Gobi desert, an African village, the very bottom of the Grand Canyon, or someplace less exotic but nevertheless out of cell phone range, like a suburb in Montana or a commercial fishing boat. After some of the people in our satellite-manufacturing division did their research, my management team and I were convinced there was a growing demand for satellite-based phones that would provide wireless voice, data, fax, and position-locating services to users around the world.

And so it was that in 1991 Loral teamed with Qualcomm, a pioneering developer and manufacturer of cell phones that had originated the code division multiple access (CDMA) technology that still dominates the industry, to create a satellite phone service that would incorporate CDMA for commercial and military use.

Globalstar started out small, but it was never meant to be a modest sideline or a venture that promised a fast and easy payoff. Although the idea for it flowed naturally from our entrance into the satellite business with the purchase of Ford Aerospace in 1990, we were well aware of the many challenges that lay ahead of us. We were in a very real sense going someplace where almost no one had gone before, and we knew that Globalstar would involve major commitments of time and money. We didn't anticipate being operational until some time in 1998, and at the start we were anticipating an investment of at least $1.8 billion.

I knew I wouldn't have trouble raising the money for Globalstar. Loral's track record meant that bankers always took my phone calls— satellite, cellular, or landline—and, if I may quote the *New York Times*, "Mr. Schwartz has many admirers in the world of high finance." Speaking to a reporter from a financial magazine, Sam Ginn, the CEO of a cellular services company called AirTouch, said, "The first rule if you're going to do a project where you have to invest a lot before you get a dollar of revenue is that you have to have someone in whom the investor community has immense confidence. And Bernard Schwartz came out of Central Casting for that role."

No, the initial challenges would come in areas beyond investment capital, and they would not be insignificant. Many were technological. We would need to design, build, and launch a constellation of forty-eight low-earth-orbiting satellites and determine how to build and operate a worldwide network of thirty-eight gateways to transmit voice and data, a project that promised numerous logistical and political hurdles. Together with Irwin Jacobs, cofounder and CEO of Qualcomm, and his team, we would need to design the handsets and determine how they would interface with the gateways' satellite dishes and with the orbiting satellites. And last but hardly least, we needed to conceive and execute a plan for getting our phones in the hands of consumers so they could begin using our service.

Loral and Qualcomm weren't the only companies that saw potential in this area. Iridium, a Motorola-sponsored company, was planning a similar effort with an initial investment of about $4 billion, and TRW was also targeting the same market with a multibillion-dollar effort. The competition didn't bother me, and the fact that there was more than one company betting on satellite phones shored up the credibility of the product among consumers and investors. Having competition was also good in that it helped spur the creation of a global web of interconnectivity.

In spite of the obvious difficulties, I was excited about Globalstar, and with good reason. We were on the edge of an important technological advance. We never expected Globalstar phones to be especially ubiquitous in New York City or Paris, perhaps, but at that time half the world's population lived beyond the reach of landline or cellular systems. Tens of millions were on waiting lists for affordable telephone service. And millions of existing wireless users often found themselves in areas where there were gaps in cellular service or where the service was incompatible with their "home" cellular systems.

There were enough advantages to the Globalstar idea, and enough disadvantages to the cell phone concept at that time, that we could imagine profitability within a few years after the service's introduction. And one of the best parts of such a business is that once you have a capital investment in the sky and on the ground and customers for your service, almost all the revenue falls to the bottom line. Any way you looked at Globalstar in the early 1990s, it was a good idea. We were providing a dial tone without borders, linking the caller to the world—simply, dependably, clearly, and more securely and affordably.

Several times I have mentioned the importance of knowing what you know and what you don't know. One thing I did know was that because Loral lacked expertise in several areas key to the success of the company, Globalstar would need to be constructed as an alliance with a large and far-flung group of equipment makers and service providers. Qualcomm was an important first step in that direction. Its CDMA technology worked well in the small frequency band that the FCC had recently opened for data-transmitting satellites. It could provide a clear, highly secure signal, allowing the system to carry a greater number of calls per minute than our competitors' version. The key was not in the satellites themselves but in the gateways, which housed the intelligence of the system. They were a brilliant stroke because they were more accessible for maintenance and upgrading than satellites in orbit and because they were designed to be scalable, making it easy to expand their capacity in step with market demand.

I realized from the start that Globalstar would need many different kinds of partners in our alliance: an amalgam of telecom and aerospace companies that could do things Loral, and Qualcomm, couldn't do by themselves. After all, we had tasked ourselves with the design and manufacture of fifty-two satellites (the forty-eight in orbit plus four spares); we needed to get regulatory approval from more than a hundred countries; and we needed to forge a connection to consumers—something a defense company like Loral had never done before. And we had to accomplish all this at a reasonable cost.

The only smart way to proceed, it seemed to me, was to sell our satellite service through a consortium of local providers—companies already established in their individual areas that understood the retail end of the business and viewed Globalstar as a valuable extension of their cellular service—and to insist that all its members have financial equity. The innovative way that we were structuring Globalstar drew praise from the national press. An article *Fortune* magazine published about Globalstar around this time said:

> *Everyone who's building any part of the system is invested in the company, and all the major telcos that will be selling the service are invested in Globalstar, too. This virtual corporation outsources nearly everything to take advantage of its partners' core competencies, which makes it more responsive to customers, more adaptable to changing markets, and more efficient at using capital. But it also makes Schwartz's job of holding the company together a perpetual high wire act.*

The writer of that piece, James Surowiecki, wasn't kidding about that.

In March 1994, Globalstar announced an alliance with nine different companies that had invested nearly $40 million each. Surowiecki's *Fortune* article trumpeted their arrival:

> *From the U.S. came cellular provider AirTouch, while from abroad came telcos Elsacom (Italy), Dacom (Korea), France Telecom and Vodafone, as well as Alcatel (the French telecom equipment maker), Alenia (part of an Italian aerospace giant Finmeccanica), DASA (Daimler-Chrysler's aerospace division) and Hyundai (the Korean industrial conglomerate).*

Assembling this group involved one of the most complicated negotiations I've ever participated in. Loral and its subsidiaries retained a 45 percent interest in Globalstar and operational control, but many of these companies were run by superstars who were accustomed to getting their own way, and no one was shy about asking for what he wanted. Although the partners were theoretically united by their significant investments, there was a good deal of competitiveness. Like my first car, the consortium did not steer easily. When China Telecom joined the alliance a few years later, it insisted that it pay for its equity at the 1994 price and that it have the right to buy wholesale satellite service from suppliers other than Globalstar. I didn't like doing that, but as I said at the time, "It was unfair, but we gave something to get something."

The aerospace partners had to be handled with care as well. As Surowiecki observed:

> *Each has a healthy slice of the business of building Globalstar's satellites. Alcatel built the antennae, while Hyundai made the electronic subsystems. Aerospatiale built the structures that house the satellite's innards. Daimler-Benz Aerospace created the propulsion system. Alenia put everything together at a factory in Rome.*

As the CEO of Globalstar, I sometimes felt like one of those jugglers on *The Ed Sullivan Show*, with a lot of plates spinning on a lot of sticks. Dealing with the members could sometimes be exhausting and exasperating. "I'm not sure I would say I like alliances," I said back then. "They're costly and they're time-consuming." But they were also necessary.

Wherever we told the Globalstar story—and I traveled the world at this time, explaining our idea to investors, industry leaders, government officials, and members of the media—we found strong support. In 1994 the total initial investment from members of the consortium, Loral and other sources, reached $1.8 billion, and the next year our IPO brought in $200 million more. One of the things I was always questioned about, though, was how our unprecedented alliance worked. How did I manage all these huge egos? Was everyone really always on the same page? Some observers had their doubts. I remember an analyst meeting we had at the "21" club in Manhattan at which I described a mechanism we had in place whereby the service providers, as we called the alliance members, would be fined a considerable sum if they failed to make certain deadlines. One of the analysts in the audience raised his hand and said, "But, Mr. Schwartz, since you're a partner with these companies, isn't fining them just cutting off your nose to spite your face?"

I paused a moment and then turned to show the room my profile.

"Have you ever seen this nose?" I said.

It got a big laugh, but the point was that we were in Globalstar for the long haul. I believed in Globalstar, and it was with great excitement that I looked forward to the launch, at that point less than two years in the future, of the first satellites in our constellation.

CHAPTER 22

The Chinese Contract and Its Aftermath

Imagine standing before a high-ranking official of the federal government—a cabinet secretary, in fact—who is speaking very emphatically and jabbing his finger in your face. This happened to me around 1990, and the finger belonged to Secretary of Commerce Robert Mosbacher. He was saying, "Listen, Bernard, I want you to tell me the truth!"

I already had. So all I could do was tell him the truth again, louder. But I'm getting ahead of myself.

Though we were still new to the satellite business in 1990, Loral had the opportunity to procure a major contract with the Commerce Department for a technologically advanced satellite for weather monitoring. This was an extremely competitive area of the business, and we were vying with large and well-established companies such as Lockheed, Martin Marietta, Hughes, and others. Still, by December of that year, we had made such good progress with the design and with cost projections that we expected to be awarded the contract.

At Secretary Mosbacher's request, I traveled to Washington for discussions that I hoped would seal the deal. The meeting was held in a room large enough to accommodate the secretary, about twelve members of his staff, and me. As we got into the particulars, the atmosphere grew quite heated at times. This was not because of anything to do with

Loral but rather because Commerce had in the recent past had some bad experiences with satellite manufacturers. Consequently, they looked upon the entire industry with a suspicion verging on anger.

After about an hour, Mosbacher abruptly stood up and asked me to come to his office, just down the hallway. The secretary, a Republican, was a wealthy Texan, a yachtsman with a patrician air, and when he wanted to, he could be a bit imperious. It was while we were standing there in his office, just the two of us, that he pointed his finger and said that he needed to be reassured—man to man and in no uncertain terms—that if Loral got the contract it would live up to its stated obligations.

"Yes, we will," I said, and not for the first time that morning. "You'll get what you paid for, and on time too!"

He just looked at me for a moment and then said, "Bernard, you better damn well do this—or I will get you!" I wasn't sure what he meant by that, but in the end Loral did win the contract, and we built the Department of Commerce a satellite that worked to its exact specifications.

Sometimes when I tell people that story, they ask if I was offended by Secretary Mosbacher's tone. I was not. He was being straightforward and honest about his concerns, operating in the interest of the office he represented. Meanwhile, I was being straightforward right back. Each of us was defending our position and in the process creating a better, fairer deal for all concerned. That's the American system, functioning at its best.

But deals in the international arena are often another matter entirely. Mistrust between parties is sometimes a given. Directness and transparency are often trumped by foreign policy, and if things don't go according to plan, domestic politics can play a role as well. Still, such huge opportunities loomed for Loral in various overseas markets that we had to accept and even embrace the challenges that came with being a global company, since the potential rewards often outweighed the frustrations.

In January 1997 SS/L secured a contract from the Chinese government to build a communications satellite called China Sat-8. The cost to China would be $250 million. Normally a satellite customer would pay half the price at the time of signing and the other half upon delivery, but I negotiated to get the full amount in advance. I knew how complicated doing business with a secretive and suspicious nation like China could be, and if there were bureaucratic or political problems down the road regarding the delivery of the satellite, I didn't want Loral to bear the burden of those delays and complications. The Chinese government was not happy with my insistence on full payment up front, but they ultimately agreed.

China Sat-8 was built strictly for commercial telecommunications uses, but when you sell China anything that has any possible military applications, you need to get a waiver from the federal government. In those days it was the Department of Commerce that had to sign off on the deal. During the eight years of the Clinton administration, American manufacturers were routinely granted waivers for projects like China Sat-8 once the proper paperwork and checking was done, just as they had been under President George H. W. Bush and would be under George Bush the younger and President Barack Obama. Our government in most cases realized that such deals had a favorable effect on the balance of trade with China and created thousands of American jobs.

Getting a waiver, though, didn't mean we could just build a satellite, send it to the People's Republic, and let the Chinese do with it what they wanted. Under the rules of the Commerce Department, we would need to get a license to ship the satellite once it was completed, and then we'd have to ensure that when it arrived in China, it remained completely under our control until launch in order to prevent anyone there from gaining knowledge of either satellite or launching technology as a result of the transaction.

We had done business with the Chinese before, and we were aware of the rules. Everything went well at first: We received our payment up front, the satellite was completed, and we were preparing to ship it. A launch date had been set. But before we could obtain a shipping license from the federal government, a tragedy occurred in China:

Intelsat, a multinational telecommunications company of which the US government was a member, experienced a systems failure in what was known as the Long March rocket during a satellite launch. This caused the rocket to crash in a remote village, killing several people.

The Chinese quickly conducted their own investigation, gathering up whatever bits and chunks of the satellite they could recover and no doubt inspecting them for any technological information they might yield. What they found scattered on the ground was in bad shape, but this was the first time they had ever gotten a chance to inspect such equipment. In time, they announced that the cause of the accident had been a failed solder joint. Then, as is usually the case after a crash, the industry created a committee to investigate and issue an independent report. Loral was invited to be a part of this review board, and we voluntarily agreed to participate. Ultimately the industry representatives concurred with the Chinese report, saying that a failed solder joint had indeed been the cause of the crash.

The review committee's written verdict did not contain any new information about either satellites or launches that might have been especially valuable to the Chinese. Nevertheless, in keeping with the strict security measures that governed dealings with the People's Republic, the report was not supposed to be shared with the Chinese until the US representatives had a look at it. The unfortunate fact of the matter, however, was that because of an administrative error made by a Loral engineer who was serving as the committee secretary, the report was mistakenly given to the entire review committee, including the Chinese members. Although the clerical error resulted in absolutely no threat to American security, it constituted a clear violation of the rules.

While all this was going on, the State Department, which had assumed control of the export licensing program, was doing nothing about granting Loral a license to ship the China Sat-8, and it was not explaining why our application was being held up either. I was extremely frustrated by this because we had operated completely by US government rules, and we naturally preferred not to alienate a customer that potentially meant hundreds of millions of dollars in future business as well as many American jobs.

To see if we could make some headway with the State Department, I called the Washington law firm in which former senator Howard Baker was a partner. At first they said they weren't interested in representing us, but when I went to Washington and personally told Baker, a Republican, how anti-business I thought the State Department was being, he changed his mind. Not that it mattered much in the end. Whatever he attempted on Loral's behalf was not effective, and the satellite remained in its crate in our Palo Alto plant.

My next step was to approach the State Department directly, and I went to John Bolton, a high-ranking official there. I visited him several times, making my case for a shipping license, and each time he said the same thing: "I'm trying my best to get an exception made for you." As it turned out, that wasn't true. Politics had taken over.

The Chinese government was at least as frustrated as I was. Eventually they asked me to give them their $250 million back. I wasn't about to do that and told them so directly. "We fulfilled our end of the bargain," I said. "We built you the satellite that you ordered. It's not our fault that we can't ship it." I think they understood the bind we were in. Still, eventually they sued us for the purchase price but lost the lawsuit.

Then things got truly bizarre. As my discussions with the Chinese grew more contentious, an article appeared that accused me of disloyalty to America. Writing in the *New York Times* on April 3, 1998, reporter Jeff Gerth picked up on the mistake the Loral engineer had made two years earlier in sending a copy of a harmless document to the Chinese and distorted it into a charge that Loral had given China access to information that threatened national security. He also said that Loral, by virtue of my support of Bill Clinton, had received special treatment in the form of a waiver to sell technology to the Chinese and in escaping any sanctions for our alleged security breach.

All of this was complete nonsense. Gerth, who had a history of unfairly attacking the Clintons that dated back at least as far as the

Whitewater controversy, had apparently been fed misinformation by a political opponent of the president, and he was overly eager to run with it. So were some Republicans once Gerth's article appeared. Newt Gingrich demonized and denounced me on the House floor, and the California congressman Dana Rohrabacher referred to me as a "pinko," reviving an ugly McCarthy-era term. Conservative *New York Times* columnist William Safire said Loral had participated in "the sellout of American security."

I knew Loral and I were completely innocent, and hearing my name associated with espionage or anti-Americanism felt surreal. At a party I attended in the Hamptons around this time, a woman came up to a man I was speaking to, gestured toward me, and said, "What are you doing talking to *him*—the man is a *traitor!*" The controversy shook my faith in both journalism and government. Though he would eventually be discredited by his peers, Gerth actually won a Pulitzer Prize for his poorly researched articles, and Congress created the Cox Committee, named after California Republican Christopher Cox, to investigate Chinese espionage in hopes of embarrassing the Clinton administration. (After a year, they produced only a lot of hot air.)

Through all of this, Bill Clinton could not have been more supportive of me. While he never dignified the accusations by addressing them directly, he went out of his way during this time to invite me to meetings and other events and to appear with me in public. I defended myself aggressively, too, denying all the charges. Both Lou Dobbs and Sam Donaldson invited me on their shows to discuss the accusations. Even though I knew Donaldson could be really tough, I chose to go on his Sunday morning show, *This Week*, because it had a bigger audience.

The panel, which included Cokie Roberts and George Will in addition to Donaldson, couldn't have been more civilized in their questioning, and I felt I was able to get my message across. One of the things I said was, "No good deed goes unpunished. The reason the company's in this struggle is because we tried to be helpful to that investigation. We could have easily abdicated that responsibility, saying we had nothing to do with it." I felt confident telling my side of the story, live, to a national audience of millions. I had the truth on my side.

I can't say the same for Jeff Gerth. In 1998 the *Times* reporter once again distorted facts, with sad consequences for a Taiwan-born American citizen named Wen Ho Lee, a scientist at the National Laboratory in Los Alamos. Gerth and a coauthor named James Risen wrote a piece, which the *Times* ran on page 1, saying that Lee had given the Chinese government "nuclear secrets for bombs." Reacting to the unfounded story, Republican senators Trent Lott, John McCain, and Richard Shelby demanded an investigation into what they saw as another "White House cover-up."

An astonished Lee denied all the charges and spoke to the FBI without a lawyer. Lee was initially charged with mishandling nuclear secrets and denied bail; he spent most of a year at home under surveillance. But when the government's case was put to the test at bail hearings for Lee, it quickly fell apart, and the lead FBI agent was forced to recant his testimony. The judge who freed Lee castigated government officials whom he said had "embarrassed our entire nation" in the handling of the case.

In the wake of that debacle, Gerth faced similar criticism from his peers for the stories about Wen Ho Lee, Bill Clinton, and me. "It looks like a terrible injustice was done to a guy, and his name first surfaced in the *New York Times*," said *60 Minutes* producer Don Hewitt, of Lee. Wrote Walter Pincus of the *Washington Post*: "It starts out with allegations, none of which turn out to be true."

My reputation was never seriously threatened, but if any doubt lingered about me, it was erased by an internal Justice Department memo that was made public in 2000. That document, authored by Charles G. LaBella, a department official with Republican leanings, said that after an initial look into the question of how Clinton and I behaved in regard to the Chinese, the prosecutors had turned up "not a scintilla of evidence— or information—that the president was corruptly influenced by Bernard Schwartz." The *Los Angeles Times*, in reporting on the memo, said,

"Far from urging an investigation of Schwartz, the documents show LaBella regarded the Loral executive as a victim of Justice Department overreaching. He criticized the ranking Justice officials for relying 'on a whiff of information' to justify their initial Schwartz inquiry. And in an addendum to his original report, LaBella flatly advised that the Schwartz case 'was a matter which likely did not merit any investigation.'"

As for China Sat-8, it never got shipped. Under the terms of the settlement with our Chinese customer, we didn't have to pay back the $250 million and were free to retrofit the satellite and sell it to someone else, which we did several years later. Still needing a communications satellite, the Chinese purchased one from a company in France. The French company put the satellite directly into the hands of the Chinese, to do with as they pleased. I'm sure the emerging superpower got an education in satellite technology as a result. If the State Department had allowed Loral to ship the satellite when it was built, that, of course, would never have happened.

CHAPTER 23

Selling the Defense Business and Rewarding Shareholders

By the summer of 1996, I had been Loral's chairman for twenty-four years, and we had enjoyed that many years of growth and success. Several times during that span, friends in the investment community had said, "Listen Bernard, I'm not saying this because I have any interest in representing you, but I think you ought to consider selling Loral. The company is at a high point, plus the future looks bright. You'd get a terrific price and you'll be rich."

My answer was always the same to these well-meaning people. "I have what I want, and what I really want to do is to continue to run Loral." I had built something of which I was proud, and I enjoyed the work, even when it was demanding. In fact, I enjoyed my life in general—my family, all the many cultural benefits of living in New York City, the constant travel for business and pleasure. I was not ready to cash in my chips. So I stayed in my chairman seat, and we continued to post quarters of ever-increasing earnings.

Nevertheless, I recognized that the defense industry was continuing to retrench and that Loral's military business might be leveling off in the growth of its market value. It might be a good time for Loral's shareholders to examine alternatives. I suppose my age might have had some impact on my thinking. At seventy, I was ready to consider a change. But there were two important considerations for me. The first was: Could I receive a price for the military portion of the business that would reflect real value for our shareholders? The second consideration was: Would Loral's employees be safe, continuing to have jobs that would provide them with the opportunity for growth and reward?

So after much reflection, I decided I would sell the defense portion of the business if I could achieve four conditions: one, a sales price of 9.5 times EBITDA of the military division, or $9.3 billion, a price that put the value of Loral as a whole at $13 billion; two, to sell to a company that had a compatible spirit to Loral, such as Lockheed Martin under CEO Norman Augustine; three, the distribution of cash from the sale to the stockholders of Loral; and four, I wanted to retain Loral's satellite, space, and communications division, and Globalstar, which after the sale would be run by Loral's surviving management. The shareholders of Loral would become the new shareholders of Loral Space & Communications. The failure of any one of these conditions would be a deal breaker.

And so in the summer of 1996, I called Norm Augustine and asked if he would meet me for lunch in a small diner not far from Lockheed's headquarters in Bethesda. I told him what my plans were for Loral and advised him that I had not approached investment bankers or other companies about my plan. If Norm was interested, I'd be willing to sell the defense division to Lockheed, but if not, I would not pursue the issue further.

This wasn't a retirement move; I still wasn't ready to cash in my chips. But I was in a different place, intellectually and emotionally, than I had been, say, ten years before, and selling the defense divisions under the right circumstances felt like a good idea. At my age I could see the upside of no longer running a large international defense company, and I thought it was time to step away from that particular set of demands— and to reward the stockholders of Loral for their faith and commitment.

Of all the requirements I had for the deal, Norm's involvement was especially important to me. He was a true visionary: the only person

I thought worthy of overseeing our assets and making sure they were properly fitted into his larger corporation. He and I were very different people. He was an engineer by training, and a Midwesterner, and I was a New York businessman who enjoyed working with great engineers. But fundamentally we were similar in that we had visions for our companies that were built around the people we employed, and we had philosophies that emphasized fairness for everyone we dealt with, even our competitors.

In short, I liked the way he did business. I also thought that even though his company was about twice as big as ours, Loral's defense divisions generally fit well with Lockheed Martin. As defense contractors we complemented each other, which meant that the respective pools of employees should be able to blend fairly easily with an absolute minimum of job loss. As alike as Norm and I thought in most ways, we weren't in quite the same set of businesses, and that was what I thought made the combining of our companies such an elegant and powerful idea.

The deal Norm and I made in 1996 was by no means the result of a classic negotiation. I told him at the outset of our lunch at the diner that I would be talking to no other companies, but I also told him that our satellite divisions were off-limits and that the price I had in mind was not negotiable. It's not that we never discussed the number; we did then, in the restaurant, and afterward. His first reaction, I remember, was that my price was on the high side. I assured him that the figure represented what I would be willing to pay for the company if I were acquiring it. I argued that at $9.3 billion, Lockheed would be accretive almost immediately and would continue to be accretive every year thereafter, and meanwhile he'd be in some great new businesses. "This is a real opportunity for Lockheed," I said. But I quickly added that if he wasn't happy with the price, we could all walk away from the deal and go back to being friendly competitors, and there would be absolutely no hard feelings.

Norm was an effective negotiator and ultimately felt good about the deal. Apart from Loral's defense divisions being a good value, the timing was right for him too. The Department of Defense had recently told its suppliers that because of the continuing shrinkage of defense budgets, the industry as a whole would get smaller, and some companies would need to, as one general put it, "go away." Neither Lockheed nor Loral was under any grave threat of extinction—we were both thriving, in fact—but by making the deal with Loral, Lockheed became an even stronger company at a time when almost everyone else in the defense business was getting weaker.

Still, not everyone at Lockheed Martin immediately signed on to the asking price. I felt that there were some on the board who felt disrespected by Loral's "nonnegotiable" price and who thought that Lockheed was an industry leader and should have been more assertive. Others on Norm's board felt that an investment banker should be involved in a deal this size. Norm, however, understood the value of this transaction and was aggressive in moving the transaction to the Lockheed board.

We announced the sale of the Loral divisions on Monday, January 8, 1996, one of the snowiest days in New York's history. Manhattan was virtually shut down like I've never seen it before or since. In anticipation of the blizzard, a small crew of key Loral people who would be responsible for disseminating the news but who lived outside the city came in the night before, stayed in a midtown hotel, and got together to raise a toast to past glories and future successes. It was a bittersweet time for most people at the company: the end of an era and a fork in the road. We would part ways with more than thirty thousand of our employees, who would be going off to work for Lockheed Martin.

I knew that the president of Loral, Frank Lanza, who was one of those new Lockheed employees, wasn't terribly happy about what was happening, even if he didn't say much about it. No one was happy that our record-breaking run was coming to an end. I understood perfectly well what was happening and why everyone felt the way they did. There was always a real sense of family at Loral, and now the patriarch was acknowledging that he no longer wanted to preside over this kind of business. It made us all a little sad to break up the old team.

On April 11, 1996, I sent a letter to everyone at the company:

Dear Loral Employee:

I expect the Lockheed Martin/Loral transaction to close shortly. I am certain that you share the mixed emotions that I am feeling about this event.

For 24 years, Loral has been a most extraordinary odyssey—filled with challenge, reward, frustration, and satisfaction. Together we have created new opportunities for individual growth. We created new products, invested in new technologies, found new businesses, achieved almost unparalleled financial performance—and throughout maintained our corporate culture.

We were not always able to resist the ravages of the defense industry decline, but Loral has been among the most stable work environments in the industry, and I truly believe we have kept faith with our employees, our customers, our communities, and our shareholders. We not only did the right things, we did things right.

The Lockheed Martin/Loral transaction was structured to provide maximum future opportunities for the employees of both companies. The merger is truly a strategic combination of people and resources, which allows a strengthened Lockheed Martin to pursue its markets, and Loral Space and Communications to focus on a bright and emerging future. As a result, I am convinced we have mitigated whatever risks we might have faced in the continuing industry downsizing. In fact, this transaction provides a more certain course than any I could have contemplated. It is only through your achievements that Loral was positioned to enter into an arrangement in which each of you has renewed and strengthened opportunities.

Both Loral and Lockheed Martin have strong cultures, which are the foundations of two enviable records of outstanding performance. Proud of our people, proud of our competence, proud of our reputations, both companies are innovative and dynamic.

I am confident that you will carry over our heritage of excellence and commitment to your new assignments. I am confident that Loral Space and Communications and Lockheed Martin will each forge new paths of excellence, and that you will be a part of it.

Even as we should be proud of our past accomplishments we should look forward to new successes. The odyssey is not over, but we have come to a turn in the road.

Bernard Schwartz

I meant what I said when I told my employees, from Frank Lanza on down, that I felt good about their futures at Lockheed Martin. Some things you can write into a merger agreement and other things—like a promise to make sure your employees are well taken care of in their new environment—you can't. But I trusted Norm implicitly when he said that he had great respect for our personnel and would continue to look out for and support Loral's people. Norm even agreed to establish a separate electronics division of Lockheed that would be run by Frank Lanza as a vice president and invited me to become vice chairman of Lockheed, a move that was meant in part to assure the former Loral people that they were safe and secure. I gladly accepted the position.

Within a year, however, some unfortunate things happened in regard to this commitment. The first was that Norm retired, as scheduled, as CEO of Lockheed Martin, though he remained on the board. The second was that Dan Tellep was chosen by the board to move up from his former post as president to the CEO spot.

Soon after that transition occurred, I was asked to come to a meeting with Norm and Tellep. Tellep handed Norm and me a sheet of paper showing his proposed new structure for the corporation. According to this organizational chart, Frank Lanza's job would be eliminated, and the electronics division that Norm had created would be absorbed by another division of the company.

I was, to put it mildly, unpleasantly surprised by this development, and I explained to Tellep that what he was proposing was contrary to our agreement. I couldn't accept this, I said, and Norm agreed that it amounted to backtracking on our deal. "We just paid $9 billion," he said, "and that was mostly for *people*." Norm didn't think Lockheed should blithely reorganize those valuable people right out of the company.

Tellep, however, was nonplussed. "This represents my view of what is best for the company," he said, "and I intend to run the company by my own lights." He added that if I disagreed, I should feel free to convey my feelings to the board. I thought that would be futile, though, since the board was likely to rubber-stamp all decisions made by their new CEO.

The first thing I did after the meeting was to call Frank Lanza and tell him about what had happened. I told him I intended to resign from the board immediately and that I would support him in any way he wished. He said he wanted to think about his next move, and for the time being we left it at that.

The second thing I did was to go back to my hotel room and write a long letter of resignation from the Lockheed board, outlining why I thought the restructuring was a mistake for the company. The next morning, though, instead of handing in the letter at the board meeting, I decided to call Jack Welch for advice.

I didn't know the chairman and CEO of General Electric, America's premiere industrial company, especially well, but I did know that GE owned 25 percent of the common stock of Lockheed and had one member on its board. And I also knew that Welch was someone whose career I'd followed and greatly admired.

When I called Jack I just said I would like to meet with him on an important business matter. He immediately said, "Sure," but noted that he was headed to Europe that weekend for an extended business trip and asked if he could see me when he got back.

"I'm sorry, Jack," I said, "but this is time sensitive."

"Okay," he said without missing a beat. "Let's meet on Friday, then. But I'll be in at GE's executive offices in Connecticut and don't know what time I can get to New York City to see you. Can you be flexible? I can probably be there in the late afternoon."

"Jack, you are doing me a great favor. I will come to see you."

So I drove to Connecticut and got to Jack's office that Friday at five-thirty. He had his jacket off, his tie was open at the neck, and he seemed to be involved in several simultaneous meetings and phone calls. Yet, from the moment I walked in, he was gracious and cordial. I told him about Loral's merger with Lockheed, about the oral agreements we had to safeguard the Loral employees, and about Tellep's decision to do things another way. Jack said that although he knew almost everyone worth knowing in American business, he didn't know Tellep, but that it indeed seemed strange to jettison people and assets that you'd just paid so much to acquire. He also said that he didn't think he could do much about the development, since he himself didn't have a seat on the board and he had rarely if ever gotten involved in Lockheed's business. But he promised to look into the situation and see what he could learn.

"Do you mind if I call Norm Augustine?" he asked me.

"Certainly not," I said.

As things turned out, I never heard from Jack Welch again on this matter. But I did get to see the results of his influence. Several days later Norm called me and invited me to a meeting with him, Tellep, Frank Lanza, and another Lockheed executive. Norm used the occasion to announce that Lockheed's management had agreed to reverse their recent decisions about corporate restructuring, that they would return Frank to his position as the head of the defense electronics division, and that they would restore virtually everything else that Norm and I had originally agreed upon. I was immensely gratified.

Tellep did not say anything at the meeting, but when I left the room, he was standing in the hall. He told me that he had never been so disturbed by any business matter before, that he regarded it as disloyal for me to go outside the company to discuss company policy, and that he would never speak to me again. He never did, either, but I always considered this a small loss.

Quite a few people have asked me why I went into my own pocket and gave a group of my former employees a total of $18 million to provide them with a cushion in case new jobs at Lockheed failed to materialize or endure. Such a move, I have to admit, is unusual and probably unprecedented in American business. But Loral was an unusual company. The people there had a sense of being part of something special, and we all looked out for each other. I even considered the shareholders part of the extended Loral family, which is why I passed along a total of $7 billion, or $38 a share, to them in the form of a special distribution that, like the money I gave my former Loral colleagues, was not something required or expected. As I mentioned earlier, I'm still delighted almost twenty years later to get their letters of support and thanks.

Not long after the meeting at which Norm Augustine told me his company was keeping its electronics division, he called me to say that it appeared that, after assessing the situation for some months, eight divisions that had been part of the Loral package of assets did not fit with Lockheed after all and would need to be sold. "All the rest we're retaining," Norm said, "but I just wanted to make sure this was okay with you."

At this time I was about to resign from my position as vice chairman of Lockheed and from the board, but Norm knew of my attachment to the companies and the people in them. "It's not up to me to object," I said, "but who are you planning to sell them to?"

"We don't know," he said. "We may go to Goldman Sachs to help us find a buyer."

"May I make a suggestion?" I said. "Why don't you sell those divisions to Frank? You two can sit down together and come to a price, and I will help Frank get the financing."

"Okay," Norm said to me. "That might not be a bad idea."

Frank and Norm worked out a deal that valued Frank's new company, L-3 Communications, at $525 million. When we brought up the idea of selling the divisions to Frank at what would be my last board meeting, it got a lot of resistance. There was an extraordinary amount of personal bias expressed against Frank for all sorts of things—being a Loral person, *not* being a Lockheed Martin person, not fitting the image of a typical defense industry executive. There was also some residual anger about the price that Lockheed had paid for the Loral divisions, and Frank to some extent was bearing the brunt of how they felt about me.

About the only defender I had on the board, besides Norm, was a brand-new member, a retired three-star admiral from the navy who said, "Look, this is my first meeting. I don't want to attempt to interfere. But you should know that I've had dealings with Loral over the years. I've never known them to do anything that was not straight up. They stood by every contract. I depended on them totally. They were good people."

At one point in this very tense discussion, Norm turned to me and said, "Bernard, do you have anything to say?"

I knew that under the terms of the deal that Norm had discussed with Frank, Lockheed would retain a 35 percent interest in the new company composed of these eight divisions, so I said, "I don't know how much you're valuing that asset in your deliberations, but I can tell you if you think it's worth $100 million, under Frank's leadership it will actually be worth $200 million."

Eventually Norm got the board to approve the sale in principle. Frank and his partners retained 15 percent of the company and Lehman Brothers 50 percent. Although Frank is gone now, L-3 Communications lives on as a leader in the field of defense electronics, a true success story in a still-challenging business.

Like a lot of people involved in the "old" Loral, the L-3 partners did more than just land on their feet, and certainly the shareholders of Loral Corporation did extremely well: They received a cash dividend and the opportunity to retain their position in an exciting and expansive satellite communications company. It was another opportunity for a win-win-win.

CHAPTER 24

A Day No One Can Ever Forget

I had arrived in Washington on the evening of September 10, 2001, for a meeting the next morning at the US Capitol building with Congresswoman Nancy Pelosi. I got to the Capitol meeting room about fifteen minutes early and sat down with some others who were watching television and chatting. I was there about a minute when the regular broadcasting was interrupted. We saw an image of a plane crashing into the south tower of the World Trade Center. Suddenly the room full of senators, congressmen and women, and their aides and guests grew very quiet. Was it a small commercial plane or an airliner? Was it an accident? Had there been any casualties? For many long minutes no one knew.

Like the others in the room, I couldn't take my eyes off the screen. Then the second crash occurred. Now we surmised that the first crash had not been an accident, but I am not sure at that moment that we understood the gravity of the situation. No one was referring to it yet as a terrorist attack. Very soon, Congresswoman Pelosi and some aides came into the meeting room and told us that it was an act of terrorism. She advised us to leave the Capitol building as quickly as possible. I immediately called my driver and asked him to meet me outside the main entrance. Luckily, he made it there through the already tightened security, and I directed him to drop me at my hotel, the Four Seasons in

Georgetown. The streets were filled with pedestrians walking away from the Capitol building. Because we got out relatively quickly, I was able to get within two blocks of the hotel.

It was a truly strange scene and one I'll never forget: Every other corner was already occupied by an army vehicle with two, three, or four soldiers in full military gear. On the car radio, we soon heard that the Pentagon had been attacked and, of course, the streets of Georgetown were full of confused and frightened people. I was able to get out of my car and walk to my hotel. I went to my room, turned on the television, and tried to call my office in New York. It was very difficult to get through on a cell phone or even on a landline. I stayed in the hotel room for most of the day, watching the events unfold.

Like most travelers on 9/11, I felt cut off, unable to call my family or my office. Luckily, I had brought my Globalstar satellite phone. With that I was able to call Lisa Stein in my New York office directly, because she had a Globalstar phone on her desk. That was the only public communication line that was working.

I asked Lisa to try to reach my wife and tell her that I was all right. I didn't know when I would be able to return, I said, but I would do so as soon possible. I was a minute or two into our conversation when I realized Lisa was in a state of shock. As she was talking to me, she was looking out of the window of her office on the fortieth floor at Thirty-Ninth Street, with a clear view of the World Trade Center towers. She described the smoke that was billowing from the buildings, and she said, "Bernard, people are jumping out of the windows." I tried to calm her, without much success. I do not remember another moment of such confusion and despair in my lifetime. I stayed in my hotel room for two days and nights, not going anywhere. It was a somber time.

On Friday, September 14, I returned to New York on my own plane, and as soon as I landed, I called the mayor's office and said I wanted to visit the site of the tragedy. I was in the satellite communications business, I explained, and I might be of some assistance. A deputy mayor arranged for a sheriff's car to pick me up and drive me downtown at five that afternoon. On the West Side Highway south of Fourteenth Street, everything was blocked except for official vehicles. I noted as we drove downtown that at almost every corner there were people with supplies of food and clothing and other things that New Yorkers were offering to those who were working on the site. Besides the material goods, they were also offering encouraging words. It was an extraordinary moment in the city's history, but painful too. The officer driving the sheriff's car drove me directly into the site, and within a block of the destruction, he let me out to walk around alone and unattended. By this point it was about six o'clock in the evening. Because I had come directly from my office, I was still wearing my jacket and tie, but everyone else was dressed for emergency rescue work.

The people I saw were firemen, policemen, soldiers, and volunteer workers, many who had come from far-off places to do what they could to help. Many had been up for days and had not slept except for brief catnaps at the site. Restaurants in Manhattan and Brooklyn were keeping the rescue workers fed at no charge. What struck me was the fatigue of these people, visible in their faces and their posture. But that was to be expected. What was extraordinary was that as I walked around, only yards from the hot molten steel and the destruction, many of these rescue workers thanked me for coming down to see them and to be with them. I stood out because of the way I was dressed, and they were sincerely grateful for whatever moral support I could bring to them. Firemen or policemen would march by me carrying one of their colleagues on a stretcher, wounded or dead, and when that happened, men and women stopped working and silence fell until the stretcher had passed. Since then I have never been able to pass a fireman or a policeman on the streets of New York City without saying hello. I hope America does not forget these noble men and women who did so much. I know I will not.

CHAPTER 25

A New Chapter

I retired as chairman and chief executive of Loral Space & Communications on February 1, 2006, and when the announcement appeared in the *New York Times* and other places, the response was gratifying. Hundreds of employees wrote or called to wish me well, to recall fondly the years they had spent working at Loral, and just to say, as employees and shareholders, they appreciated how I had managed over the decades to increase the value of their investment.

The press was kind, too. Under the headline "An Icon Departs," *Space News*, a leading industry publication, wrote:

> *Top satellite industry executives have come and gone over the years, but Bernard L. Schwartz has been a fixture . . . The ultimate survivor, Mr. Schwartz has both driven and weathered the upheavals that have shaken and shaped the satellite telecommunications landscape for the last decade and a half. With his departure, the industry loses perhaps its most visible representative and certainly one of its most committed statesmen and advocates.*

Was I sad to be leaving Loral? Yes, but it was the right thing to do; it was time. I was ready to move on to other endeavors: infrastructure reform, involvement in certain think tanks and cultural institutions, and managing my family's investments. I had also become disappointed in the way that the business environment had changed in the years since I'd entered the workforce: Corporate executives more often thought in terms of mining existing companies for whatever profit they might yield rather than of building something, not caring whether they destroyed them in the process. But although I left Loral Space & Communications in good shape, with our stellar management team in place, I did not, because of circumstances beyond my control, leave the chairmanship in very good hands.

Because of a perfect storm of events—the failure of Globalstar, adverse conditions affecting the satellite industry, auditors' disclosure requirements, and even bankruptcy laws—Loral Space & Communications was forced to file for reorganization under the federal bankruptcy laws. After decades of ever-increasing success, such a setback was an aberration for me. But how we got to that point, how we handled the situation according to the lights of the Loral culture, and how we emerged a stronger company than we were before—all that is necessary to tell as part of my story.

Earlier I related that Globalstar was structured as a consortium of ten telecom companies from around the world, each of which had a major financial investment in the concept of a global satellite phone network of separate companies. This made it viable but also challenging to handle. In 1997 Globalstar revised its financial needs upward from $2 billion to $2.5 billion. While that price tag was relatively modest for a system of Globalstar's size and scope, it was nevertheless a significant sum to raise in advance of service. Still, in 1997 and 1998, we sold $1.5 billion in senior notes, raising a total of $2.9 billion.

I knew the financial requirements would continue to grow and that dealing with the CEOs in the consortium wouldn't get any easier, yet I was unflaggingly optimistic. Satellite communication was an important and exciting business to be in, connecting millions of people to vital services and to each other via highly advanced technology. The potential upside was impressive.

At the annual Globalstar shareholders' meeting in April 1997, I said, "The countdown, the fiery exhaust of the rockets, the slow initial reaching upward off the launch pad, the powerful vibration radiating outward, the exhilaration as it takes flight, the wonderment that human beings can and do defy the laws of gravity, that we can through genius, invention, and collaboration actually extend our reach to the heavens and harness this miracle for the welfare of all the earthbound residents of this small planet—all of this is what our space adventure is about." One month later I announced that, right on schedule, we had received orders for thirty-three gateways to support the more than one hundred countries the Globalstar system would cover. I also revealed our new slogan: "We'll have the whole world talking," part of an advertising plan aimed to establish the company's identity as the high-quality, low-cost global communications tool for people without access to other phone service in underserved areas of developed and developing countries.

Apart from its own intrinsic merits, the venture, which was 35 percent owned by Loral Space & Communications, seemed to fit neatly into the company we had become after 1996. SS/L, our satellite manufacturing and technology division, was the second-largest business of its kind in the world. We had started our second operating business—fixed satellite services—by acquiring Skynet from AT&T in 1996 and, a year later, had further extended that arm of the company by teaming with our Mexican partner to purchase a 75 percent interest in Satmex from the Mexican government.

These divisions became the foundation for the Loral Global Alliance Network. With the acquisition of Orion Network Systems in 1998, we added transatlantic and transpacific satellite services. A year later we acquired from APT Satellite Holdings the Apstar-IIR satellite, which provided coverage over Asia. Customers rated Skynet, which managed the alliance, "best in industry" for service and reliability. While these operations were distinct from Globalstar, they also were synergistic with it.

But the fact that it fit naturally with our other assets did not mean that everything about Globalstar fell smoothly into place. Our troubles began as soon as we launched the first of the planned fifty-two satellites—forty-eight working ones, plus four spares—into their low-earth orbits. Our initial launch, from Cape Canaveral in November 1997, didn't happen as scheduled. Instead of popping champagne corks and announcing that we had taken a giant step toward the realization of our goal, we had to put out a press release saying that Globalstar was postponing the launch eight weeks to allow for further testing and rehearsals of the tracking, telemetry, and control ground equipment that would monitor the deployment of the satellites. In September 1998 we had a true disaster. A Ukrainian-built Zenit-2 rocket carrying twelve Globalstar satellites took off from the Baikonur complex in Kazakhstan, veered in a wrong direction, and moments later crashed and exploded in a remote area. No one was injured, but a quarter of our satellite constellation was destroyed.

Launch failures are an unfortunate part of the satellite business, and we had to factor them into our business plans, but for us, the Zenit episode was especially painful, and not just because the equipment we lost was worth $100 million. I knew immediately that the financial setback would not be as harmful to our efforts as the time lost. We needed to move expeditiously with Globalstar because, while we were working toward our goal of being fully operational by 2000, rapid advances were being made in cellular technology.

Cellular systems allowed for broader and cheaper phone service as well as such now-familiar, consumer-friendly features as call waiting, voice mail, and pocket-sized equipment that Globalstar didn't offer on its less compact and more basic satellite-based handsets. I wanted to concentrate on getting our system up and working before we addressed the issue of the phones themselves, but the telecoms whom we'd partnered with, partly for their knowledge of consumer marketing, insisted that we had to offer more features on our phones if we were going to be competitive. Their reasoning was sound in theory, but by turning our attention to those issues, we further delayed our entry into the marketplace.

Despite all the difficulties, however, I remained excited by the possibilities. In late 1999, six months before we were due to be fully operational, we went to Geneva Telecom, a major telecommunications technology exhibit held every five years. Globalstar was the hit of the show. People were walking around the grounds using our service and our satellite phones, and everyone thought the experience was terrific. But we needed additional funds to get us through those final months: money for our ground stations, increasingly advanced handsets, marketing, licensing, and other things.

So I went to our partners and said, "We must raise another $1 billion. If you put up your share, Loral will put up $500 million." Alcatel, the French company, responded by kicking in $200 million, China Telecom invested an additional $37.5 million, and other members of the consortium contributed as well. In 1998 Loral bought out two partners for $420 million, representing 16.8 million shares, and then sold half those shares to Soros Partners for $245 million—a strong endorsement for a high-profile investor. It seemed my consortium members were betting with me. But if I had known then what I know now, I would definitely not have invested that last half billion dollars.

As I've mentioned, by that point Globalstar had suffered several setbacks and was already later than projected in getting to market. Also, the system budget had risen several times, from approximately $2 billion to more than $2.5 billion, and now the cost was going up farther. The public debt market, which had already contributed almost $1.5 billion, was closed to us, and most of our partners were not willing to put up additional equity. Globalstar had lived up to all of its promises; our technology, in space and on the ground, worked wonderfully. But market conditions beyond our control were changing as advances in cellular technology meant that truly remote parts of the world became fewer and farther between.

But in 1999 we were still forging ahead. In March of that year, Loral approached one of its primary banking relationships with a structure that would allow Globalstar to borrow the money it needed to get operational at a very good price. The banks would commit to a loan to Globalstar for the full $500 million if Loral Space & Communications would agree to guarantee the loan and give the banks collateral in Loral Skynet's Telstar 6 and Telstar 7 satellites, currently under construction. In return for providing the guarantee and collateral, Loral would get warrants to purchase additional partnership units in Globalstar.

The loan closed in late 1999, and within a year, it was clear that because of the advances in cell phone technology, Globalstar was not going to be able to adhere to the terms of the loan and would default. In order to protect the investment in Telstar 6 and Telstar 7, Loral went to the same bank group in late 2000 and borrowed $500 million with the understanding that it would use the proceeds to purchase the Globalstar loan from the banks. This would allow Globalstar to continue to operate and would allow Loral to avoid foreclosure on two of its most valuable assets.

Loral's guarantee of the Globalstar loan had allowed us to finish the system and begin commercial operations, but now Loral had also taken on an additional $500 million of debt. In 2000 Loral ended its financial and management commitment to Globalstar. Still, Loral was by no means insolvent or even in a distressed situation. Although the failure of Globalstar led Loral to report a net loss of $1.5 billion, or $5.20 a share in 2000, our core business showed signs of strength and vitality.

At the same time, though, the satellite business was seeing dramatic changes. Consider that from 1997 through 2001, SS/L booked twenty-eight awards for geostationary satellites. In addition, at year-end 2001, SS/L had backlog of $1.6 billion. But largely because of the bursting of the telecom bubble and a recession in Asia, from late 2001 through 2002 the satellite industry experienced a drought of bookings unprecedented in its more than forty-year history.

This downturn left many of SS/L's customers uncertain of the future competitive landscape for communications services. There was a general feeling that communications infrastructure was going to become a very competitive business with a severe overcapacity. More problematic still for SS/L customers was that the financing markets that had been wide open to telecom and Internet companies for the past several years were now all but closed. Even those customers who had a compelling business plan and wanted to build a satellite would have found there was little or no external financing available. In 2002 only four commercial satellite programs were awarded industry wide, as compared to an average of twenty-eight programs per year over each of the prior ten years. By the time SS/L booked a new program in September 2003, it had been two years since its last award.

Sometimes when it seems as if things can't get any tougher, they do. In early 2003 Loral's independent auditors advised me that because the People's Republic of China had a claim against us for around $150 million over the nondelivery of its China Sat satellite and because Alcatel had made a claim for another $350 million over Loral's termination of an agreement with them, we had to show the total of $500 million on our books for fiscal 2003 as a "loss reserve." I told the accountants that there was absolutely no validity to either of those claims, but they were at that time particularly risk averse.

Taking that write-off put Loral in a precarious financial position, which had the further result of the auditors giving us what's called a "Going Concern" qualification—which automatically triggered calls for all of Loral's more than $2 billion in outstanding debt. We would, in fact, eventually prevail over the China Sat matter. As for Alcatel, we paid $13 million to settle with them, but that charge was completely offset by an accounting gain of $14 million in Loral's favor that arose from the reversal of losses recognized earlier.

Just before all of this happened, I got a call from a man named Mark Rachesky who asked me if we could get together to talk about Loral. I had never heard of him before, but it turned out he'd been acquiring our bonds quietly but aggressively. It wasn't unusual for me to meet with investors who expressed an interest in our company, so we arranged to have dinner the next night in Palo Alto. "Can it just be the two of us?" he asked, and again I agreed.

In the meantime I did a little research and found out that Rachesky was a private capital banker who made his money by buying bonds low and converting them to stock—often by forcing the target company into bankruptcy. This allowed him to take control of a company, after which he would methodically strip out and sell off its assets and cease making investments in things like R&D in order to increase his short-term profit. Under his control a company might undertake a large dividend recapitalization, meaning it would borrow money and return Rachesky the amount he'd invested.

Firms like his ordinarily cared nothing about the employees or the long-term goals of the companies they were dismantling. For him it was all about the short term: how much he could extract from a situation before moving on to fresh meat. He was, in other words, a classic corporate raider in the style of his former boss, Carl Icahn. Rachesky smiled a lot at dinner and was very charming. He didn't say, "I want to take over your company" in so many words. Instead he said, "I'm a big bond-holder. I think we can work together."

"Really?" I said. "I don't think we would work together very well at all."

"Why is that?"

"Because we have diametrically opposed views. My view is to keep building the company, to think in the longer term. Your view is get the stock price as high as possible as fast as possible for your own benefit as a major stockholder. Sometimes those two philosophies can be successfully blended—but not in this case."

"Well, think about it," Rachesky said.

I smiled. I had a lot to think about in those days.

The next day when I was meeting with Jeanette Clonan, who was by then Loral's investor relations officer, she asked me, "How did dinner with Mark Rachesky go?"

"That guy is trouble," I said. "He wants our company."

I detested the idea of bankruptcy, and in fact Loral was really not a good candidate for Chapter 11 reorganization. We had enough assets to cover our debts—approximately $2.3 billion in total at that time, $1 billion of which was secured bank loans—and as we tried to get through this difficult time, business was actually improving. In mid-2003 we came to an agreement with Intelsat to sell them our six satellites serving the North American market: a $1 billion deal with a $50 million down payment on an order for a new SS/L-made satellite for Intelsat. That obviously was great news for Loral. It broke the order drought and kept our factories open. It was also a signal of confidence in Loral from a major satellite provider.

The catch was that, although this transaction would significantly reduce Loral's total debt load, Intelsat was concerned that Loral could suffer financial difficulties in the future that could lead to bankruptcy. Under bankruptcy law, any asset sale completed shortly before a Chapter 11 filing can be challenged in court by the remaining debtors, thus making Intelsat vulnerable to losing the satellites. As our discussions progressed, Intelsat inserted a condition that would require the transaction to be completed with the approval of the bankruptcy court. I agreed that we would swallow hard and file for Chapter 11 protection. This allowed the Intelsat sale to happen on schedule, but it also had the unfortunate consequence of ultimately allowing Rachesky to convert his bonds to common stock; he owned 35 percent of the outstanding shares after the reorganization.

I planned to pay back our debts in full and to make sure that all our employees and even the local merchants we did business with—the deli that catered our occasional in-house breakfasts and lunches, the pizza guy—didn't get hurt or left out of any settlement. Rachesky, on the other hand, wanted to pay back cents on the dollar and gouge the employees at every turn. I once had an argument with Rachesky's lawyer, who said, "Why don't we just take the assets from the pension fund? Money's money, right?"

"Wrong," I said. "This is the employees' hard-earned money, and it's going to stay where it is."

What Rachesky wanted defied common decency. It was unthinkable to me to take advantage of your employees, to cut or eliminate their pensions or reduce their compensation just so you could enrich yourself.

I fought Rachesky at every turn. He had the largest block of votes on any plan of reorganization because he had bought those bonds. But I always had leverage over him because of the way I'd structured my companies. Loral Space & Communications owned and operated SS/L but was a separate entity from it, which was debt free and solvent following the repayment of the secured debtors. Rachesky had no claim on SS/L other than an equity claim as a shareholder. If Rachesky pushed too hard, I always had the option of separating the SS/L bankruptcy case from the case of the parent, thus maintaining control of it and depriving him of one very significant asset. My legal advisors were not a hundred percent behind my view, but I felt it gave me leverage. Rachesky's concern that I would do that kept him sufficiently out of the way so that I could get the important things done: battling for my employees and the long-term good of the company.

Rachesky took me to court, trying to have me forced out or at least have my decisions overturned. The judge ruled in my favor. My own lawyer sometimes disagreed with me about sticking to my principles. "Bernard, you owe Bank of America a billion dollars," he said. "They'd be happy to get back $800,000."

"I don't care," I said. "We owe it, and we'll pay it *all* back." And sure enough, there came a day when I repaid Bank of America $1 billion.

We emerged from the reorganization on November 21, 2005, a much stronger company than we had been before the filing. Both Space Systems/Loral and Loral Skynet were intact, with their management in place; I made sure all the top executives had two-year employment contracts. Employees also received new stock options that would allow them to benefit from the growth in value of the new Loral. All creditors were satisfied, either through the full payment of their claims plus interest, as in the case of SS/L and Skynet creditors, or through the issuance of new Loral equity, as in the case of the bondholders. SS/L was debt free, with assets of $872 million, up from $362 million before the reorganization.

And the future looked solid, provided the assets were managed smartly. Both Space Systems/Loral and Loral Skynet came out of the reorganization with strong customer bases and healthy backlogs. Regrettably, the one group that gets hurt in a reorganization like ours is the shareholders. Although many of them had benefited greatly over the years as Loral shareholders, they lost the value of their current holdings in the bankruptcy. To my everlasting regret, there wasn't a thing I could do about it.

With this one exception, I was proud of the way we had handled ourselves during the reorganization. But with Mark Rachesky controlling the board, it was not the same Loral for me. Running the company wouldn't be fun anymore, and that was one of the main reasons I resigned.

I have a couple of original Globalstar phones on a shelf in my office; occasionally I take them down for closer inspection and think about those troublesome times. I'm embarrassed by the failure of Globalstar, which set off a chain reaction of events that ultimately led to some people losing their investments. People trusted me, and in this instance, I did not reward their trust; I am sorry for that. But everyone involved knew it was a high-risk, high-reward investment. If I take any consolation, it is that I failed while trying to grow the company. I hoped to build a worldwide network of interconnectivity, foster a new technology, and, in the process, create tens of thousands of jobs. (Globalstar still exists and is still providing satellite phone service to remote locations.)

You can't win every battle; the best you can do over the course of a career is fight bravely and hope you win more than you lose. I judge myself on my overall record. Some investors lost money as the share price of Loral Space diminished to a virtual vanishing point. But there's a big difference between the independent stockholders who purchased shares from their brokers and, say, Alcatel, Vodafone, France Telecom, Qualcomm, and the other large companies that were partners in our Globalstar consortium and made an investment.

Most of the individual investors who owned Loral over the decades had long since reaped the fruits of the enormous value we created between 1972 and 1996 as the stock rose steadily in price and split three times.

Ultimately, relatively few "little guy" investors were hurt by the failure of Globalstar. The brunt of the loss, rather, was borne by the high-yield debt investors and Loral, as well as by the telecoms that used our satellite technology as insurance against cellular technology and accepted the price of that insurance as a cost of doing business. If someone had to get hurt because Globalstar didn't work out as we had hoped and expected, I preferred it would be them.

It's hard to sum up a career of more than fifty years in one newspaper story, but I was honored and flattered by what the *Wall Street Journal* wrote about my departure:

> *Loral Space & Communications, Inc. Chairman and Chief Executive Bernard Schwartz said he will step down next month at the age of 80, ending a flamboyant, sometimes contrarian 34-year run at Loral that mirrored the ups and downs of the U.S. aerospace industry.*
>
> *A former accountant and New York City native who was a darling of Wall Street throughout his career, Mr. Schwartz's personal and management style bucked industry trends in various ways. He maintained close ties to Bill Clinton, even as the Democratic former president slashed defense spending . . . Mr. Schwartz's retirement as chairman and chief executive of the pared-down New York satellite firm, effective March 1, also marks the exit of one of the industry's best-known elder statesmen and an ardent booster of commercial-space businesses. But his outspoken, freewheeling style may not be a good fit with the private-equity interests now in charge of Loral . . .*
>
> *Mr. Schwartz, who said he wrote his letter of resignation two months ago to ensure an orderly transition, declined to talk about a successor. But in an interview he said, "there probably will never be a more appropriate time to turn over the reins."*

PART V

Creating Jobs and Sharing the Wealth

"Bernard is a classic, Roosevelt-influenced New Dealer,
unabashed, but not ideological. He's very focused on jobs, very
concerned about the losers in the financial crisis, but with a
very pragmatic outlook. Frankly, the Obama administration
would have done well to spend more time listening to him
because events have vindicated his views. The best evidence
of that is that Bernard was talking about the value of infra-
structure investment as a response to the country's competitive
challenges even before the financial crisis in 2006–2007."

—STEVE COLL, PULITZER PRIZE–WINNING
JOURNALIST AND DEAN OF THE COLUMBIA
UNIVERSITY GRADUATE SCHOOL OF JOURNALISM

CHAPTER 26

Bill Clinton and Infrastructure

Not long ago, while I was in my office on Fifth Avenue dictating a chapter of this book, I got a call from Bill Clinton. I took it immediately, of course, but the nice thing about it was that it was not terribly important; my favorite president in the last sixty years was just keeping in touch. "Hey, Bernard, how are you doing?" he said in his familiar Arkansas drawl. "It turns out I was at a meeting yesterday and something came up about infrastructure legislation, and the speaker mentioned your name in connection with it. People were reacting with a lot of enthusiasm and excitement. I thought you'd like to know that, and I made a mental note to give you a call." He paused, and then his tone became less breezy. "Tell me, how do you think things are going on the infrastructure front?"

Bill Clinton knows well the history of my involvement with what used to be called public works. One reason the issue is so dear to me, I think, is that I have always been more interested in the manufacturing economy than the Wall Street economy. I like the idea of conceiving, designing, and making *things*, rather than, say, buying and selling derivatives. But the real reason I push for infrastructure reform is that America desperately needs it.

In an age when more than 20 million people are unemployed or underemployed and our nation struggles with dangerously outmoded road, rail, and water systems—not to mention a seriously inadequate electric grid and aging, hard-to-secure ports—putting people to work rebuilding our nation is an obvious, efficient, and even elegant solution to two of America's most urgent problems: unemployment and structural renewal. Yes, federal, state, and local governments are strapped for cash. But I'm embarrassed by the apparent denial about this obvious problem. Proper legislation could result in both private companies and the federal government hiring people to create what's needed, fix what's broken, and bring the country into the twenty-first century.

If you go to Hong Kong, South Korea, or Europe, you'll find broadband speeds and air traffic control systems that are generations ahead of what we've got here. If you fly from the airport in Beijing to JFK in New York, you could be excused for thinking you are going from a first-world nation to a third-world one. It's a shameful situation, and it has only gotten worse since I began talking about it in earnest in the late 1990s.

I am a lifelong Democrat—an angry Democrat, sometimes, but a Democrat nevertheless. I don't hate Republicans or think they are crazy. What they believe in—smaller national government, limited governmental participation in peoples' lives, smaller budgets and expenditures, a lack of restrictions on industry, a strong defense but limited international involvement—are all reasonable objectives. They just don't happen to be mine. I believe in individual freedom, equal opportunity, the dignity of the individual, the social contract and government responsibility for investments in personal development, and, yes, the national infrastructure—ideals that are better served, in my experience, by the Democratic Party.

Believe it or not, I have on occasion voted for Republican candidates. I even voted against a Democratic presidential candidate once when I went for Ronald Reagan over Jimmy Carter. I didn't share Reagan's philosophy of government, but he did use his office to project hope for America, and I was attracted to that. The way our system works, we don't vote for the perfect candidate but for the better of two choices.

Mind you, I was not a stranger in the Carter White House. On one occasion I was one of six business and political leaders, Republicans and Democrats, whom he invited to the Oval Office to give him advice on whether the federal government should advance loans to Chrysler Corporation. At the start of the meeting, which included Bob Strauss, the former chairman of the Democratic Party and then a special envoy to the Middle East, President Carter took his chair from behind his desk and brought it around to the front so we could sit in a circle, as equals. I thought that was a gracious thing to do.

As it turned out, all the people at the meeting except the president and I were against extending help to Chrysler. I spoke up strongly in favor of what I called a foundation stone of the American economy, not just an important automobile company. In the end with Carter's support, Chrysler got the help. But what was interesting, I thought, was that what wound up being advanced to Chrysler was not a loan, per se, but a loan *guarantee* for which the government could charge an upfront fee. Ultimately, the company recovered on its own and never called upon the guarantee—and the government nevertheless made a substantial profit on the fee.

Some people have wondered how I can reconcile my Democratic beliefs with building and running a Fortune 200 company. How can I be both a progressive *and* a capitalist? There really is no conflict. I'm all for capitalism, but just as I would not want to live in a New York City that had no traffic lights and stop signs, I would not want to live in an America where capitalism went unregulated. I think it's part of the federal government's responsibility to oversee economic growth and direction; to move in and spend money when it's necessary to provide balance or to stimulate growth; to make the winners pay their fair share of the tax burden; and to give the losers the opportunity to get back on their feet, so the system can keep going and provide opportunities for people in its imperfect but ultimately reliable way. If the ultimate goal is to guarantee equal opportunity (but not equal results) then I'm all for big government, and I'm not ashamed to say it.

When I was running Loral, a major defense contractor, I would occasionally run into people who, because I am a Democrat, treated me like I had a communicable disease. I occasionally got some static, too, from shareholders who didn't understand how I, one of the few Democrats in the industry, could actively work for presidential and congressional candidates who were openly against increased defense spending. Shouldn't those people be my avowed enemies? It was a fair question to ask since Loral was a public corporation, but my response was polite and always the same: "If you don't like it, you are free to sell your stock. We are not the only company in the defense industry. This is who I am, and ownership of our stock does not give you the right to alter my basic beliefs."

I like politics: the intellectual sparring and all the old-fashioned hoopla that goes with it. I have been attending the Democratic National Convention for some time, and both the nature of conventions and my participation in them have changed over the years. On many occasions Democratic conventions have had a significant impact on our political results. The demonstrations that took place in support of various candidates, some of them taking as long as an hour, actually affected the outcome, and the convention often determined the party platform that expressed the visions and expectations of the Democratic Party. Over the years, however, the practice was changed to a primary system that chooses the candidate long before the convention; even discussions with respect to party platform take place before that event.

I believe this is unfortunate. The primary system in the United States is broken. Often, primary delegates are chosen by a minimum of elections or caucuses, and very often only the most extreme positions of each party choose convention delegates. This results in an overwhelming majority of incumbents being reelected, with some new candidates selected by the most extreme ideological philosophy. This is not a good system.

My first convention experience took place in 1947, while I was still in college, when I was invited to the Democratic National Convention to support Henry Wallace as a presidential candidate. I went there innocent, enthusiastic, and excited, but I came away informed, disappointed, and wiser. That was the convention that was taken over by a political crowd, dominated by a very extreme, leftist position. There was no democratic mechanism to express the viewpoints of the delegates; it was completely dominated by the convention organizers. I came away devoted to the Democratic Party and to Harry Truman as a candidate.

My subsequent experiences at these conventions, however, reinstated in me a belief in the Democratic philosophy. The demonstrations, flag-waving, shouts of approval and condemnation, partying till the wee hours of the morning, brushing shoulders with all types, from delegates to superstars—this was exciting stuff.

I try to enjoy the political process as much as I can. Irene and I have been throwing gala election-night parties since 1968, when Richard Nixon beat Hubert Humphrey. We always have a particular candidate whom we are personally pulling for, of course, but the purpose of the parties has always been to celebrate the American democratic process and make the point that the election or reelection of a president is a cause to rejoice and to give thanks—a nonpartisan salute to the way our country works.

The election-night parties started as small gatherings in a restaurant near our home, but they grew every four years and became a strictly black-tie affair. For a while we had them in a Horn & Hardart Automat (we provided our guests with nickels, dimes, and quarters so they could "buy" their dinners), and then the Cipriani on Forty-Second Street, Brasserie 8½ on Fifty-Seventh Street, the Rainbow Room, and later the New-York Historical Society, where in 2012 we hosted more than four hundred people—friends and employees as well as local and national political figures.

The menu has evolved into something I call "American traditional": hot dogs, baked beans, turkey, roast beef, ice cream. There are always plenty of TVs on which to watch the election coverage, and nonstop live music from the Great American Songbook: Cole Porter, Rogers and Hammerstein, George Gershwin, Irving Berlin, and, naturally, we couldn't get by without Frank Sinatra's "New York, New York." Not to be overlooked is the immeasurable contribution made by my right-hand woman, Lisa Stein, who oversees every detail of these celebrations with precision and elegance.

I'm also an avid political donor; Irene and I have given more than $10 million to Democratic causes and candidates in the last dozen years. Yet as enthusiastic as I am in my giving, I'm not the sort who just writes a check and says "Good luck!" I like to get involved. Several times I've had the honor of addressing the House and Senate Democratic caucuses, and when I get behind a person or an idea, I'm usually an activist. As part of my push for infrastructure reform and renewal, for example, I've flown down to Washington many times, met with people from both political parties, organized groups of policy makers, and commissioned papers and used them to brief key people. I've made lots of speeches, thumped a few tables, buttonholed a few lawmakers, and bent a few ears. I want to win on this issue, and I believe I will, because I've got a plan and I'm executing it.

House Minority Leader Nancy Pelosi said in a recent interview, "The Democratic Party doesn't have a more active, emphatic, or passionate supporter than Bernard Schwartz," and even though I know there have probably been times when she wished I was a little less active, emphatic, and passionate, I'll take that as a compliment.

I think most Democratic political leaders understand who I am by now. They know I tend to participate in the process, and they also know I'm not a believer in Super PACs, those organizations that are allowed to collect money for political campaigns virtually without restrictions. At first President Obama, living up to his 2008 campaign promise, refused on principle to accept the help of Super PACs. I wholeheartedly agreed with him.

But then, in early 2012, the president changed his mind, reasoning that to not accept Super PAC money would give Republicans an unfair advantage. When that happened, I had a little debate with my conscience and, before I figured out how I really felt about the matter, wound up giving a few hundred thousand dollars to organizations supporting

Democratic congressional candidates led by House Minority Leader Pelosi, Congressman Steve Israel, and Senator Chuck Schumer. But I hadn't thought the matter through at that point and eventually, after I did, I didn't feel comfortable with Super PACs. I really did feel that they tended to make elections a contest of spending, not of ideas. So I changed my policy and just said No to Super PACs. Now when their representatives call and say, "Not contributing gives the Republicans an edge," I say, "Work harder for your cause, but stay within the restraints. This is a matter of principle. Sorry."

The ever-growing importance of money in the political process is something we must be vigilant about. Once you get involved with Super PACs, it's a slippery slope. In late February 2013, the *New York Times* ran a page-one story that made me both angry and sad. It said:

> *President Obama's political team is fanning out across the country in pursuit of an ambitious goal: raising $50 million to convert his re-election campaign into a powerhouse national advocacy network, a sum that would rank the new group as one of Washington's biggest lobbying operations.*
>
> *But the rebooted campaign, known as Organizing for Action, has plunged the president and his aides into a campaign finance limbo with few clear rules, ample potential for influence-peddling, and no real precedent in national politics.*

This is nothing more than a thinly veiled attempt to circumvent federal limitations on campaign contributions and other laws and rules that would make political parties accountable for how they raise money, how much they raise, and what they do with it. That's why Organizing for Action will be set up as a tax-exempt "social welfare group" when it is really a political fund that allows wealthy people to pay for access to the president of the United States. President Obama has the bully pulpit, and he should be using it to denounce ideas like Organizing for Action. His aides admit that, as the *Times* said, "a small number of deep-pocketed donors" will drive the organization. There is even a menu: For $50,000 you get to go to a "founders summit" with high-level White House staff; for $500,000 or more you can buy entrance to a "national advisory board" and have quarterly meetings with the president. Really? Count me out.

What about the people who don't have that kind of money? And what about the special interests of the super rich, many of whom are not at all concerned with "social welfare"? Organizing for Action is *not* the American way.

My position on Super PACs hasn't made me a pariah—not so far, anyway. I still get invited to dinners with the president, and elected officials and others still call to ask my advice. One reason I maintain my status, I believe, is that legislators and political organizers know that when they hear from me, it's about infrastructure legislation or some other issue that I believe in, and not because I want a favor. I have never once asked any office holder for preferential treatment or a benefit for a business I was running. President Clinton has said as much publicly, and so has Senator Bob Kerrey, a good friend of mine who was head of the intelligence committee when I was running Loral and was in a position to do me a lot of favors. He didn't, because neither of us ever wanted government to work that way. "I've known Bernard Schwartz a long time," Senator Kerrey once said, "and I've been in this job for a long time. Bernard Schwartz has never once asked me for special treatment."

President Clinton, likewise, has never taken an action that would help me financially, but that doesn't mean he hasn't shown his friendship and loyalty in meaningful ways. I've mentioned how, during the Chinese satellite dust-up, President Clinton quietly stood by me. During a period when I was being unfairly pilloried on television by the Alabama Democratic senator Richard Shelby and by California Republican congressman Dana Rohrabacher on the House floor, the president made sure I was invited to the White House and seen in photographs with him.

His behavior must have left Gingrich and his friends bewildered, because at the same time they were trying to taint President Clinton by connecting him to me, Bill was more than willing to publicly demonstrate our connection. We never talked about what was happening, and to me that made it all the more amazing. Bill Clinton made a powerful statement of support and trust with his actions, and for that I am forever grateful.

The first time I met Bill Clinton was at a small party in New York City at the home of the investment banker Alan Patricof, an old friend of mine. It must have been about 1988. The future president was still the young and not terribly well-known governor of Arkansas, and if he had any presidential plans, I didn't know about them—at least not when Irene and I arrived that evening. The party wasn't a fund-raiser, just a gathering of about twenty New York Democrats for a dinner and conversation.

At one point when people were mixing and mingling between courses, the woman who'd been seated next to me at dinner got up to talk to someone else, and Bill Clinton sat down in her place. It was immediately clear that he'd done his homework and knew who I was. "You know, Bernard, I'm thinking in terms of seeking national office," he said, "and to be honest, I don't really know much about the defense industry and defense policy in general. In Arkansas that's not a priority, so I've never had to learn about it. I've got a lot of questions on the subject, and if you don't mind, I'd like to call on you sometime and get your views."

Although I barely knew who he was, I was instantly impressed. I liked that he was straightforward about his political ambitions, and—this is even rarer in a politician—willing to admit what he knew and didn't know. What I especially liked about him, though, was the way he was seeking out someone who had strong practical knowledge of the defense business and the challenges it faced. I wound up talking to him for about twenty minutes that night, giving a smattering of information and opinions on a wide variety of defense topics. He listened closely, asking the occasional question, and then thanked me and returned to his seat.

After dinner he was asked by Alan Patricof to say a few words and take a few questions—one of which happened to be about the defense industry and the defense posture of the United States, and how it did or didn't fit his own philosophy. I'll never forget his response. "I don't have a lot of expertise in this area," he told the group, "but let me tell you some of the things I've recently heard and want to check out further." He then, in about five mesmerizing minutes, put forward a succinct and perfectly accurate version of my rambling remarks of perhaps an hour earlier. He spoke off the cuff, but in a series of beautifully shaped paragraphs. It was like watching him compose an essay in thin air. He didn't mention my name, but as he wrapped up he said, "I don't know if these ideas are right or wrong, but I'm going to find out. The next time you see me, I'll have the answers." Everyone at the dinner applauded warmly.

I would, in December 1992, see Bill Clinton put on a similar performance when, as president-elect, he hosted an economic conference at the Robinson Center in Little Rock. As he stated in his opening remarks, he had called together "a diverse and talented group of Americans who make this economy work" to provide input on where the US economy stood and how the economic plan should be shaped. The group consisted of his vice president, Al Gore, and numerous members of Congress, captains of industry, economists, and academicians. After each topic was discussed—often disputed—he would extemporaneously summarize what he and all the participants had covered, leaving out no significant detail or nuance. He has an amazingly supple and absorbent mind.

As he said at the conference, it was his intent "to begin through this very public process to reconnect the American people to their government, and to ask for their help, too, in making economic progress." It was a powerful and effective gesture. Just as he had at Alan Patricof's house, Bill Clinton struck me as both down-to-earth and self-assured, and I knew then and there that I'd be solidly in his corner, whatever he decided to do next. I wound up working hard for him in his run for the presidency—people forget what a long shot he was at the start of that first race against Bob Dole—and his reelection, and I became a major contributor to his and eventually his wife Hillary's campaigns.

I'm not one of Bill Clinton's most intimate buddies, but I'd like to think that over the years we have become friends. We've certainly shared some great times together. In June 2002, for instance, Irene and I traveled with the former president to England for a meeting of a small group interested in a progressive approach to politics and economics, often referred to as the Third Way. Prime Minister Tony Blair, the president's old Oxford buddy, was there, as were Christiane Amanpour and her husband, James Rubin, a former assistant secretary of state and spokesperson for the State Department. In one of the most magnificent settings I could ever imagine, the English countryside home of Evelyn and Lynn Rothschild, we discussed the important matters of the day and listened to the president and prime minister engage in a lively exchange about NATO's relationship with and responsibilities toward the Arab world.

In 1998 the Clintons had a Christmas dinner at the White House for about two hundred people. It was on December 13, which happens to be Irene's and my birthday. Somehow Bill and Hillary had found out, and they added a little celebration for us. It was beyond thoughtful—almost overwhelming, really.

I didn't get to know Hillary very well until about a year and a half into Bill's first term. Then one day I got a call from the First Lady's office saying, "Mrs. Clinton would like to invite you to the White House." I went, of course, but at first I didn't figure it would be anything out of the ordinary. The First Lady and the president frequently hosted gatherings where there were small groups of people, often from the same state or with a common interest in a particular issue. I figured I'd be mingling with some of my Democratic friends from Manhattan and maybe having a few words with the First Lady and getting to know her a bit, if I was lucky.

Instead, it turned out that it would be just the First Lady and me having tea and a freewheeling, open-ended conversation. Two and a half hours later I was still there. We talked about everything—politics, the economy, parenting, international events, plays, movies, the infrastructure, the joys and challenges of living in New York City. It was like a Schwartz family dinner without all the debating. Hillary is a remarkably open and well-grounded woman. I found her completely captivating and do still.

I sincerely believe the Clintons are in politics for two simple reasons: They have a commitment to public service, and they like people. I realize they are often said to be "master politicians," and they certainly know their way around that world, but their secret of success is that they follow their gut. I remember President Clinton striding into one White House dinner a bit late and announcing, "I've just begun overhauling the welfare system. The liberal wing of my party isn't going to like this one bit, but I didn't do it to make friends. I did it because it's the best thing for the country. We're going to change the welfare system as we know it." (Later, he would say that publicly.) I was really impressed to hear him talk that way in a private conversation.

Over the years I've been fascinated to watch the Clintons interact with others on a one-to-one basis. When you see Bill and Hillary at a dinner, greeting guests warmly and seeking those same people out later to find out more about them, you know their interest in others is genuine and not based on any agenda or quid pro quo. I've heard so many people say, "I can't believe I met the president of the United States and he looked me in the eye and talked to me like I was somebody important!" or "I can't believe Bill Clinton remembered me from the last time we spoke and quoted back to me several things I'd said!" Bill Clinton is a genius when it comes to dealing with people, largely because he loves doing it and doesn't consider it work.

On New Year's Eve of 1999, President Clinton presided over a huge gathering at the White House to celebrate the millennium. I was there with Irene and our daughters, Karen and Fran, and their husbands, John and Matt. At some point in the evening, the president said, "Hey, Bernard, what are you doing on New Year's Day? Want to come by tomorrow and watch some football?" I'm a sports fan, but Clinton is a genuine football nut. "Can you be at the White House at around two o'clock?"

"Can I bring—" I started, but before I could finish he said, "Sure, bring Irene, we'd love to see her."

"Honestly, Mr. President," I said, "I don't think we're going to get my wife to watch a football game, even at the White House. What if I bring my son-in-law?"

"See you guys at two," he said, clapping me on the shoulder and moving on.

When John and I got to the White House on January 1, 2000, we were ushered to a small theater in the family wing. About ten people were gathered around a large-screen TV, watching . . . well, what most of us were doing, to be precise, was watching Bill Clinton watch football. If you've never seen this spectacle, all I can tell you is that to me, anyway, it was more interesting than the Rose Bowl. The leader of the free world was jumping up and down, screaming at the screen—"Pass the ball, for God's sake!" "Hey, ref, that's your second dumb call in a row!" "Go for the first down!"—and constantly changing the channel.

At one point President Clinton walked by me, tapped me on my shoulder, and said, "Follow me, Bernard—and bring John." He took us on a private tour of the Oval Office, which was not far down the hall. He showed us the paintings and statuary and talked to us at length about each piece and why he found it so significant. Then he took us into his private office and did the same thing: showing us his books, picking up personal mementoes from his desk, and telling us the stories behind them.

We were off with him for at least a half hour. At one point John asked President Clinton, "Which president from the twentieth century do you most admire and why?" The president thought for about ten seconds and then said, "Harry Truman—because he knew who he was as a person and did not back away from making tough decisions." That little tour was something neither John nor I will ever forget.

Soon after we returned to the party, Hillary drifted in, and a few minutes later I saw from across the room that she and Bill were engaged in conversation the way any couple might do. She was sitting on the arm of his chair and leaning against him affectionately. The moment was, in other words, altogether unremarkable. Then Chelsea popped in, and during a break for halftime, she and her father quickly got into a debate about some matter of public policy. He seemed confident in his opinion, as a president of the United States should be, but Chelsea wasn't giving an inch. When I saw them interacting that way, I thought, "This is a solid family."

When Bill Clinton called me on that recent morning while I was dictating this book and asked how things were going with the infrastructure, I knew he was referring in large part to our progress on the political front.

"I haven't given up by any means—I have reason for hope," I told him. "Now, when President Obama sees me at a dinner or some other function, he usually comes over and talks about our infrastructure initiative, and though he doesn't make any promises or say anything definite, he assures me he understands the value of what I've been pushing for."

It's really a shame that infrastructure reform—an issue I've been fighting for since 1995—is viewed as a political issue. In the almost twenty years that I've been pushing for it, not one person on either side of the aisle has said to me, "I'm against that!" The federal government's investment in infrastructure projects that the private sector has been unable or unwilling to undertake has been a key factor in the growth of America. From the Louisiana Purchase, the building of waterway systems, the funding of land grant colleges in the 1860s, the electrification of rural America in the 1930s, the building of dams like Grand Coulee, Hoover, and Glen Canyon, which brought irrigation and new life to large land areas of the West, the building of our national highway systems under Eisenhower, and the repair and improvement of our road systems—these were investments made by our government to enrich America.

Prior to the 1970s, annual infrastructure investments in the United States aggregated about 3 percent of our gross domestic product. During the 1970s and thereafter, the annual aggregate infrastructure investment declined to about 2 percent of GDP, causing a continuing and growing infrastructure deficit in America. The American Society of

Civil Engineers has estimated that an investment of about $1.7 trillion is required to bring our national infrastructure to a point where we will regain our competitive leadership and improve our style of living. Additionally, such a program would create tens of thousands of new jobs. Yet despite these realities, national, multiyear-infrastructure programs fail to win the support of our political leaders.

The push for a new and improved infrastructure policy is neither Democratic nor Republican, liberal nor conservative at its core. In fact, senators John Kerry (a Democrat), Kay Bailey Hutchinson (a Republican), and Mark R. Warner (a Democrat) introduced a bill in 2011 called the Building and Upgrading Infrastructure for Long-Term Development, or BUILD, Act. "This is a bi-partisan moment to make a bi-partisan issue bi-partisan once again," Senator Kerry said at the time.

I know from my own personal experience with the shaping of the BUILD Act that John Kerry and his staff (particularly Heidi Crebo-Rediker) put a tremendous amount of effort into it—and they came up with something that's miles ahead of anything we've ever had in this area before.

The purpose of the BUILD Act is to create a special infrastructure bank, politically independent and fiscally responsible, that will allow us to leverage public and private capital from the United States and abroad for the rebuilding of America and the creation of 6 to 8 million jobs. In addition, since the funds advanced are loans or loan guarantees, interest and fees would be charged to the project. The only cost that would be scored as an expenditure would be the bad-debt potential associated with the loan—offset, in turn, by the interest and fees earned by the bank. Only a minimum, if any, amount would be scored as an expense and added to our deficit. This is a very important point because it addresses the concerns of legislators who fear that such investments, as vital as they are, would add too much to our ballooning debt. In fact, they would not.

By providing loans and loan guarantees instead of grants, the infrastructure bank would allow us to tap into pools of funds available globally in sovereign wealth and in hedge and pension funds that are seeking long-term, stable avenues for investment. The BUILD Act envisions a modest initial investment of $10 billion in each of the first two years, followed by $140 billion spread over the next seven years. The bank would finance no more than 50 percent and more typically 25 percent of any project. As a result the $160 billion invested by the government over almost a decade could result in a leveraged amount of up to $640 billion available to repair, modernize, and expand our ailing infrastructure system—without adding appreciably to the national debt.

Because the projects will be selected by an independent, bipartisan board of directors and a CEO appointed by the president and confirmed by the Senate, politics are minimized. Loans and loan guarantees ultimately will be repaid to the US Treasury, and since they will be paid back with interest and fees will be charged on guarantees, loan recipients—not the government—will ultimately bear the cost, and the bank will generate revenue and become self-sustaining over time.

The BUILD Act is backed by people with real clout: Kerry has run for the presidency and is now the secretary of state; Hutchison, now retired, was a ranking member of the Commerce, Science, and Transportation Committee; and Warner is a member of the Banking, Housing, and Urban Affairs Committee. On the House side, Representative Rosa DeLauro, who serves on the Appropriations Committee, has introduced her own infrastructure bill, as has Maryland representative John Delaney. Other prominent proponents of infrastructure investment include Representative Steve Israel, current head of the Democratic Congressional Campaign Committee, New York's Senator Kirsten Gillibrand, former governor of Pennsylvania Edward Rendell, and Felix Rohatyn, the esteemed banker and one-time savior of New York City.

You'd think that a bill with that kind of support—a bill that so many could have bragged about voting for—would have sailed through Congress and already have the president's signature. But that would mean Washington was functioning a lot better than it actually is. As we've seen time and again since Barack Obama became president in 2008, it has grown increasingly difficult for our lawmakers to rise above political partisanship and actually get anything accomplished. Because the BUILD Act would almost certainly result in good economic news during a Democratic administration, burnishing the president's legacy—and because it's the rare politician who is willing to be seen by his constituents as being in favor of raising the national debt—it has been strenuously and continuously opposed by many Republicans (and even some Democrats) with the sad consequence that it is stalled in the legislative pipeline.

We can't just blame Republican obstructionism for the bill's failure to pass; the program failed to secure the necessary support from the president to win passage through our Congress. Although the president mentioned infrastructure reform as one of his four priorities in early 2013, and mentioned the issue prominently and repeatedly in his State of the Union Address, he has so far failed to invest sufficient political capital to make it happen. And so we continue to witness the deterioration of our critical resources, such as high-speed rail, air traffic control systems, airport security systems, and our national power grid. We are losing the chance to build efficient and technologically improved ports and to replace an ancient water-treatment system.

The principal argument most often heard against an eight-year infrastructure initiative is that the country cannot afford it. But what is ignored in the political ferment is that infrastructure investment dollars will not only create jobs but also enrich our country. Increased real estate taxes, toll road usage, user fees, and an improved economy will pay for the investments that we make. It's a workable plan. But we do not have the political leadership to get this program done, and we have failed to muster the necessary political will to advance infrastructure reform for the last thirty years.

When I want to feel good about this issue, I say to myself, "Well, this used to be an issue that was on the margins, and now we've moved it to the mainstream." But the fact remains that it's still stalled. Can we get it moving again and create a bank that would help close the widening infrastructure-funding gap? I believe we can but, ironically, only if we can convince President Obama—who so carefully picks his political battles—that infrastructure is one area where during his second term he should stand and fight. As Bob Herbert, the now retired *New York Times* columnist, wrote in March 2011, "It's not an overstatement to say that unless we atone for our infrastructure sins, the high tide of American greatness will have passed."

I trust we won't let that happen. This solution is not beyond our capabilities. America is truly the world's leader. The world is still playing by our playbook. More countries across the globe are turning to democracy and free capital systems. America commands a leading role in the area of culture. It is *our* music, *our* blue jeans, and *our* movies that are sought after throughout the world. Our medical institutions are the world's leaders in both research and performance. Our R&D centers, like those in Silicon Valley, North Carolina, Texas, and Long Island, are still the most innovative in the world. Our citizens are the most mobile and best educated. We have the greatest military power, and we devote it to saving lives and promoting democracy. We make 26 percent of the world's products. Our currency remains the leading currency of the world. And Wall Street provides the most capital and most efficient financing.

Our ability to innovate, our optimism, and our resilience are unmatched, and they provide the resources that we will employ to improve not only our own society but the rest of the world's societies as well.

"So what should we do next, Bernard?" President Clinton asked that day when he called me about the state of our infrastructure initiatives.

I couldn't help laughing. "You're asking me?" I said. "You're supposed to tell *me* what to do!"

He chuckled. This is the way a talk with President Clinton very often goes. A conversation with him is always a dialogue, something you can't say about every official in Washington. Bill Clinton, as president, was always smart, confident, and passionate about what he believed in—a man truly dedicated to service—but at the same time he was almost always open-minded and willing to listen.

I miss the Clinton years.

CHAPTER 27

Giving Back

I've enjoyed more than my share of luck over the years, and now more than ever, my family and I are actively engaged in the enormously gratifying experience of paying back to the society that has given us so much. Through my political activism, my experience working within the system to achieve increased accountability and fairness, and my campaign to increase investment in infrastructure and put people back to work, I think I can, in a modest way, influence public debate and help America and the world become a better place.

My base of operations these days is my company, BLS Investments. Leaving Loral freed me to devote more time to the management of my family's finances and to increase my involvement with some of the not-for-profit organizations we support. With the help of my longtime right-hand woman, Lisa Stein, I found office space on Fifth Avenue that looks uptown over Central Park. We created a well-equipped work environment for what would become a staff of twelve—almost all of them veterans of Loral.

This is where I sit down with the principals of the organizations I support, as well as with politicians looking for advice—and support. The walls are decorated with photographs of New York City—still my cultural "campus"—and memorabilia of my more than sixty years in business. I meet with—and sometimes spar with—various fund managers and advisors, usually accompanied by the indispensable Judy Linksman, my personal financial and investment assistant for more than thirty years. Judy's wisdom and judgment are extraordinarily effective. I should also say something about her memory: It is a steel trap. And, she's indefatigable.

It was 2006 when I retired from Loral, and at that time there was increased media focus on the condition of our veterans returning from the wars in Iraq and Afghanistan. So many of our servicemen and women were afflicted with what would be life-long physical and mental disabilities, and despite their sacrifices, many were relegated to relying on food stamps when they found the doors to employment closed to them. Our nation was not prepared for their return. This particularly disturbed me. I believe America has an immense obligation to those who defend us in military actions abroad. At the same time, I believe very strongly that our involvement in those two wars constituted bad national policy. My feeling about these circumstances led me to call my friend Bob Kerrey—Medal of Honor recipient, former governor, and former US senator—to discuss these issues with him and see if he could arrange for me to visit Walter Reed Hospital where I could meet with our wounded veterans directly to determine for myself to what degree the media reports were true. Bob made the arrangements for the two of us to visit Walter Reed.

When we arrived, the hospital authorities—all members of the military—greeted us cordially. We proceeded to visit the rehabilitation and medical facilities, and then stopped by the rooms of several of the veterans so that we could talk to them. The one persistent impression I had from speaking to these wounded veterans was their courage, commitment, and optimism. Another observation I made was that Bob Kerrey had a connection to these veterans that I did not have. As a World War II veteran, I felt a kinship with these men and women, but I had not seen military action. The much-decorated Bob, on the other hand, fought the Viet Cong and suffered the loss of part of his right leg. The rapport he had with them was immediate and intimate. It was striking.

We chatted with one fellow in his early twenties, for instance, who had lost a leg, and Bob asked him what he intended to do when he left the hospital. The young man responded that he was going back to Iraq. When Bob asked him why, he responded, "That's where my buddies are."

Bob sat down on the man's bed, gripped him by the elbows, and stared into his face. "Soldier," he finally said, "you don't have to do that. You've done your part." They sat staring at each other for a long time. I'm sure Bob got through to him.

On one other occasion, I visited Walter Reed on my own and had a chance to speak to an older veteran who had also had part of a leg amputated. He was a Marine drill sergeant—I'm guessing about thirty-five years of age. He told me he was in training to go back to his drill sergeant duties, which require marching fifteen to twenty miles in a day. I asked him why he was going to return and he said, "I can do this and I will." This kind of courage is exceptional and should be recognized—not with medals and citations alone but with timely compensation, prompt processing of disability claims, treatment for physical and mental disorders, and opportunities for education and employment that our government owes these people. Our treatment of veterans is disgraceful and we—not just Congress but all American citizens—need to press for change and afford the men and women who so ably defend us the honor and care they deserve.

My concern about issues like this is reflected in my increased involvement in the support of think tanks and educational institutes that seek to influence national policy. Back in 1990 I joined the Democratic Leadership Council, of which Al From was the CEO. Founded in 1985, the DLC, with Al and his cofounder Will Marshall, was instrumental in convincing Bill Clinton to run for president as well as in contributing significantly to his progressive political agenda and campaign strategies. As a member of the DLC and, eventually, other think tanks, I found that my personal experience in developing and growing a manufacturing company was extremely useful.

Oftentimes, I was the only person at the table who knew what it was like to manufacture things; to operate a company of thirty-eight thousand people; to design products, assess market demand, create shipping and advertising programs, hire, set compensation levels, negotiate pension criteria, and bargain with unions; to establish marketing standards and programs; to create R&D activities; and to sell things. In short, I was usually the only one present who was a businessman. As such, I think I was a useful counterbalance to those who possessed a multitude of other talents but lacked the practical experience of sweating to meet a payroll and satisfying the expectations of multiple stakeholders.

I am proud of my contributions to the DLC, which included the creation of its quarterly journal, *Blueprint*. But the organization gradually lost its relevance as other progressive think tanks proliferated. Over the years, Irene and I became less active in DLC's initiatives. Al From stepped down from his leadership role in 2009, and the institution disbanded in 2011. But I identified several other think tanks whose work contributed to the discourse on important economic policy issues and engaged with them to create programs that would grab the attention of and influence our lawmakers.

At the 2004 Democratic National Convention in Boston, a friend asked me to meet with Jon Cowan, who was starting an unusual think tank called Third Way. The purpose of this organization is to study and develop moderate policies on subjects like US economic growth, energy, immigration reform, same-sex marriage, and gun safety. Rather than employ scholars in ivory towers, Third Way creates teams of thinkers from inside and outside its organization who do research and run training programs for their customers: Democratic elected officials and candidates for public office. Its work has benefited small-town mayors, the president of the United States, and all sorts of people in between.

I was impressed with Jon's dedication, experience, and, above all, his proposal for how to best serve Democratic members of the House and Senate in establishing a political agenda. I agreed to become chairman of the board of Third Way and to provide Jon sufficient financial support to develop the institution. Along the way we established the Bernard L. Schwartz Initiative on American Economic Policy at Third Way to further an agenda that would foster long-term growth and job creation in America. Jon and his associates, including Jim Kessler, Matt Bennett, and Nancy Hale, have been extraordinarily successful in establishing a lean, extremely effective, and oft-cited progressive think tank that is an important part of the national conversation. I am now chairman emeritus of this vital organization, but still an active participant in its policy deliberations.

The Council on Foreign Relations, based in Manhattan with offices in DC, has been around since 1921 and is recognized as the world's preeminent think tank promoting America's position in the world of foreign policy. I am a member there and have tremendous respect for its president, Richard Haass. With his cooperation I established the Schwartz Senior Fellowship in Business and Foreign Policy, currently held by Ted Alden, an expert on US economic competitiveness as well as on trade and immigration policy. I also sponsor an annual Schwartz Lecture on Business and Foreign Policy there.

Back in 2004 author and journalist Kati Marton and her husband, Richard Holbrooke, then US ambassador to the United Nations, invited Irene and me to meet economist Ted Halstead. Ted spoke with great eloquence and passion about the New America Foundation, then a new public policy organization that planned to be active in a wide range of challenging issues. After the meeting Ted and I met privately to discuss how I might become involved with New America.

Irene and I made a significant, multiyear financial commitment to the organization, helping to establish and support an economic growth program and forming the Bernard L. Schwartz Fellows Program, which supported classes of innovative thinkers who focused on their areas of expertise—such as economic growth, health care, education, and technology—and during their one- or two-year stays at the organization published articles, participated in symposia, and wrote books. Along with two of the original cofounders of the New America Foundation—Sherle Schwenninger and Michael Lind—and with its second president, Steve Coll, and Steve Clemons, NAF's American Strategy Program director, we continued and expanded the Schwartz Fellows Program and pursued initiatives such as the creation of a national infrastructure bank.

In early 2013 Steve Coll resigned as president of the NAF to become dean of the Graduate School of Journalism at Columbia University and to write on the Middle and Far East, as well as on American businesses and the economy. At around the same time, I, too, concluded my relationship with New America. After nine years together, our ideological paths had diverged somewhat, and I opted to redirect my energy and support to other programs that more closely parallel my commitment to ensuring America's economic health and preeminence. I am proud of New America's achievements and am happy to have been instrumental in its start. Independent of New America, I have continued working with Sherle Schwenninger and Mike Lind, and from time to time, I am privileged to attend small, salon-type dinners run by Steve Clemons, now editor at large of the *Atlantic*. With Steve as moderator, attendees at these dinners engage in lively discussions about politics, foreign affairs, the economy, or whatever is Topic A at the moment in Washington.

David Rothkopf, a prolific writer who focuses on America's role in the world, is a visiting scholar at Carnegie Endowment for International Peace and now CEO of *Foreign Policy* magazine. He and I are of similar minds on many of the challenges facing our country today and have coauthored op-ed pieces for the *Financial Times* and the *Washington Post*. With my support, David holds frequent well-attended "conversations" with Washington, DC, thought leaders, bringing to the fore the controversial issues confronting our nation and constructing policy options to address those issues.

At the New School for Social Research, under the auspices of the Schwartz Center for Economic Policy Analysis and led by the remarkable Teresa Ghilarducci, various studies, seminars, white papers, articles, and interviews with Teresa and her colleagues address what role government should play to promote economic security, create jobs, and raise living standards in America. Teresa is the author of a book and numerous articles on retirement security and pension reform.

In 2005 Strobe Talbott, head of the Brookings Institution, a venerable liberal think tank distinguished by its age, influence, size, and budget, invited me to participate in the institution's activities. (Strobe, who managed the consequences of the Soviet breakup during the Clinton administration, was also a celebrated foreign correspondent for *Time* magazine.) I funded a $3 million endowment, and together we developed a multiyear program that would include symposia, the naming of a Schwartz Fellow, and periodic publications to advance the development of policies to secure America's economic growth and leadership. The Schwartz program at Brookings remains in place today.

Apart from the efforts I've already mentioned, we have provided general support for or formed Bernard L. Schwartz programs on economic development, job creation, and infrastructure at the School of Advanced International Studies at Johns Hopkins and at the Information Technology and Innovation Foundation. Most recently, I undertook the funding of the Roosevelt Institute's Rediscovering Government initiative under the able direction of economist Jeff Madrick. I continue to support the excellent policy magazine *Democracy Journal* and participate as a panelist or observer at conferences often hosted by economist James Galbraith that draw impressive crowds and even more impressive speakers such as Paul Volker, Robert Rubin, Gene Sperling, Laura Tyson, and members of Congress.

I intend to remain an active supporter of the efforts I've described here. It is important to me that the national dialogue includes the issues of unemployment and what I believe is a structural change in America's economics. Just as there was a transformation in our history from agriculture to manufacturing to post-manufacturing, at present we are experiencing a structural change from technology to service. Our country will continue to lead in technology and service, and although we will be able to maintain our superiority in global economic competition and keep up our steady economic growth, we will nevertheless employ fewer of our citizens to maintain this leadership position.

This is a much-overlooked structural change of grave dimension. To meet its challenges, we must be prepared to change our national behavior in support of education, R&D, immigration, trade policies, retention of foreign-born students, the elimination of the burden of student loans, the protection of our technology and patents, and the security of our currency. In other words, we must adopt a national industrial policy. It is my intention to promote change though my support of these think tanks and advocacy organizations.

Philanthropy is another part of my payback plan. Over recent years Irene and I have donated more than $125 million to think tanks and like organizations, as well as to what we consider to be among the most outstanding cultural organizations in New York City. Among them are the New-York Historical Society, whose Schwartz Lecture Series always hosts a sell-out crowd; the Film Society of Lincoln Center, of which I am a trustee; and the Asia Society, which holds a competition every year for the Schwartz Book Award. At Thirteen, New York's public broadcasting station led by award-winning television executive Neil Shapiro, we provide funding for a variety of news programs. In addition, Irene is an ardent, longtime supporter of the American Ballet Theatre, the Central Park Conservancy, and the Bard Graduate Center.

In addition to donating to the New School, our support of local higher education has included CCNY's Baruch College, Irene's and my alma mater, where I am very proud of the work of the Schwartz Communication Institute, and the Schwartz Center for Media, Public Policy, and Education at Fordham University, led by the indefatigable Bill Baker, president emeritus of WNET. My family and I are also supporters of two major medical research hospitals: the Johns Hopkins School of Medicine in Baltimore and NYU Langone Medical Center, led by CEO Dr. Robert Grossman, one of the world's leading authorities on the science and practice of radiology.

I do not recite this list of organizations other than to thank them for presenting programs that attracted our attention and provided us with the chance to "pay back." The issue of repaying society for the bountiful opportunities provided us has been an extraordinary benefit of living in our time and place.

Payback is . . . beautiful.

CHAPTER 28

A Warning . . . and a Challenge

"I want you to get up right now and go to the window. Open
it, and stick your head out, and yell: 'I'm as mad as hell, and
I'm not going to take this anymore!'"

—News anchor Howard Beale, played by Peter
Finch, in the 1979 film *Network*

"Our primary system is broken."

"Congress is dysfunctional."

"The financial system is not working."

"The government's oversight of financial institutions is nonfunctioning."

"We are not doing the right things to sustain our economic health."

I hear these comments more and more often from more and more people. It is obvious that many well-informed people are frustrated, confused, and angry—and I share those feelings, particularly since many of our country's problems and its recent decline in influence are self-imposed.

Despite the modest progress our economy has achieved as we slowly recover from the 2008 economic crisis; despite the fact that America's corporate earnings get stronger; despite the fact that we have extraordinary liquidity; despite the near-term prospect of energy independence; and despite so many other favorable economic developments, America still has approximately 20 million men and women unemployed or underemployed, with little prospect of them finding suitable work. Earnings for all but 1 percent of our population have stagnated. Graduates emerge from college burdened with debt and facing dismal job prospects.

These problems are not fundamental or endemic to our system; they are the result of a misallocation of resources. When we review the weaknesses and excesses of our banking system in America, we find that the problems causing the crisis of 2008 have, in large measure, remained unaddressed, defying regulatory solutions that are easily achievable. "Too big to fail" investment firms or banks not only continue to do business, they continue to grow. Toxic assets are still on the balance sheets of our largest companies. A proactive administrative policy could fix these problems, and that is why I describe our national economic difficulties as self-imposed.

Laugh if you want, and I know some people will, but when I was running Loral and other companies, I thought of bankers as though they were family, at least some of the time. In this I was different from my brother Harold, who also started a Fortune 500 company; if Harold could borrow money for an eighth of a point less from a bank he'd never dealt with before, he would do it. Sure, that's a legitimate method of operating, and some banks respected him for it. But it wasn't my way. I believed that a long and steady relationship with one dependable bank was worth far more than an eighth of a point. Often Loral dealt with three or four banks and had a strong relationship with each. For extended periods Loral operated without bank loans, the result of a healthy and persistent cash flow. Even during those periods, I met often with the senior bank executives to keep them up to date on our business. It was all about maintaining relationships, not just doing transactions.

A lot of people used to treat their business relationships as something precious. As I've described in earlier chapters, there was a time in this country's history that when a bank loaned you money, it was because the officers believed in you, and if times got tough and you couldn't make the payments, they might extend the loan because they knew you personally and believed you'd navigate the rough stretches and eventually be good for it.

During the early 1930s, my future father-in-law, Sam Zanderer, a salaried worker in a leather goods factory, bought a modest three-family house in the East Flatbush section of Brooklyn. A few years after the Depression set in, he lost his job, and before long he couldn't make the monthly mortgage payment. Instead of foreclosing, his bank let him live in the house, paying a modest rent. The housing market was so bad, I'm sure they would have had a hard time unloading the house, and besides, they thought he was a good, honest guy, so they thought it best for him to stay and take care of the property. As soon as he got back on his feet— by the early 1940s—he bought back the house and lived there until the day he died, in 1978.

Today there are many people in my father-in-law's position, but their stories won't resemble his. Now the banks won't even try to get to know homeowners, whose bond with the lender is broken as soon as that lender sells off those mortgages to financiers who use them to create complicated derivatives of the sort that were instrumental in the economic crisis of 2007–2008. Now, when a homeowner falls behind in his or her payments, foreclosure becomes more or less automatic.

Once, Wall Street was all about relationships. If you were taking your company public, the most important thing was that the potential underwriter believed in your story: what you were saying about your prospects of growth, of repaying debt, and of paying dividends. Indeed, an investment banker often wanted to be *part* of your story, to strengthen the connection between you and them by having a seat on your board. If things didn't go as well as you had projected, the underwriter felt it had failed its customers, and you as CEO felt that you'd failed the bank and the shareholders. But if things did click and the value of investments in your firm grew, the banks were proud of their involvement with you. They would take out one of those classy-looking "tombstone" ads in the *Wall Street Journal*, proclaiming to the world that they had worked on *your* deal, and then they would have these ads framed and hung on their office walls.

Then, sadly, the era of relationships devolved into the transactional time in which we now live. This happened gradually at first, as federal regulators allowed commercial banks to engage in a growing number of securities activities. Gambling with depositors' money was expressly forbidden by the Glass-Steagall Act, also known as the Banking Act of 1933. But, eager to increase their profits and arguing that they needed to act more like investment banks in order to compete with foreign houses, American commercial banks found a sympathetic ear at the US Treasury Department and started eroding the power of Glass-Steagall.

In 1999 the Gramm-Leach-Bliley Act repealed the Glass-Steagall Act—all but meaningless by then—and officially gave banks free rein to play with deposits at their discretion. Within a few years, Goldman Sachs, Bear Stearns, Lehman Brothers, and other Wall Street institutions had placed bets, leveraging forty or fifty times their capital—and in some cases considerably more—mostly on arcane financial instruments connected to ill-begotten subprime real estate loans. To the bankers involved, the extent of the risk didn't matter, because now that they were employees of public corporations (formerly, investment banks were partnerships or sole proprietorships), they were absolved of any personal responsibility.

A sea change had occurred. Calvin Coolidge, the president when I was born, once noted, "The business of America is business," but by the early 2000s, the business of America seemed to be all about completing a transaction and getting your commission. Your responsibility ended when you got paid. Instead of building badly needed roads and bridges or running manufacturing plants that created goods and provided jobs, businesspeople became fixated on complicated debt swaps and other abstract "products" that made money only for the broker. Some of these were so complicated and arcane, we now know, that they were beyond the comprehension of the executives running the investment houses.

In his searing book *After the Music Stopped*, Alan S. Blinder, a former member of President Clinton's Council of Economic Advisors and a professor of economics at Princeton, makes the case for just how crazy things got. "Estimates are that the notional value of outstanding privately negotiated derivatives amounted to under $1 trillion at the end of 1987," he writes, "but they grew . . . to a staggering $69 trillion by 2001 . . . and to $445 trillion by 2007."

Among US firms the lion's share of the business is conducted by just five big banks: Goldman Sachs, Morgan Stanley, JPMorgan Chase, Citigroup, and Bank of America Merrill Lynch. When subprime loans started going bad by the thousands in 2007 and 2008, some of those once-respected investment banks collapsed, nearly taking down the US economy with them. No one deserves more blame for what happened than the overseers—the SEC, the insurance companies, and the ratings agencies that allowed the poisonous conditions to develop in the first place. Some people today talk about creating a system of oversight to prevent such a collapse from ever happening again—but a system was already in place. *It wasn't our system that failed; it was the people running the system.* The regulators failed to regulate, the banks made loans to people who shouldn't have been borrowing, and the credit-rating agencies acted in their own self-interest—everyone in charge knowing that it didn't matter, because even if things went wrong, they wouldn't get hurt personally.

When the government stepped in to bail out a bank, an insurance company, or any organization considered "too big to fail," it was you and I, the American taxpayers, who paid the bill. Millions of people lost their jobs, and hundreds of thousands endured the foreclosure of their mortgages. Meanwhile, the egregious behavior on the part of government overseers and executives from private-sector banking, rating agencies, or insurance companies did not result in a significant number of convictions or terminations. For all practical purposes, no one has been held accountable.

Among the most horrendous examples of this phenomenon was the bailout of American International Group. When AIG teetered on the brink of failure because of the bad gambles it had made, the US government granted relief to the tune of $85 billion. Meanwhile, the company's management abandoned all responsibility for their performance and in fact received something like $165 million in bonuses, even as AIG was going over a cliff. As Blinder writes, "The government concluded that AIG would not be able to pay off its vast cadre of CDS counterparts and, in essence, notionalize the company—turning its huge liabilities into taxpayer liabilities."

Yet nothing has changed. After a federal bailout, the vast majority of those guilty parties are still where they were before the crisis, doing the same things in the same substandard and dangerous ways. And what have we learned from the AIG debacle? Nothing, it seems. Thanks to the government overseers and the top executives of our major banks, the transactional age goes on, with outsized compensation for the financial managers.

How could we go through the debacle of 2008 and not make fundamental changes to the way we enforce the rules? Blinder notes that "this mess did not have to happen" and calls the regulatory failure "inexcusable," but he notes that the people in charge were in denial. "In 1998, Brooksley Born, then head of the CFTC, was sternly rebuked" when she recommended regulatory oversight "by the government's financial heavyweights at that time: Fed Chairman Alan Greenspan, Treasury Secretary Robert Rubin, Deputy Secretary Lawrence Summers, and SEC Chairman Arthur Levitt . . . Treasury Secretary Hank Paulson said in an April 2007 speech that the subprime mortgage problems were largely contained. A month later, Federal Reserve Chairman Ben Bernanke told a Fed conference that we did not expect significant spillovers from the prime market to the rest of the economy or to the financial system."

But after September 15, 2008, when Lehman Brothers filed for bankruptcy, "the whole US economy fell off the table . . . We have literally never seen a labor market this bad in the post-War era." Indeed, as Blinder points out, "Job losses averaged 46,000 per month over the first quarter of 2008, but a frightening 651,000 per month over the last quarter, and a horrific 780,000 per month over the first quarter of 2009. Total employment peaked in January 2008 and then fell for a shocking 25 consecutive months—the longest such losing streak since the 1930s."

But even that "double whammy" has not significantly altered the conditions that brought on the collapse. We still read media stories about JPMorgan Chase and its failing hedging investment strategy. Deals like Facebook are promoted at IPO prices twice their assumed values. In another example of the laxity in following up on the irresponsibility of our top financial executives, the Justice Department ended its investigation of Goldman Sachs and its top executives.

The financial collapse of 2007 and 2008 did not come as a surprise to anyone who had been paying attention to what was happening on Wall Street. Many people I knew could see that the investment banks were ridiculously overleveraged, that the weird new world of derivatives was based on loans that should never have been made, and that a corrupt bond-rating system and a lax SEC had perpetuated the insanity.

I wasn't dealt a serious blow by what is frequently cited as the most serious economic meltdown since the Great Depression. In June 2008, a couple of months before it started in earnest, I entirely liquidated all the equities I held and moved the money I oversee for my family and myself into government bonds. I don't take credit for being a soothsayer—a lot of people knew that a huge market correction was inevitable.

The most I can say is that my timing was right. A few years later I'm back in the equity market again, albeit with a very conservative portfolio. What can I tell you? I believe in America. I can't help it.

The history of American economic progress shows that our success has not been linear. We've faced and overcome many challenges that restrained our economic growth in the past. But our political leadership has always summoned sufficient will and determination to overcome these challenges and continue growing. In recent years America's naysayers have wrongly predicted that the US dollar would be replaced by the euro as the international currency, or that China would become the global economic powerhouse, or that the oil cartel countries or the strength of the Japanese economy would overcome America's leadership. These predictions of our failure have gone silent.

America's supremacy is intact, and I foresee only continued growth and strength in the American system. This nation still makes up 26 percent of the world's economy. We maintain the strongest and best-equipped military in the world. America has recently become the safe haven for investment and savings. America's corporations are demonstrating sustained earnings power that continues to gain momentum. And, if we do things right, America's economic superiority and leadership will continue to grow.

The frustration, of course, lies in the cautionary phrase in the last sentence: If we do things right. The 2008 crisis was long predicted by economists of all stripes. Our leading banks aggressively pursued collateralized debt obligations and other structured financial products without restriction from regulatory overseers. Those products were often collateralized by commercial mortgages that were comingled with other products, varying in creditworthiness but receiving undeserved AAA credit ratings. This entire process, known as securitization, was conducted with full knowledge of our regulators and investment community. Sadly, despite the vicissitudes of the 2008 recession, these financial mechanisms are still in place. And our national banks have emerged from the economic crisis fewer in number, stronger and richer, but unfortunately not better.

I've touched on these issues in the earlier chapters of this book, but what I want to call attention to here in the final pages is the fact that our political system is so broken it is incapable of addressing these problems. Congress in particular is wasting opportunities in endless investigations and committee hearings, and recent administrations are incapable of pressing a growth agenda.

Part of this failure is attributable to the way our government functions. Is it possible for us to have a truly competitive electoral process when 91 percent of our 2012 congressional and senatorial elections were won by incumbents despite their abysmal approval ratings? Can we say that our system is a representative democracy when money flowing from Super PACs (including the president's recently formed $50 million slush fund) corrupts the process by putting the decision making in the hands of a wealthy few? And can anyone say that our Supreme Court works independently when in fact it comprised nine justices who elected George W. Bush president of the United States in 2000? And speaking of elections, I don't believe that the Democratic candidate won the last two presidential elections. In fact, he was elected by the failure of the Republican Party to promote any adequate candidates for the job. This administration's victories were merely success over incompetent adversaries.

One of the other concerns I have about the state of our union is the unchecked influence of two sectors of our society: the financial community and the military. Since the middle of the Clinton administration, the reins of governmental power have been held by men like Robert Rubin, Hank Paulson, Larry Summers, Alan Greenspan, Timothy Geithner, and Ben Bernanke. Not all of these gentlemen are equally responsible for the 2008 crisis or its potential repetition in the future, but there has been a pervasive conceptual thesis advanced by this group that heavily favors Wall Street over Main Street. And so, over the last three administrations (Clinton, Bush, and Obama), government policy has leaned heavily toward the interests of large banks. And unfortunately, President Obama's immediate political advisors were not experienced enough to offset this imbalance of influence.

Another issue about which I have increased concern is the extraordinary influence that our military establishment has on the formulation of national policy. This is not a new development, but the disproportionate influence of the armed services within our society has been growing. I have considerable respect for our US military establishment, particularly its culture of reward based on performance. In general, men and women enter the service on an equal basis and advance in rank on merit. It is a huge proving ground based on dedication, integrity, courage, intelligence, and hard work. But even in peacetime, the service employs huge resources; currently the 2013 military budget exceeds $800 billion, not including expenditures for Afghanistan and Iraq. I believe that the armed services can assume budgetary reductions without deteriorating its military efficiency. Of even greater significance is the influence that the military high command has on national policy.

Most disquieting of all is that neither political party has a growth agenda. With much help from other concerned citizens along with elected and appointed officials, I have spent at least twenty years developing a job creation program based on infrastructure investment that is urgently needed by our country. And while every political authority I meet understands the need to tackle our infrastructure deficit and put people back to work in the process, and despite this being the only project of scale that can put 7 to 10 million people to work in the near term, neither party has summoned the will to authorize the creation of an infrastructure bank along the lines of the BUILD Act proposed by then-senator John Kerry.

Paul Krugman wrote on March 28, 2013, in the *New York Times*: "Inveighing against the risks of government borrowing by undercutting political support for public investment and job creation has done far more to cheat our children than deficits ever did . . . our sin involves investing too little, not borrowing too much."

Indeed, the real sin is the lack of political will to dispense with "politics as usual" and respond to the demands of the American citizenry for real leadership and real fixes for what's broken in our country.

I have been lucky to be engaged in life, to have prospered, and to have obtained the economic security that allows me to pay back. The level of personal growth I attained is a reflection of our country's bountiful system and the contributions of so many mentors, friends, partners, and colleagues along the way. I hope that you, the readers of this book, will accept the challenge of ensuring that these benefits are preserved for our children and grandchildren.

Acknowledgments

This book was undertaken mainly at the urging of Karen Schwartz, Francesca Schwartz, and John Paddock, my children, who felt strongly that I should write down the story of Loral. They believed that what was created over a course of thirty-four years was a unique business culture. At Loral everyone was given the opportunity to contribute to the company's success, and in return they were applauded and financially rewarded; it was a place where anyone could succeed without diminishing his or her coworkers, our customers, or society. My children, who have inspired me and made me a better man in so many ways, convinced me that it was time to tell this story to a new generation. I cannot adequately express my gratitude to them for continuing to encourage and challenge me.

Also worthy of special comment is my senior-most assistant for thirty-three years, Lisa Stein, who helped set the standard for Loral's distinctive character and employee dedication. She literally grew up with Loral; her encyclopedic recollections of our people, transactions, and events over the years attest to that. As the company became increasingly complex, Lisa remained the calm and focused gatekeeper whose judgment I depended on to keep things rolling. And, above and beyond all of these critical qualities, she is fun to work with—another Loral hallmark. Lisa's role at Loral is cited several times in these pages, but it's fitting to mention her right at the start; she has made an enormous contribution and cannot be mentioned enough.

There are two other people whose contributions to this book deserve special mention: Jeanette Clonan and Charles Leerhsen. Jeanette has been a colleague of mine since she first came to work at Loral, in 1981, as director of communications. Jeanette featured prominently in our management team and contributed to our values as she rose to the position of vice president of investor relations and corporate communications. Although she officially retired from the BLS team in 2012, she agreed to stay on to help me edit and launch *Just Say Yes*. She urged me to recruit Charles, a writer and editor of biographies and a skilled interlocutor. Together they did prodigious work as researchers and added discipline, structure, and cohesion to the process. I am also grateful to Patrick Doehner, a former Loral executive, whose research on the Loral experience was invaluable, and to Lysa Jones, my executive assistant, who never flinched during my endless dictations and rewrites. Her consistently positive attitude and her ability to juggle "book" matters with her usual heavy workload are impressive. This book would never have been attempted without these people being part of the team.

It was on Charles's recommendation that the focus of this book be widened to include not just Loral's history but also the story of my life. I didn't mean this to be a narcissistic act but rather a chance to pay tribute to the American society that provided me with a path to success. My generation had the wind at our backs and seemingly endless opportunities ahead of us to be educated, to find good work, and to start our families. Without this enriching environment, a generous helping of luck, and the people who worked alongside me at Loral, there would be no story to tell.

Finally, the most important tribute is to my wife, Irene. As you read in these pages, my business career was anything but routine. From the very start of our relationship and my business career, through the consistent upward moves, over the various hurdles, and in the midst of all the victories, Irene's advice and support were there as a guide and as encouragement. It is Irene who set the tone for the most important part of my life. She created a home where she and our daughters provided me with their unwavering support without complaint. And she made sure we had fun together—on family trips, at holiday celebrations, or simply at the dinner table (her apple pies are without peer). Irene's intelligence, constancy, willingness to challenge me, and sense of humor have always inspired and motivated me. Ours has been a happy and loving partnership—the most important ingredient in my life—and I am indeed a fortunate man to have Irene by my side.

Index

A

Abramowitz, Elkan, 185–87
acquisition philosophy
 personnel integration, 140, 142–43,
  148–49
 synergy as key to, 6, 138–42, 170,
  203–4, 207, 221, 222
acquisitions by Loral
 Aercom, 168
 Conic Corporation, 138–39, 150,
  157–58
 Fairchild Weston Systems, 193–94, 202
 Ford Aerospace, 149, 203–8, 225
 Frequency Sources, 168
 Goodyear Aerospace, 139, 149, 169–73,
  181, 192, 193–94
 Honeywell Electro-Optics, 202
 Hycor, 169, 191
 IBM Federal Systems, 149, 221, 222
 LTV Aerospace, 149, 217–22, 221
 Narda Microwave Corporation, 168
 Randtron Systems, 151, 168
 Rolm Mil-Spec, 169, 191
 Unisys Defense Systems, 222
 Xerox Electro-Optical Systems, 169
action bias, 7, 149
Admiral Plastics (APL), 42–44, 46, 49–52,
 57, 59, 61, 63, 81
Aercom, 168
Afghanistan war, 286–87
After the Music Stopped (Blinder), 297, 298,
 299
air traffic control systems, 212–13, 222
Aircraft Braking Systems Corporation
 (ABSC), 173–79, 193
AirTouch, 225, 228
Alcatel, 228, 257, 259, 263
Alden, Ted, 289
Alenia, 228
Alpert, Leon, 5, 85, 89–90

Amanpour, Christiane, 277
America. *See also* politics
 banking and financial system, 294–99,
  300, 301
 business climate, xiv–xv, 254
 economic history of, 295–99
 economic structural changes, 291–92
 infrastructure reform, 267–68, 272,
  280–84, 285
 leadership and innovation of, 284, 300
 military establishment influence, 301–2
 military veterans, 286–87
 post-WW II, xiv, 28, 31–32
 resource misallocation, 293–94
 Vietnam War era, 5, 71, 84, 87, 91
American Ballet Theatre, 292
American Beryllium, 150
American International Group (AIG), 298
American Society of Civil Engineers,
 280–81
American Veterans Committee, 34
Apstar-IIR satellite, 255
APT Satellite Holdings, 255
Asia Society, 292
AT&T, 255
Augustine, Norman, 3–4, 7, 8, 93, 218,
 219, 240–42, 244, 246–48
Aurora Capital Group, 178–79

B

Bain Capital, 141
Baker, Bill, 292
Baker, Howard, 235
Bank of America, 262
Bank of America Merrill Lynch, 297
banking system, 294–99, 300, 301
Bard Graduate Center, 292
Bartiromo, Maria, 223
Baruch, Bernard, 33
Baruch College, 292

Bear Stearns, 296
Beijing, China, 194, 195–98
Belgian Air Force, 161
Bennett, Matt, 289
Berlind, Roger, 61
Bernanke, Ben, 298, 301
Bernard L. Schwartz Fellows Program, 289, 291
Bernard L. Schwartz Initiative on American Economic Policy, 288–89
Berry, Bob, 210–12
Biloxi, Mississippi, 23
Blair, Tony, 277
Blinder, Alan S., 297, 298, 299
BLS Investments, 157, 285–86
Boeing, 7
Bolton, John, 235
Bombardier, 174
Born, Brooksley, 298
Bossidy, Larry, 178–79
Brand, David, 175, 178
Brasserie 8 1/2, 271
Brookings Institution, 290–91
Brooklyn, New York, xiv, 11–18, 19
Brown, Ron, 198–99
BUILD Act, 281–83, 302
Bush, George H. W., 233
Bush, George W., 233, 301
Butler, Samuel, 4

C

Carey, Hugh, 135–37
Carlyle Group, 218
Carroll, Jim, 45–46
Carter, Arthur, 61, 64–67
Carter, Berlind & Weill, 61–62, 63, 64–67
Carter, Jimmy, 218, 268–69
Caxton Encyclopedia, 77
cellular communication technology, 224, 256, 257
Central Park Conservancy, 292
CFTC (Commodity Futures Trading Commission), 298
Chapin, Homer, 97
Chemical Bank, 67–71
Cheney, Dick, 147
China, 194–99
China Sat-8, 232–38, 259
China Telecom, 228, 257
Chrysler Corporation, 269
Cipriani, 271

Citigroup, 297
City College of New York, 21, 32, 33–34, 292
Clemons, Steve, 289, 290
Clinton, Bill, 233, 235–37, 267, 274–80, 284, 287, 301
Clinton, Chelsea, 280
Clinton, Hillary Rodham, 29, 276–80
Clonan, Jeanette, 154–56, 260
Cogan, Berlind & Weill, 65
Cogan, Marshall, 62, 65
Coll, Steve, 265, 289–90
Commerce Department, 198–99, 231–32
conglomerates, 5, 6, 85, 139–40
Conic Corporation, 138–39, 150, 157–58
Conway, Bill, 219–20
Coolidge, Calvin, 296
Council on Foreign Relations, 289
Cowan, Jon, 288
Cox, Christopher, 236
Cox Committee, 236
Crebo-Rediker, Heidi, 281
CTI, 67, 82

D

Dacom, 228
Dalmo Victor, 162
DASA (Daimler-Chrysler Aerospace), 228
Daschle, Linda, 213
DeBlasio, Michael, 101, 153, 175
defense industry
    budget cutbacks, 87, 95, 105, 191–93, 202–3, 220, 222, 239, 241–42
    contract process, 87–88, 119, 161
    Loral's role within, 7, 167
    Operation Ill Wind, 181–88
    production cycle, 105
    Schwartz as viewed by, 4, 101–2, 121, 270
    Schwartz's view of, 4–5, 86–88
    Wall Street's view of, 6, 84, 87, 138–39, 170
Delaney, John, 282
DeLauro, Rosa, 282
Democracy Journal, 291
Democratic Leadership Council, 287–88
Democratic Party, 16, 38–39, 71, 186, 268, 269–72
Democratic Progressive Club, 38–39
Desert Storm, 201–2
Dobbs, Lou, 236
Dole, Bob, 276

Donaldson, Sam, 236
Drexel Burnham, 170–72

E

economic crisis of 2008, 297–99, 300
economic policy issues, 287–92
Elsacom, 228
Emanuel, Rahm, 1, 148
Embraer, 174
Engineered Fabrics, 193

F

Facebook IPO, 299
Fahd, Prince, 213–14
Fairchild Weston Systems, 193–94, 202
Federal Aviation Administration (FAA),
    122, 212–13, 222
Federal Bureau of Investigation (FBI), 181,
    183–85, 237
Film Society of Lincoln Center, 292
Financial Times, 290
Fingeroth, Jim, 154
Finmeccanica, 228
Fishman, Harry, 28, 42–43, 44, 45–46, 49,
    50–51, 52, 53, 61
Ford, 139
Ford Aerospace, 149, 203–7, 225
Fordham University, 292
Fortune magazine, 227–28
Fox, David, 82
France Telecom, 228, 263
Frankfurter, Felix, 33
Frequency Sources, 168
Frohmann, Jules, 119, 120
From, Al, 287–88
Fuld, Dick, 176

G

Galbraith, James, 291
Galvin, William M., 181–88
Gates, William F., 151
Geithner, Timothy, 301
General Electric, 7, 19, 245
Gershwin, Ira, 33
Gerth, Jeff, 235–37
Ghilarducci, Teresa, 290
GI Bill, xiv, 33, 109
Gillibrand, Kirsten, 282
Gingrich, Newt, 236, 274
Ginn, Sam, 225

Gittis, Howard, 97
Glass-Steagall Act, 296
Globalstar, 224–29, 240, 250, 254–58,
    263–64
Golan, General, 128–29
Goldman Sachs, 296, 297, 299
Goldsmith, Sir James, 169
Goodrich, 173–74
Goodyear Aerospace, 139, 149, 169–73,
    181, 192, 193–94
Gore, Al, 276
Gramm-Leach-Bliley Act, 296
Great Depression, xiv, 11–14, 16, 28, 295
Greenspan, Alan, 298, 301
Grossman, Robert, 292

H

Haass, Richard, 289
Hale, Nancy, 289
Halstead, Ted, 289
Hardy and Company, 44
Harris, Townsend, 21
Hauer, Arthur, 46–47
Heath, Edward, 107
Heft, Ed, 43
Herbert, Bob, 284
Herman, Bernard, 98
Hewitt, Don, 237
Hewlett-Packard, 209
Hodes, Bob, 5, 44–46, 64, 69, 84–86, 89,
    97, 174, 185
Hodes, Jim, 44
Holbrooke, Richard, 289
Hollings, Ernest "Fritz," 214–15
Honeywell, 173–74
Honeywell Electro-Optics, 202
Horn & Hardart Automat, 271
Hughes, 7, 184
Hussein, Saddam, 201
Hutchinson, Kay Bailey, 281, 282
Hycor, 169, 191
Hyundai, 228

I

IBM, 7, 54–55, 57, 62–63, 82–83, 139
IBM Federal Systems, 149, 221, 222
Icahn, Carl, 260
Ideal Rubber Company, 53–54
Information Technology and Innovation
    Foundation, 291

infrastructure reform, 267–68, 272,
    280–84, 285
initial public offerings, 41–46, 299
Intelsat, 204, 234, 261
Iraq war, 286–87
Iridium, 225
Israel, Steve, 273, 282
Israeli Air Force, 124–31, 161
ITT, 7

J

Jackson, Fred, 108
Jackson, Steve, 156
Jacobs, Irwin, 225
Johns Hopkins University, 291, 292
Johnson, Les, 182–84
JPMorgan Chase, 297, 299
Justice Department, 185–88, 237–38, 299

K

K & F, 176–79, 181
Kay, Avery, 24–25
Kekst, Gershon, 5–6, 97, 154
Kekst & Company, 154
Kent State University, 71
Kerrey, Bob, 274, 286
Kerry, John, 281, 282, 302
Kessler, Jim, 289
Keynes, John Maynard, 4
Kissinger, Henry, 196–97
KKR, 141
knowledge gap, 81–82, 85, 86, 98–99, 107,
    226
Kolitz, David, 125–29
Kresa, Ken, 219–20
Krugman, Paul, 302
Kuwait war, 201–2

L

L-3 Communications, 247–48
LaBella, Charles G., 237–38
Lanza, Frank, 129, 160–65, 181, 242,
    244–48
Lazard Frères, 172
Lazarus, Charles, 66, 97
Leasco Data Processing Equipment Corpo-
    ration
    assets and revenue, 58, 62
    business model, 54–58, 62–63, 82
    Chemical Bank takeover attempt by,
        67–71

culture of, 82–83
diversification of, 62–67
Pergamon Press acquisition troubles,
    76–80
Reliance takeover by, 62–67, 82
Schwartz as accountant for, 56–59
Schwartz as president of, 63, 67–71
stock price, 67, 70
Lee, Wen Ho, 237
Lehman Brothers, 172, 173–78, 206–7,
    248, 296, 299
Levitt, Arthur, 62, 298
Lind, Michael, 289, 290
Linksman, Judy, 286
Litton Industries, 162, 164, 182–83
Lockheed Martin, 3, 7, 101–3, 110–12,
    184, 217–20, 240–48
Loral. *See also* acquisitions by Loral; defense
    industry; Loral employees; Loral
    stockholders; satellite business
    air traffic control system, 212–13, 222
    board of directors, 97–98, 154, 184
    branding, 150–51
    chairman's meetings, 146–48, 150
    core business, 84–86, 105–6, 193–95,
        202, 204, 207
    culture of, xv, 7, 99–100, 134, 142–44,
        148–49, 156, 162, 192, 207–8
    Defense Department contracts, 4, 88,
        101–3, 110–12, 121
    Desert Storm contribution by, 201–2
    dirigibles project, 181–88
    entrepreneurial spirit of, 134, 142, 149,
        152, 207–8, 223–24
    Galvin's contract with, 181–88
    growth of, 7, 133–34, 135–37, 138,
        167–69, 170, 191–94, 202–3,
        220–21
    history, 5, 85
    international business, 123–31, 161,
        194–99, 210–14, 232–38, 259
    management team, 7, 99–100, 142–44,
        149, 160
    manufacturing facilities, 96, 113, 135–37
    missile business, 217–20, 221, 222
    nonmilitary customers, 205
    radar warning systems, 88, 118–23, 125,
        129–30, 160–61, 168, 193, 221
    Schwartz's purchase of, 4–7, 84–92, 154
    Schwartz's sale to Lockheed, 3–9,
        239–48
    Schwartz's vision for, 85, 88, 95–96
    staff meetings, 83, 100

Loral Aerospace, 173
Loral Aerospace Holdings, 203–7
Loral American Beryllium, 150
Loral Conic, 138–39, 150, 157–58
Loral Defense Systems, 181–82
Loral Electronic Systems (LES), 88, 96,
    135–37, 160, 181
Loral employees
    compensation and benefits, 149–50, 262
    firing of, 157–58
    hiring of, 98–99, 100
    interviewing, 153–57, 162–65
    labor strike by, 113–15
    promotion of, 152
    quality of, 86, 88, 96–97
    Schwartz's concern for, 8, 140, 142–52,
      240–46, 260–62
Loral Global Alliance Network, 255
Loral Randtron, 151
Loral Skynet, 255, 258, 262–63
Loral Space & Communications, 8, 240,
    253–64
Loral stockholders
    cash distribution from sale, 8–9, 240,
      246–48
    letters to, 109–10, 117–18, 133, 145,
      167–69, 191–92, 194–95, 201–3,
      220, 221–22
    Loral Space & Communications, 253,
      263–64
    Schwartz's politics and, 270
Loral Vought, 221
Lorenz, William, 5, 85, 89–90
Los Angeles Times, 237–38
Lott, Trent, 237
LTV Aerospace, 149, 217–20, 221
LTV Corporation, 217
luck, xiv, 28, 32, 81, 109, 285, 302

M

Madrick, Jeff, 291
Malamud, Bernard, 33
Manheimer, Matilda, 16
Manufacturers Hanover, 57–58, 69
Mao, Zedong, 198
Markel, Arnold, 35–36, 37, 46–48
Markel, Schnee (company), 32, 34–37,
    41–48
Markel, Schnee, and Hauer, 46–48
Marshall, Will, 287
Martin Marietta, 217–18
Marton, Kati, 289

Massachusetts Protective Association,
    49–51
Maxwell, Robert, 74–80
McCain, John, 237
McClellan, George B., 149
McCracken, Frank, 82–83
McDonnell Douglas, 7, 88, 101, 118–19,
    124, 174, 177
McGillicuddy, John, 68–69
Meggitt PLC, 178, 179
Merchants Bank of New York, 36–37
Metz, Robert, 68
Mickey Mouse, 147–48
military establishment, 301–2
military veterans, 286–87
Milken, Michael, 170–73
Miller, Harvey, 189, 220
Milton, John, 26
Minard, Sally, 97
Mitsubishi Electric Corporation, 210–12
Moren, Nick, 149
Morgan Stanley, 297
Morgenthau, Henry, 38
Mosbacher, Robert, 231–32
Motorola, 225
Murdoch, Rupert, 74–75

N

Narda Microwave Corporation, 168
National Student Organization of America,
    34
Netter, Ed, 61–62, 63
New America Foundation, 289–90
New School for Social Research, 290
New York City, 11–18, 33, 96–97, 113–14,
    135–37, 249–51, 271–72
New York Times, 68, 225, 235–37, 273, 284,
    302
New-York Historical Society, 271, 292
Nixon, Richard, 71, 87, 107
Northrop Corporation, 7, 219
NYU Langone Medical Center, 292

O

Obama, Barack, 233, 272–74, 280, 283–84,
    301
Office of Education, 122
Operation Ill Wind, 181–88
Organizing for Action, 273–74
Orion Network Systems, 255

P

Paddock, John, 146, 278–79
Parsky, Gerald, 179
Patricof, Alan, 275, 276
Paulson, Hank, 298, 301
Pelosi, Nancy, 249, 272–73
performance as strategy, 41, 46, 95, 138,
　　202, 221
Pergamon Press, 74–80
Perle, Richard, 147
Pincus, Walter, 237
politics. *See also* Democratic Party
　as broken system, 300–301
　China Sat-8 project and, 232–38
　election process, 270–72, 301
　infrastructure reform and, 267–68, 272,
　　280–84, 285
　Super PACs, 272–74, 301
Powell, Colin, 33, 115
property insurance business, 62–63
Proxmire, William, 121–22

Q

Qualcomm, 224–27, 263

R

Rabin, Yitzhak, 130
Rachesky, Mark, 259–63
radar warning systems, 88, 118–23, 125,
　　129–30, 160–61, 168, 193, 221
Rainbow Room, 271
Randtron Systems, 151, 168
Rapport system, 129–30, 160–61, 193
Reagan, Ronald, 199, 268
relationship era, xv, 11, 36–37, 58, 294–96
Reliance Group, 5, 58, 67, 81, 107, 223
Reliance Insurance Company
　Chemical Bank takeover attempt by,
　　67–71
　culture of, 82–83
　financial problems, 107–8
　Leasco takeover of, 62–67, 82
　Pergamon Press acquisition troubles,
　　76–80
Renchard, William, 68–70
Rendell, Edward, 282
Republican Party, 268, 301
research and development (R&D), 87, 130,
　　135, 141–42, 192
Rich, Merry, 70–71

Risen, James, 237
Robert Maxwell Communications, 79
Robert Maxwell LTD, 77, 79–80
Roberts, Bill, 82
Roberts, Cokie, 236
Rohatyn, Felix, 172, 282
Rohrabacher, Dana, 236, 274
Rolm Mil-Spec, 169, 191
Roosevelt, Franklin, xiv
Roosevelt, Jimmy, 24–25
Roosevelt Institute, 291
Ross, Diana, 171
Rothkopf, David, 290
Rothschild, Evelyn and Lynn, 277
Rothschild, Jacob, 75
Rubenstein, David, 218–20
Rubin, James, 277
Rubin, Robert, 291, 298, 301
Ruderman, Mal, 97

S

Safire, William, 236
satellite business. *See also* Globalstar
　Chinese contract, 231–38
　Ford Aerospace acquisition, 203–7, 225
　Loral Space & Communications, 8, 240,
　　253–64
　Mitsubishi contract, 210–12
　weather applications, 214–15
satellite telephones, 224–29, 240, 250,
　　254–58, 263–64
Satmex, 255
Saudi Arabia, 213–14
Schnee, Abe, 35–36, 46–48, 52
Schnee, Hauer, Schwartz, 48, 52, 81
Schrafft's restaurant, 14
Schumer, Chuck, 273
Schwartz, Benjamin, 16
Schwartz, Bernard. *See also* Leasco Data
　　Processing Equipment Corporation;
　　Loral; Reliance Insurance Company
　ABSC acquisition by, 173–79
　action bias of, 7, 149
　advocacy organizations support by,
　　287–92
　at APL, 49–52, 57, 59, 61–63
　business philosophy of, xiv, 4, 7, 134
　Carter's mistrust of, 64–67
　childhood, xiv, 11–15
　confidence of, xiv, 22, 134
　contentment of, xiii, 73–74, 81–82, 239

decisiveness of, xiii–xiv, 99, 100, 142,
    152, 189
education, xiv, 21–22, 32, 33–34
empathy and compassion of, 146,
    148–49, 150
ethics, xv, 147–48
family background, 15–18
on knowledge gap, 81–82, 85, 86,
    98–99, 107, 226
as Lockheed vice chairman, 244–47
on luck, xiv, 28, 32, 81, 109, 285, 302
at Markel, Schnee, 32, 34–37, 41–48
marriage, 37–38
media coverage of, 225, 235–38, 253
Mickey Mouse and, 147–48
military service, 32–33
need to run own company, 5, 83–84
personal visits to customers, 195–99,
    209–15
personal visits to divisions, 98, 143–44,
    157–58
philanthropic activities, 292
political activism of, 38–39, 71, 186,
    287–92, 301–3
problem-solving abilities, 27, 43–44,
    118, 152
retirement of, 8–9, 253–54, 264
Steinberg's relationship with, 54, 58–59,
    73–74, 91–92, 106–8
as tough negotiator, 89–90, 120–23,
    125–29, 148, 174–76, 179, 220
travel schedule, 73, 143–44
on wealth, 38, 96, 108–9
Schwartz, Beth, 178
Schwartz, Francesca, 17, 46, 73, 90–91,
    146, 176–77, 278
Schwartz, Hannah, 12–13, 15, 18, 25
Schwartz, Harold
    business career, 28, 42, 44–46, 49,
        50–52, 61, 63, 113, 294
    childhood, 13, 17, 18–19
    military service, 19, 22–28
Schwartz, Harry, 12, 16–18
Schwartz, Ilana, 178
Schwartz, Irene
    advocacy organizations support, 288,
        289
    Clintons and, 275, 277–79
    courtship and marriage, 32, 34, 37–38
    election-night parties, 271–72
    family life, 46, 48, 52, 71, 73, 90, 91,
        126, 163

philanthropic activities, 292
    travels, 8–9, 79, 195–97, 277
Schwartz, Jonathan, 178
Schwartz, Jules, 13, 14–15, 17, 18–19, 21,
    177
Schwartz, Karen, 17, 38, 46, 73, 90–91,
    146, 177, 278
Schwartz, Kenneth, 177–79
Schwartz Book Award, 292
Schwartz Center for Economic Policy
    Analysis, 290
Schwartz Center for Media, Public Policy,
    and Education, 292
Schwartz Communication Institute, 292
Schwartz Lecture on Business and Foreign
    Policy, 289
Schwartz Lecture Series, 292
Schwartz Senior Fellowship in Business and
    Foreign Policy, 289
Schwenninger, Sherle, 289, 290
Securities and Exchange Commission
    (SEC), 43–44, 297, 299
September 11, 2001 terrorist attacks,
    249–51
Shapiro, Donald, 97
Shapiro, Neil, 292
Shavit, Yalo, 128–29
Sheffield Farms, 12
Shelby, Richard, 237, 274
Shinn, Allen, 97, 120, 123, 184
Simon, Al, 118–20
Simon, Art, 97
Skynet, 255, 258, 262–63
Smith, Red, 133
Soros Partners, 257
Space News, 253
Space Systems/Loral (SS/L), 206–7, 232–38,
    255, 258–59, 261, 262–63
Sperling, Gene, 291
Stanton, Tom, 86
State Department, 234–35, 238
Stein, Lisa, 157, 250, 272, 285
Steinberg, Bob, 107
Steinberg, Gayfryd, 223
Steinberg, Jonathan, 223
Steinberg, Julius, 53, 55–57
Steinberg, Michael, 53–55, 56
Steinberg, Saul. *See also* Leasco Data
    Processing Equipment Corporation;
    Reliance Insurance Company
    character, 54–56, 223
    decline and death of, 223

family dynamics, 55–56, 58–59
Milken and, 171
Schwartz's relationship with, 54, 58–59,
    73–74, 91–92, 106–8
Steiner, Jeffrey, 176
Stern, Ed, 157–58
Stevenson, Adlai, 38–39
Strauss, Bob, 269
Summers, Lawrence, 298, 301
Super PACs, 272–74, 301
Surowiecki, James, 227–28
synergy, 6, 105, 134, 138–42, 170, 203–4,
    207, 221, 222

T

Talbott, Strobe, 290–91
telecommunications industry, 232–38, 253.
    See also Globalstar
Tellep, Dan, 244–46
terrorist attacks of September 11, 2001,
    249–51
Thanksgiving stories, 146, 163
think tanks, 287–92
Third Way, 277, 288–89
Thirteen, 292
This Week, 236–37
Thomson-CSF, 218, 219
Tiananmen Square, 194, 196
Towbin, Bob, 175–76
Townsend, Rich, 153–54
Townsend Harris High School, 21–28, 33
transactional era, xv, 37, 58, 296, 298
Truman, Harry, 271, 279
TRW, 225
Tyson, Laura, 291

U

Unisys Defense Systems, 222
University of Pennsylvania, 33
US Air Force, 88, 90, 96, 101, 118–23, 160,
    182, 183
US Army, 121, 130–31, 141
US Army Air Corps, 19, 23–27, 32–33
US Navy, 88, 90, 96, 101–3, 110–12, 118,
    160–61, 181–88
US Senate, 214–15, 218, 219

V

venture capitalists, 6, 141
Vietnam War era, 5, 71, 84, 87, 91
Vodafone, 228, 263
Volker, Paul, 291

W

Wall Street Journal, 264
Wall Street's view of defense industry, 6,
    84, 87, 134, 139
Wallace, Henry, 270
Walter Reed Hospital, 286–87
Warner, Fred and Simone, 195–97
Warner, Mark R., 281, 282
Washington, DC terrorist attacks, 249–50
Washington Post, 290
Washkowitz, Alan, 178
Weill, Sandy, 61–62
Weizman, Ezer, 125
Welch, Jack, 7, 149, 245
Wharton Business School, 33
Wilder, Don, 101–3, 110–12
Will, George, 236
Willkie, Farr, and Gallagher, 44–45
Wilson, Ed, 156
Wilson, Harold, 74
win-win-win situations, 217–20, 248
Wordsworth, William, 9
World Trade Center attacks, 249–51
World War II, 18–19, 21, 22–28

X

Xerox Electro-Optical Systems, 169

Y

Yankelovich, Daniel, 97
Young, John, 209

Z

Zanderer, Irene. *See* Schwartz, Irene
Zanderer, Sam, 295

About the Author

BERNARD L. SCHWARTZ is an investor, retired industrialist, progressive public policy advocate, and philanthropist. He is currently chairman and CEO of BLS Investments LLC, a private investment firm. Mr. Schwartz also manages the investments of the Bernard and Irene Schwartz Foundation, which supports think tanks and economic policy advocacy organizations, universities, medical research centers, and New York City–based cultural organizations.

Prior to establishing BLS Investments in March 2006, Mr. Schwartz served for thirty-four years as chairman of the board and CEO of Loral Corporation and its successor company, Loral Space & Communications, formed in 1996. Loral, a Fortune 200 defense electronics firm, employed as many as thirty-eight thousand employees at its twenty-five locations. At its height Loral attained annual revenues of nearly $7.5 billion and had a market value of $13 billion.

In addition, from 1989 to 2005 Mr. Schwartz formed and served as chairman of the board of K&F Industries, a worldwide leader in the manufacture of wheels, brakes, and brake control systems for commercial transport, general aviation, and military aircraft. He also served until 2001 as chairman and CEO of Globalstar Telecommunications Limited, a low-earth-orbiting global mobile satellite telecommunications network launched under his leadership in 1991.

Reflecting his interest in American competitiveness and growth, Mr. Schwartz has established programs that promote the development of US economic policy initiatives at a number of think tanks, universities, and advocacy organizations, among them Third Way, the New School, Johns Hopkins University's School of Advanced International Studies, the Council on Foreign Relations, Carnegie Endowment for International Peace, Economists for Peace and Security, the Roosevelt Institute, and the Brookings Institution.

A lifelong New Yorker, Mr. Schwartz also serves as a trustee of the New York University Hospitals Center, the New-York Historical Society, Thirteen/WNET Educational Broadcasting Corporation, and Baruch College. He is vice chairman of the New York Film Society and sponsors a program at the Asia Society. Mr. Schwartz's wife, Irene Schwartz, is a longtime supporter of the Bard Graduate Center, the American Ballet Theatre, and Central Park Conservancy.

Mr. Schwartz graduated from City College of New York with a bachelor of science degree in finance and holds an honorary doctorate of science degree from the college.